# Facilitating Meaningful Contact
# in Adoption and Fostering

*of related interest*

**Attachment, Trauma, and Healing**
**Understanding and Treating Attachment**
**Disorder in Children and Families**
*Terry M. Levy and Michael Orlans*
ISBN 978 1 84905 888 9
eISBN 978 0 85700 597 7

**Mindful Therapeutic Care for Children**
**A Guide to Reflective Practice**
*Dr Joanna North*
ISBN 978 1 84905 446 1
eISBN 978 0 85700 840 4

**Life Story Books for Adopted Children**
**A Family Friendly Approach**
*Joy Rees*
ISBN 978 1 84310 953 2
eISBN 978 0 85700 190 0

**Life Story Work with Children Who are Fostered or Adopted**
**Creative Ideas and Activities**
*Katie Wrench and Lesley Naylor*
ISBN 978 1 84905 343 3
eISBN 978 0 85700 674 5

**Direct Work with Vulnerable Families**
*Audrey Tait and Helen Wosu*
ISBN 978 1 84905 319 8
eISBN 978 0 85700 661 5

**A Child's Journey Through Placement**
*Vera I. Fahlberg*
ISBN 978 1 84905 898 8
eISBN 978 0 85700 631 8

**Understanding and Working with Parents of**
**Children in Long-Term Foster Care**
*Gillian Schofield and Emma Ward*
ISBN 978 1 84905 026 5
eISBN 978 0 85700 489 5

# Facilitating Meaningful Contact
# in Adoption and Fostering

*A Trauma-Informed Approach to Planning,
Assessing and Good Practice*

LOUIS SYDNEY, ELSIE PRICE *and* ADOPTIONPLUS

Jessica Kingsley *Publishers*
London and Philadelphia

First published in 2014
by Jessica Kingsley Publishers
73 Collier Street
London N1 9BE, UK
and
400 Market Street, Suite 400
Philadelphia, PA 19106, USA

*www.jkp.com*

**Library of Congress Cataloging in Publication Data**
Sydney, Louis.
  Facilitating meaningful contact in adoption and fostering : a trauma-informed approach to planning,
assessing and good practice / Louis Sydney, Elsie Price and Adoptionplus.
     pages cm
  Includes bibliographical references and index.
  ISBN 978-1-84905-508-6 (alk. paper)
  1. Adoption. 2. Foster parents. 3. Birthparents. 4. Child development. I. Title.
  HV875.S95 2014
  362.73'3--dc23
                         2014006408

**British Library Cataloguing in Publication Data**
A CIP catalogue record for this book is available from the British Library

ISBN 978 1 84905 508 6
eISBN 978 0 85700 924 1

Printed and bound in Great Britain

# Contents

# Foreword

As the title suggests, this is a book providing guidance on managing contact for children who are adopted or fostered. However, it is much more than this. This is also a book about suffering and compassion for children and their families when there is a need to hold multiple families in mind. I am fond of a quote by priest and psychologist Henri J.M. Nouwen that I have used in my previous writings and trainings. It gets to the heart of what children, hurt by their early experience, need from all of us. It is worth repeating here as it sums up what I believe is the central message of this book:

> Let us not underestimate how hard it is to be compassionate. Compassion is hard because it requires the inner disposition to go with others to places where they are weak, vulnerable, lonely, and broken. But this is not our spontaneous response to suffering. What we desire most is to do away with suffering by fleeing from it or finding a quick cure for it. (Nouwen, 2011)[1]

The formulaic use of contact set up with little planning and at a frequency which is 'what we do' rather than individually tailored for the child seems to me a very good example of the quick cure that Nouwen refers to. We have contact in place and therefore we do not have to confront the pain, fear and suffering of the child who is caught in a web of relationships that are hard to make sense of.

How does a child understand not living with birth family; the hurt and pain that was inflicted upon them; the loss of later carers who felt like lasting parents but weren't; and the fear that ultimately there is something so wrong with them that these current 'forever parents' must discover this also and then will be gone too? In this book Elsie

---

1    Nouwen, J.M.H. (2011), *Out of Solitude: Three Meditations on the Christian Life* (as cited in GoodReads) available at www.goodreads.com/author/quotes/4837.Henri_J_M_Nouwen, accessed 10 February 2014.

and Louis discuss how we can manage contact head on; arguing that we should reflect on rather than prescribe contact, with compassion for all involved. In this way we can help the child find a way through the suffering; learning to live in a world that is more complex than any child should have to deal with.

As Elsie and Louis illustrate, contact can be a positive force helping the child to disentangle the web and live comfortably with those in their life, whether directly or indirectly. Much compassion is shown for the child at the centre, but Elsie and Louis go much further. They also have compassion for the adopters, foster carers, other family relations and the birth parents, where it all began. Their sensitive and moving case examples show us that contact can be healing for all involved; leaving the child stronger and those touched by this child healthier.

Fleeing from suffering is often done through our reactions to it. We look for someone to blame. The child is misbehaving; the parents are unreasonable; the birth parents were responsible. In this book we are gently taken beyond such reactions to a place of compassion; we learn that with some thought, time and planning we can facilitate contact that allows everyone to be connected; the child is no longer caught in a web but is cushioned by the joined hands of those who ultimately do want to do what is right for them.

I have worked with many children living in foster care, adopted or living with kin. They all in their own unique way are struggling with the same issue: am I good enough? For some they seek answers in the rejection of their mother and the idealisation of the birth mother – 'when you are mean to me I will run to her'; others seek to angrily test their birth families' commitment to them during the contact sessions arranged in each school holiday; still others seek to reassure and take care of the birth parents who appear to hold their 'goodness' in their hands. I have met children who are yearning, seeking and reconciling their feelings about their original family whether or not they are having direct contact with this family. I have met parents who are struggling to manage caring for their child whilst carrying the knowledge of the other family at the edge of theirs. They feel angry, sad and anxious. They worry that perhaps the child would have been better off with their birth family or that the child will one day choose to return to them. I have witnessed the dilemma of parents who don't know whether to let a child go or fetch them back when they have discovered their first family on Facebook and run off to be with them. As I have supported these families in their distress I have experienced first-hand how difficult contact can be and how hard it is to find a way of keeping children connected that is healing for them and helpful for all.

Conflict of loyalty, a need to be claimed, fears of failure and fantasy of what might be are at the centre of the lives of children adopted, fostered or looked after away from their family of origin. Contact can confirm or resolve these depending upon how thoughtfully and seriously we take our responsibilities to facilitate these arrangements. Whether direct or indirect, contact is a reality that we have to confront; removing children from their birth families is a responsibility that does not stop when permanence is secured. If we don't take this responsibility seriously then permanence will be compromised. The trauma of removal, done in the best interests of the child, will be compounded by the further trauma the child experiences as they try to discover who they are and where if anywhere they deserve to belong.

We may not always be able to get contact arrangements right, but that does not mean we should not try. It will take resources, time and energy. These can be hard to find alongside the demands of front-line social work as practitioners work to safeguard children. Children will not be fully safeguarded, however, if we cannot follow through and ensure that we do the very best for them in their journeys through the care system. The children have continuing contact with birth families whether through face-to-face arrangements, indirect letterbox contact or through the ongoing life story exploration that allows the child to comfortably keep all their families in mind. This is a central part of the ongoing care we must give to children when the state has intervened so dramatically. With thoughtful, flexible and carefully reviewed contact arrangements we can secure emotionally healthy lives for the children. This can have an impact in helping to reduce the breakdown of permanent arrangements all too familiar during the complexities of adolescence.

This book is well informed, evidence based and thoughtful, providing much wisdom that can guide practitioners and commissioners to make their services 'contact sensitive'. The case examples provide beautiful examples of what can be achieved and attention is given to contact in all its forms, not forgetting siblings, past carers and separated families. Rachel writes thoughtfully about the use of 'letterbox' and Elsie and Louis are mindful of current technology and practices whether it is the difficulties of social networking or the benefits of video and facilitated letter writing. The advice is also realistic; even with best intentions, sometimes the preferred option is just not possible. This is all underpinned by consideration of child development and the impact of trauma on the developing brain.

So thank you Elsie and Louis for allowing us to give such careful consideration to the issue of securing successful contact for children who have experienced hurt, separation and loss early in life. You remind us that we are not only present at the start of these children's journeys into a safer future but that we have a continuing responsibility throughout their childhoods. Adopters, foster carers and birth family members deserve the thoughtful, compassionate support you advocate to ensure that contact arrangements facilitate the health and wellbeing of the children as well as those caring for or thinking about them. It is too easy to assume a job is done and not to confront the ongoing suffering that can be a part of growing up outside of the family of origin. By guiding our compassionate response to this suffering we can be more hopeful that contact can be a beneficial and constructive way to help the child keep multiple families in mind whilst learning to live healthily in their 'for now' and ultimately 'forever' family.

*Kim S. Golding, Clinical Psychologist*
*February 2014*

# About Adoptionplus

Adoptionplus is a voluntary adoption agency registered in 2008 to find families for older, harder to place children with complex needs.

We offer a new type of adoption service in the UK, one that recognises how essential responsive effective adoption support is. As part of our placement service we decided to recruit a therapy team, which would be available to all of our families whenever they needed support. Our team is headed by a consultant clinical child psychologist, and offers a range of trauma and attachment-based therapies. We want to ensure that the children we place for adoption not only have secure, loving and happy homes, but that they truly have the opportunity to heal from their early trauma, learn how to have relationships, manage their feelings and live satisfying lives.

As part of our work we were aware that children need a coherent sense of their past, an understanding of what has happened and why it may have happened. Many children often believe that it is their fault that their birth parents couldn't look after them, or abused and hurt them. They think that they are unlovable or bad and that they are responsible for all of the pain they have suffered. We believe that leaving children with these distorted self-beliefs will not only negatively impact the development of new healthy attachment relationships with their adoptive or foster parents, but is also likely to lead to a life of ongoing emotional pain, not being able to gain the comfort and support of healthy emotional relationships with others, as it is difficult for children to believe that they are lovable. It becomes difficult to trust that other people genuinely care for them. Additionally, children may have a distorted view of their birth parents, and may attribute positive qualities to them that they do not have. In turn these fantasies can be very unhelpful in the development of healthy attachment relationships with adoptive parents.

Adoptionplus sees contact as an opportunity to clarify the myths and promote a realistic and helpful understanding of past events. Seeing for themselves and understanding why their parents may have behaved as they did can correct children's distorted self-beliefs. We believe that this is enormously important to long-term emotional health.

As an agency, Adoptionplus also works with birth parents who have had their children removed and placed for adoption. These parents are often themselves confused about how they have ended up in the situation they are in, let alone knowing what to say to their children about it. In our experience many parents would welcome support and guidance to help them help their children. With the right support, some parents are keen to apologise for mistakes they have made and clarify that none of it was their children's fault. In lots of ways we believe this can also be beneficial for the birth parents' emotional health. Their sense of self-worth can increase if they can feel that they are truly offering their child something that is helpful to them. Offering some feeling of resolution is better than the pain of none at all. This pain can often leave birth parents stuck in the trauma of losing their children and make it very difficult for them to move forward in their lives, and can in fact lead to further deterioration of emotional health.

The more emotionally healthy birth parents are, the better it is for their children. In the current age of Facebook and the internet, there are clearly many benefits of investing in addressing unresolved issues as early as possible. Local authorities already spend resources on arranging and delivering contact services. We believe that this investment can be so much more beneficial if local authorities consider how they use contact time. Instead of it just being a space where resources are used to monitor and assess, it could be used to significantly benefit the emotional health of both the children and their birth parents. We are really interested in encouraging local authorities to review their understanding of their use of contact sessions, and to consider how it could be so much more beneficial. In a time of limited resources, it seems sensible to look at improving something that local authorities are already doing and to consider how some changes could encourage numerous benefits.

*Joanne Alper, Director of Adoptionplus*
*April 2014*

# Preface

The authors of this book, Elsie Price and Louis Sydney, met some years ago when they were both working at the adoption support agency, Family Futures, and have since worked together in supporting many adopted, fostered and permanently placed children and their substitute parents. In doing so, they have come to understand that the internal world of the child, their relationship with their birth mothers, fathers and other relatives has needed recognition and attention. Not infrequently these developmentally disadvantaged children have had contact arrangements with these same relatives who have been failing to meet their needs, exacerbating confusion, distress and, at worst, perpetuating trauma. Having observed what happens when contact is poorly managed, we have developed plans and found ways to intervene in these arrangements in a bid to support a child's recovery and their capacity to integrate and make sense of their life story. This has involved working with, supporting and guiding not only the child but also their birth parents (or other birth family members) and their adoptive parents and foster carers.

In this book it is our intention to offer ways of thinking about, planning and facilitating contact for babies and children who are in substitute families due to experiences of maltreatment. We intend to make the child's needs and interests central. We are also mindful that not all the children who have histories of early trauma are adopted, or are in foster or kinship care; many are continuing to live in chronically stressful family circumstances.

Client confidentiality has been rigorously protected in the reconstruction of cases through changing names and other identifying information. Where possible client permission has been obtained; in other presentations we have developed composite case studies based upon recurring themes encountered when working with our client group.

## CHAPTER 1

# Introduction

## What is Contact and What is It For?

Some years ago, as part of an assessment for care proceedings, Louis was taken to observe a contact between a boy in foster care and his birth father. This was typical of many contacts he had been involved in over the years.

Louis recalls the following:

## Case study: Ian

The contact venue was way out of a city centre and had seen better days. The facilities were poor and the place as a whole had a feeling of tiredness about it. The room where the contact was to take place lacked good seating and a nearby table was covered in wasted food (crisps, chocolate and stale bread) from the previous contact.

The background to the contact involved a history of domestic violence and frequent separations between the parents, alcohol abuse and pervasive neglect. Since the 9-year-old boy (whom I shall call Ian) had been taken into care, his parents had separated and their relationship was so acrimonious that arrangements had to be made for Ian to have separate contact sessions with each parent. A date had been set for an observation of Ian's contact with his mother for the previous week; however, this had to be rescheduled as she had phoned to cancel due to ill health – the suspicion was that she had in fact been drinking. Both the mother and the father had been known to social services as children. The mother had been sexually and physically abused by her stepfather and Ian's father had witnessed severe domestic violence until the age of 12 when his alcoholic father died as a result of liver failure.

Ian was brought to the contact by the foster carer and dropped off at reception. Once in the room, he waited nervously and was offered a drink by a staff member who greeted him cheerily, saying 'Hi Ian! Here to see Dad and Nan... you must be excited!'

He did not look excited to me. He could not settle, tried to get into the garden and went to the toilet repeatedly. When the father and paternal grandmother arrived, it felt to me as if we existed in a nether world. In this world, nothing much happened, no one really spoke about anything much and the unspoken rule was only to use social niceties such as 'You OK? Good! How's school? OK? That's good. Do you want some crisps; they're your favourite flavour!' I tried to imagine what it must be like for this 9-year-old boy who had frequently not been fed, and had experienced sudden scary separations without repair by an adult. From social services records it appeared that no one had tried to sit with Ian and help him make sense of what had happened in his shocking life to date. Certainly, no one had said 'sorry' for the fact that he had suffered for so long and seen more terrors than many adults have in their entire lives.

Admittedly, my background is in child and adult psychotherapy but it was shocking to witness the extent of avoidance of any *meaningful* or *purposeful* conversation with Ian about his early life trauma. It seemed 'crazy-making' that a boy aged 9, who had been taken into care because his parents had barely fed him, had witnessed his mother being beaten to the point of unconsciousness by his father, experienced the family home being raided by the police, had an older half-sister who had been sexually abused by 'an uncle' and yet no one spoke about anything. During the 14 years I have been regularly involved in contact between children, young people and their birth family, it has too often been the case that there is an enormous 'elephant in the room' which everyone steps around saying nothing!

This prompted me to wonder *what is contact for?*

## Contact today

The contact described above is not unlike many contacts that are happening today, in the sense that children in care and children who are adopted (or living in kinship care) are having contact with birth family members with whom they share a history of trauma which is left unspoken and unacknowledged within the relationship. The contact may be in person or via confidential 'letterbox'. In his article on contact, Loxterkamp[1] describes his concern regarding the many cases 'where the child has suffered maltreatment and contact is considered safe'. In social care, the dominant view is (often despite some misgivings) that contact should be promoted to support a positive connection to the birth family, to help ameliorate a sense of loss, reassure children about the wellbeing of family members and promote a sense and understanding of their own identity.

We must also consider the number of sibling contacts regularly taking place where traumatic life stories are avoided and left 'for when they feel ready to talk about it'. Similar to the concerns highlighted by Loxterkamp above, our experience is that fundamental information about a child's history has sometimes been withheld, minimised or glossed over by professionals, who advise adoptive parents and long-term foster carers to take a similar approach with the child. In attempts to present 'neutral and non judgemental' accounts of birth parents, fostered or adopted children are offered sanitised explanations such as 'your mum and dad loved you but couldn't look after you', 'she wasn't well', 'she was too young' or 'no one taught your mother how to care for you'. These nebulous descriptions, although well intended, can obscure reality and prevent children from grappling with core truths about their developmental experiences and lives. As is the way with exploring such painful material, many children and adults rarely feel ready to confront these issues and need some form of outside support to help them manage, and a framework for thinking about their history.

Ian, the boy Louis introduced at the beginning of this book, was the subject of an interim care order and saw his parents in the same contact centre over many months whilst his future was being decided by the court. Interim contact arrangements are recognised as necessary to support and sustain relationships between children and parents and are often the only means available to assess for reunification.[2]

However, concerns have been raised about the variable quality of some of the professional supervision, and the recorded observations which are submitted to the court during care proceedings. Others have proposed ways to change, improve and maximise the potential benefits of supervised contact, both for the children and parents.[3, 4, 5] The disruption and distress such arrangements can cause to the children and particularly babies and toddlers who experience 'high frequency contact' has also been the subject of increasing challenge and comment.[6] Similarly, the previously asserted contribution such high frequency contact makes to reunification has been challenged by more recent research studies.[7]

Interim proceedings that conclude with the making of a full care order and the decision that children are in need of permanent alternative care will involve care plans that include future contact arrangements.

Whilst most academics and researchers who consider the needs of children in permanent placements appear to agree that contact recommendations and plans for individual children need to be case-specific and reflect their unique experiences and circumstances,[8, 9] social workers, children's guardians and other professionals involved in making recommendations to the court tend to use a formulaic approach that is based upon the type of order being recommended.

The contact research studies that are referred to later in this chapter all highlight the dynamic nature of contact, the changing needs of the children and the need for regular reviews. The current system where contact arrangements are largely decided by the court at one particular point in time can make flexibility difficult, particularly if a cessation or reduction in frequency is indicated. When considering the timing and the way in which views about direct contact in adoption are made, Dr Peter Dale[10] advocates for the recognition of 'natural parents' role and needs and the long-term needs of the child as best being served by allowing for a period of independent therapeutic assessment of the birth parents' capacity to manage direct contact, which should occur following the making of a placement order.

Within the current legal framework, the decision about the frequency, structure and support of contact arrangements depends on whether the plan is for adoption, long-term foster care, residential care or kinship care. The expectation of the frequency of such contact changes, depending on which legal solution has been agreed, with those children placed for adoption most often (although not always) having minimal arrangements for contact with adult birth relatives (often indirect via a letterbox). Plans that are made and agreed for other permanent solutions are much more likely to include direct professionally supervised meetings, typically occurring at a frequency of six to eight times a year and sometimes significantly more. This is particularly the case with a kinship placement where the kinship carer is much more likely to supervise contact than is the case where a child is placed with agency foster carers to whom the child is unrelated.

However, as Caroline Lindsey states: 'The distinctions between the different forms of care are not always the most relevant factors for the child, despite the differences in the legal framework that play a part in determining how much and whether contact occurs.'[11] In other words, the wishes, feelings and thoughts the child has about contact and the impact the decisions have upon the child will not be determined by the legal framework.

The longer maltreated children have lived within their birth families the more significant their relationships with parents and other family members are likely to be. It is also likely that these same children have been exposed to chronically adverse and stressful experiences which in turn have shaped their neurological development, their ability to form (or allow formation of) meaningful attachments, their beliefs about themselves and others and their capacity for behavioural and emotional regulation.

Contact should be planned and managed primarily in the interests of the child and in supporting them in their recovery and need to develop a coherent narrative relating to their history of loss and trauma. It should be aimed at helping the child make the psychological adjustment required in being part of two families as well as facilitating an improved capacity for self-regulation. This is not a once-and-for-all process and presents an ongoing challenge for many children who are unable to grow up and live safely with their biological parents.

## Attachment theory

Considerations about the child's attachment to their caregivers, be that birth parents, foster carers or adoptive parents, are central considerations for professionals when planning for and supporting the children who are the subject of this book.

John Bowlby's attachment theory postulates that babies have an innate behavioural system designed to elicit the care and protection of caregivers (usually mothers). Given the level of helplessness of babies, these behaviours help to ensure survival of the species. Mothers have a reciprocal system designed to help them bond with the baby and meet their needs. When babies and young children are feeling safe within their environment, their attachment behaviours are complemented by exploratory behaviours, which are also instinctive. Therefore, the internal sense of security instilled (or downloaded) from the primary attachment relationship is transformed into a drive to explore the external world and all that comes with it.

Bowlby also developed the theory of the internal working model, which begins to emerge pre-verbally as the child forms general inferences about themselves and others based upon how they are treated by primary caretakers. As babies grow older their care-eliciting behaviours become more sophisticated and purposeful. The responses and behaviours of caregivers produce differing internal working models and attachment behaviours in children, which eventually organise into an attachment style. In the case of abuse and neglect, these inferences and the developing internal working model are likely to be negative, both in relation to the self and others. A child's perception of the world is prone to expecting threat, harsh responses or indifference.

The infant's internal working model develops within the context of a multisensory communication. This working model evolves within the developing right brain and is encoded in implicit unconscious memory. The sensitivity, tone and appropriateness of the parents/ caregivers' vocalisations, eye and body movements, sounds and smells all contribute to the development of the model and profoundly inform beliefs, which affect the child's ability to form loving relationships and healthy connections with others.

Attachment theory and methods of researching attachment security have played a significant role in illuminating our understanding of the psychological development of children and adults. Research into non-clinical populations has shown that 55 per cent of the adult population have 'secure' attachment status, therefore at least 45 per cent of us have an insecure style of relating. There are three insecure attachment presentations that have been identified as developing during early childhood. In non-clinical populations, the prevalence of insecure ambivalent resistant attachment is around 8 per cent, insecure avoidant 23 per cent and disorganised 15 per cent. Research into children brought up in neglectful or abusive environments shows that as many as 80 per cent develop disorganised attachments. These children behave unpredictably and have difficulty regulating their emotions. Disorganised attachment is strongly associated with later psychopathology.[12]

## Neuroscience and attachment

Bowlby hypothesised that an infant's capacity to manage stress is developed within the relationship with the mother, with her responses shaping the infant's developing coping responses. The work of clinicians and neuroscientists such as Allan Schore are affirming Bowlby's theories and have deepened our understanding of the mechanisms and areas of the brain involved in the infant's developing capacity for affect regulation (which develops in the right hemisphere of the brain) and the central importance of the attachment relationship and role played by the mother or primary caregiver.[13]

Research into the stress responses of toddlers who exhibited a disorganised attachment revealed that these children had higher cortisol levels and higher heart rates than all other attachment classifications.[14]

Neuroscience informs us that babies and toddlers' brains develop rapidly and sequentially, from the bottom (brain stem) to the top (cortex) and from the inside out. The neural systems which mediate social interaction, communication, empathy and the capacity to bond with others are all shaped by the nature, quantity and timing of early life relationships. Interpersonal experiences with primary caregivers literally shape the developing brain. The more a neural system is 'activated', the more that system changes to reflect the pattern of activation. Children exposed to significant threat will 're-set' their baseline state of arousal such that even when no external threats or demands are present they will be in a physiological state of persistent alarm. This means that when they do encounter even relatively small relationship stressors, the traumatised child will be more reactive and easily triggered into fight, flight or freeze responses. This increased baseline of arousal and response to perceived threat plays a major role in the various behavioural and cognitive problems associated with the traumatised child.

Whilst young children may initially respond to fear by becoming hyperaroused, showing and acting out their distress through their behaviour, a second, later-forming reaction to infant trauma is seen in dissociation, in which the child disengages from the stimuli in the external world. The child's dissociation in the midst of terror involves numbing, avoidance, compliance and restricted affect (the same pattern as adult PTSD).[15]

Van der Kolk *et al.* advocate moving away from labelling children with diagnoses such as reactive attachment or conduct disorders to using the term 'developmental trauma disorder'. This concept more accurately describes the consequences for babies and young children of living with day-to-day exposure of multiple/chronic forms of developmentally adverse experiences, including neglect, physical/ sexual abuse, witnessing domestic violence and abandonment.[16]

The insights that attachment theory and neuroscience bring to our understanding of the needs of the developmentally traumatised and emotionally troubled child informs the work of some of our most eminent therapeutic clinicians and practitioners, such as Kim Golding and Dan Hughes.[17, 18]

If developmentally traumatised children are to be offered a realistic opportunity of developing an improved capacity for regulation and increased resilience, they first need to be placed within a low stress, safe and secure environment. Caregivers need to understand that new experience is 'filtered' through past experience, as the brain makes associations between sensory signals co-occurring in any given moment in time. The child needs sensitively attuned carers who understand and meet the feelings that generate reactive behaviours. The child also needs a predictable, consistent, nurturing and structured routine, which is aimed at addressing their developmental stage (and needs) rather than chronological age (and needs). Change occurs through consistent, nurturing, patterned, right-brained experiences, which require multiple repetitions as a means of supporting the development of new healthier neural connections. An image to describe this process is of layer upon layer of healthy interactions that eventually create a more solid foundation to a child's lived experience.

## Adoption and attachment

Children who are placed for adoption between the ages of 4 and 8 are considered 'older and hard-to-place'. A longitudinal study carried out by Kaniuk, Steele and Hodges[19] into the changes in 'attachment representations' or 'internal working models' of children who were placed for adoption in this age group concluded that previously maltreated children were able to develop internal working models of parental figures that were more responsive and caring. However, the previous internal working models of neglectful, abusive or rejecting parent figures continued to exist alongside, although with diminishing potency. During times of stress and change, however, the earlier working models are likely to be activated, evoking feelings of confusion and anxiety. On this point these researchers conclude, 'It is not possible to wipe out or remove memory traces of early negative experiences. Indeed, neurobiology indicates that traces of early traumatic experiences will remain indefinitely in the primitive structures of the brain.'[20]

Although the studies we have read in relation to this research do not specify whether or not the children were having direct contact with the birth parents from whom they had been removed, a personal communication with Jeanne Kaniuk, one of the researchers/authors, indicated that such contact arrangements would have been highly unlikely.

Summarised below are Howe and Steele's[21] comments on contact arrangements for permanently placed children who have suffered 'severe maltreatment' and demonstrate disorganised attachment behaviours.

- Children with such experiences may be re-traumatised by contact with maltreating parent(s) and therefore experience the permanent carers as unable to protect them.

- When such children feel unsafe and insecure they will continue to employ psychological measures of defence which involve aggressive, controlling and distancing behaviours. Such behaviours place great strains on the carer–child relationship and increase the risk of placement disruption.

- However, if adopters possess high levels of sensitivity, empathy and reflective attunement they help children feel both safe and emotionally understood and such parenting capacities promote secure attachments and increase resilience.

- Secure and resilient children are better able to cope with the emotional challenges of difficult relationships, including those which evoke feelings of distress.

- Where children suffer re-traumatisation through contact the need to make the child feel safe and protected becomes the priority. Therefore, contact in the 'medium term would not be indicated'. However, some form of contact could be instigated at a later date, depending on whether or not the child has achieved the levels of resilience, psychological autonomy and reflective function that help equip them to deal with the emotional arousal the renewed contact with the once traumatising parent will trigger.

We might ask how the difference between 'maltreatment' and 'severe maltreatment' can be judged, given the research quoted earlier where 80 per cent of abused and neglected children go on to develop disorganised attachments which engender significant developmental and health risks throughout the lifespan. It is also possible that not all children who experience contact as traumatising display the reactive and disoriented behaviours typically associated with disorganised attachment; rather they could revert to the dissociative, shut down, compliant responses associated with earlier experiences of fear and terror.

## Case study: Sam

We recently worked with Sam, a young boy who had first been subject to care proceedings during his third year, where the court on recommendation of the guardian had directed ongoing contact with his birth father whilst the local authority sought an adoptive placement. Sam was in his third foster placement at that point, largely due to his challenging behaviour. A psychologist had assessed Sam as having a disorganised attachment. He knew that Sam had made disclosures to his foster carers about feeling scared of his father who he also said had abused him. The psychologist recommended that contact should cease. Yet when having contact with his father, Sam's behaviour was observed as being calm and appropriate by contact supervisors and the guardian, who therefore viewed this relationship as having a positive and stabilising influence, recommended contact continue. However, before and after contact he was very distressed, aggressive and oppositional, and continued to recount memories of abuse, telling his foster carer he was 'scared of daddy and did not want to see him'. In our view, what had been observed during contact was overcompliance and restricted affect, which were triggered by fear. Sam has since experienced a further three disrupted placements, making the prospect of the security that adoption could offer very remote.

## Contact research

Some research studies into contact report it to be a largely beneficial experience.[22, 23] On the other hand, a number of other studies into the impact of contact on children who are adopted or permanently fostered have reported that many children had unsettling experiences. For example, Macaskill[24] found that the impact of the experience for 57 per cent was both positive and negative, while 25 per cent experienced it as very negative. Wilson and Sinclair[25] found that nearly six out of ten fostered children experienced contact as distressing. Selwyn[26] found that 21 per cent of the children in her study were physically/sexually abused during unsupervised contact whilst in the care system and in adoptive/long-term foster placements. The most recent study into direct contact in adoption was conducted by Neil et al.[27] during which they ascertained the adoptive parents' views on how contact was working at two points in time. At time point two, 45 per cent (slightly more than at point one) of arrangements were working well, with the remaining 55 per cent experiencing unresolved issues. Fifty-one per cent of the children in this study were having contact with a birth relative (all but one of whom was a parent) who had been their main carer and had been implicated in neglecting and abusing them. Sixty-seven per cent of the arrangements that were not working well involved these adults.

Many children whose birth parents are unable to care for them safely are not placed for adoption. Sadly, it has been our experience that too many children who are placed in permanent foster care experience regular contact that risks re-traumatisation, undermines capacity for recovery, or for developing improved affect regulation and a more secure 'internal working model'.

## Triangles and quadrangles – relationships in adoption and foster care

The term the 'adoption triangle' emerged out of early research and therapeutic support for adoptees, their adoptive parents and birth mothers.

Early research and clinical comment on adoption focused on relinquished babies and their psychological adjustment as children and adults. Research also began to focus on the psychological adjustment of the other key people in the child's developing sense of self: their adoptive and birth mothers, the impact of loss and the interlinking ways they and the adoptee thought about and acknowledged one another and how each of them adapted. 'Genealogical bewilderment'[28] was a term developed to describe the negative effects on many adoptees who grew up in closed confidential adoptions. Along with the fact that as adults many adoptees wanted information and the possibility of tracing their birth mothers, this eventually changed adoption laws and practices and informed the evolution of 'open adoption'. This in turn led to an increasing number of adoptive families and birth mothers maintaining a level of direct or indirect contact.

In *The Adoption Triangle Revisited: A Study of Adoption 'Search and Reunion Experiences'*, the authors sum up the issues facing the relinquished adoptee, adoptive and birth parents as: 'communication and openness are two of the key challenges and dilemmas for all parties in the adoption triangle.'[29]

During the last decade there has been growing interest in the interplay of the adoptive and foster carers' attachment status[30] and the effect this has on the child's adjustment in placement. In Kanuik, Steele and Hodges' study of attachment representations referred to earlier,[31] a small percentage of the children's sense of attachment security did not improve, a finding that correlated with the adoptive mothers' 'unresolved attachment status'.

Most contact studies highlight the fact that foster carers and adoptive parents (and kinship carers, come to that) can experience contact arrangements as stressful. Research into contact has highlighted the adoptive parents' level of communicative openness and willingness to accept the child's shared 'kinship' and connection with the birth family in maintaining contact arrangements. The attitudes of foster carers in managing contact is also considered. For those researchers interested in the dynamics of attachment, connections can be made between the attachment status of the substitute parent and their capacity to manage the process of contact, both for themselves and their children (as highlighted in Howe and Steele's recommendations on contact for 'severely maltreated' children).[32]

Others have pointed out the significance for adopters of not being adequately prepared in anticipating their own feelings when managing contact arrangements.[33]

Research into contact has also taken account of the attitudes and experiences of the birth parents and other relatives involved in the arrangements, including focusing upon their adjustment to the loss of their child to adoption or permanent foster care.

Openness and communication about a child's birth family, history and experiences are very important for children who have been removed from birth parents due to maltreatment and are being permanently parented by others. The what, when, how and by whom this information is communicated to the developing child is much more complex *and* is intrinsically linked with issues of contact.

We believe that the roles professionals play in deciding on, preparing for and supporting contact can and does have a significant impact on whether or not children can benefit from contact arrangements and the way their adopters, foster carers and birth relatives experience it.

In *The Ecology of Adoption*, Palacios[34] explored the complexity of the systems involved in adoption and the importance of the

'Process-Person-Context-Time' and used the term 'adoption quadrangle' to emphasise the centrality of the role professionals play in the adoption process. This looks at 'what we know and don't know' as a result of various research in the field of adoption. Palacios makes a number of points about the role and knowledge base of professionals within the field of adoption, for example:

- Poor professional follow-up and lack of adequate support were implicated in studies of disrupted placements.

- Professional decisions are based on consensus or on personal or cultural biases.

While these comments were not referring specifically to the professionals' role in relation to contact, they are nevertheless pertinent to the debate. As Logan and Smith state, 'Decisions about contact must…be made in relation to the needs, characteristics and circumstances of particular children and their families rather than in response to general evidential rules or ideological commitment.'[35]

Harris and Lindsey (2002)[36] carried out a small qualitative study using interpretive phenomenological analysis to explore the meanings and beliefs that professionals involved in making decisions and recommendations about contact brought to the task. The professionals involved in the study included judges, guardians *ad litem* (now replaced by children's guardians), psychologists and psychiatrists. They found that while these professionals were using similar ideas and terms, for example, attachment and bonding, they were using them in different ways. Participants also described contradictions within their own beliefs that led to dilemmas about recommending contact or not.

Children and families need professionals and agencies that can offer informed and reflective assessments in relation to contact plans and implementation, including support that enables children to benefit. Contact arrangements need to be mindful of the impact and enduring nature of early relational trauma. Contact should be structured and supported in ways that empower and work towards enabling children to make sense of their past and 'the emotional arousal' that is triggered when meeting with a parent who was previously neglectful or abusive.

Adopters and foster carers are often uncertain about the best way to talk with their children about their early experiences. A frequent concern is how to explain and talk about what their birth parents did or didn't do and not sound negative, overwhelm the child, or set the child up for experiencing conflicts of loyalty. These children and their foster and adoptive families need professionals who are 'open and communicative' about the child's early life experiences, are open to listening to how the child feels and thinks about those facts and about their contact experiences. Although explanations need to be kept simple for young children, they still need information delivered in a way that helps authenticate their *felt* experiences. Even young children like Sam, who was still in his third year when he began making disclosures about abuse, have confused and fearful memories they want and need to communicate. Importantly, children should have time and support to prepare for contact and support to reflect and debrief afterwards. Essential to this process is the role of attentive, curious adults who do not 'move children away' from the authenticity of their thoughts, feelings, hopes, doubts, fears or concerns which require active exploration. Educating children and parents about the physiological responses of trauma and fear, opening general discussion on the kinds of thoughts and feelings fostered or adopted children might experience, also builds reflection and helps to 'normalise' reactions that can trigger overwhelming shame for the maltreated child. Involving adoptive parents and foster carers means they are on hand to offer support, co-regulation and to facilitate a shared understanding and reflection between parent and child.

Contact with birth parents has the power either to support the child's journey of recovery or hinder it. Making contact beneficial also means working with birth relatives in a way that prepares and enables them to do the best they can to help and support their child on the journey of recovery.

All contact arrangements should be regularly reviewed, particularly at key ages and stages of development for children and young persons. We have developed a reference chart (see Appendix) which could help inform contact reviews and the information and support that might be required and helpful at particular stages.

Often there are a range of professionals involved in assessments and delivery of services to adoptive and fostered children. These various professionals such as social workers, guardians, contact supervisors, foster carers, Independent Reviewing Officers, psychologists and psychiatrists have varying responsibilities and actual or perceived authority and/or power. In such circumstances there is huge potential for disagreement and splitting.

Paula Conway, a clinical psychologist and psychoanalytic psychotherapist, addresses such issues. When describing the coping strategies of children who have experienced abuse and neglect, she states that:

> to protect themselves and to find some order in chaos these children can fall back on creating a world of clear cut 'good objects' versus equally clear cut 'bad ones'. From moment to moment, the world – or a particular figure in it – either holds the longed-for promise of perfection or turns devastatingly bad.[37]

She goes on to explain how professionals and services working with such disturbed but understandable patterns of communication may find themselves affected by these powerful processes:

> Processes which interfere with clear rational thinking... professionals can find themselves convinced that this really is an awful birth parent/adopter/foster carer/social worker/guardian/teacher...and that they are the only one who understands, has got it right.[38] (p.21)

When we provide training or consultation on contact, questions we often ask participants are 'What is contact for?' or 'Is contact a good thing?' These simple questions begin to tap into core beliefs about contact. They are questions that lead us into thinking about our families and what they are for, the nature of sibling relationships and what is often described as 'blood ties', a person's belonging to and connection with a biological 'other'. Conversely, views can be dismissive on the value of contact with people who have played a significant role in relation to a child but who do not have a blood tie. In discussions about contact in our training and consultations, statements by participants often begin to introduce words such as should, ought, always, never and must. These words are rooted in belief systems that are framed as 'right' or 'wrong' and black or white. The ability to tolerate the grey areas of decision making and integrate one's thinking is challenged by anxiety. The thoughts, feelings and experiences that are evoked by contact with our own parent(s), siblings, grandparents and family are often complex, powerful and as one course participant described 'rarely beige'!

These charged feelings and belief systems can create difficult dynamics between professionals working with maltreated children, particularly when contact is an issue. These same professionals are not only dealing with the unbearable experiences of the child but also those of the birth relatives and, particularly, the birth mother and father. These dynamics can create increased potential for splitting and have in our experience led to the making of inappropriate contact plans where the needs of birth parents have taken priority, and direct contact arrangements have been agreed as a means of offering consolation. The split within the professionals working with and on behalf of Sam (the 3-year-old referred to earlier), for example, has had serious implications for him and his potential recovery.

Individuals or teams who are working with issues related to trauma, neglect, violence and family disruption can find taking an integrative position immensely challenging when conflicting grey areas are being debated. The following list may provide some insight into identifying when splitting could be taking place:

- Are your opinions becoming entrenched?

- Do you find yourself taking a particular dislike to a family member or professional? Is this dislike out of proportion to the event?

- Is it difficult to hear both sides of a particular discussion?

- Do you find yourself interrupting or 'switching off' with the family or professionals?

- Can you observe a process of polarisation in either your discussions or in the group you are with? Does the atmosphere appear charged or heated?

- In what way does the dynamic being acted out in your (or the group's) discussion mirror the dynamic of the family you are intervening with?

- Is there a way in which the dynamics of the drama triangle (perpetrator, rescuer and victim) are being acted out in the support network? Which position are you taking? What different position or approach could you assume?

- What might be the way that you could share this insight (if appropriate) with the colleague, family member or group you are dealing with? Is there an image you could also share that somehow describes your experience (such as 'I have an image of two teams pulling in a tug of war and neither team is giving an inch!')?

- What needs to happen to integrate this splitting process? What needs to be named?

Finally, although there are many who advocate the benefits of ongoing direct contact, there is in fact no long-term study (i.e. into adulthood) of the impact of contact on children who have experienced abuse or what makes such contact beneficial in the longer term. The long-term research available in respect of contact in adoption was carried out with adoptees who were relinquished.[39] On the basis of this research, practices and philosophies have developed that encourage ideas of the child being at the centre of an extended kinship. This includes the importance of the adopters (and also foster carers) embracing this reality and therefore being ready and willing to enter into routine, regular and amiable contact arrangements. This can involve, for example, visits to zoos or museums, picnics or going to restaurants.

On the basis of this research the practice of agreeing to a routine of contact has been developed for the maltreated child. Even when it is clear that such contact needs professional supervision, it is still viewed as being essentially beneficial. Whilst the relinquishing birth mother and the birth mother whose children have been removed on the basis of neglect and abuse do share some similarities, for example disenfranchised grief, there are also many differences in how their lives progress and evolve. Significantly, there are also differences within the developmental experiences of their children. The relinquished baby experiences the trauma of separation. While the maltreated child may experience the trauma of separation too, they have also experienced developmental adversity as a consequence of abuse and or neglect. Currently the research that is available indicates that as many as 50 per cent of children experience distress as a result of contact. We risk doing a disservice to both the maltreated child and their birth parents if we start out by agreeing a routine of direct contact which may later have to be halted in the interests of the child or because a birth relative is unable to manage the arrangements. However, we also do a disservice to both if we rule out the possibility of any direct contact. It is our view that birth relatives should always be encouraged to join and take part in a letterbox arrangement, with the understanding that there may well come a time when a facilitated direct contact session will be necessary and helpful for the child. In any event, any agreement for direct contact should include a statement that it is not possible to know in advance how the child will experience contact and how their needs and wishes in relation to contact will change over time; therefore, all arrangements will be regularly reviewed. A decision that no direct contact is indicated should not result in the birth parents and other significant relatives being left without information about their child, and services should be developed that offer direct access to support from an informed professional, say once or twice each year. An effectively run and proactive letterbox system is the lynchpin that enables all future possibilities of contact for the adopted child.

## Contact and the internet

Prior to the development of the internet and social networking sites, an adopted child's desire for 'reunion' and 'the search' was unlikely to be acted upon until the adoptee reached the age of at least 18. Today, the developing adoptee is no longer protected by this age barrier as they and members of their birth family can seek and find each other using one of many routes available via the internet, including social networking.

The Evan B. Donaldson Adoption Institute, based in New York, issued a report in December 2012 on the impact of the internet on adoption. Entitled *Untangling the Web: The Internet's Transformative Impact on Adoption*, the report opens with the following summary:

> It is difficult to describe the extent to which the Internet is changing the everyday realities of adoption – and the lives of the millions of people it encompasses – without using words that sound hyperbolic. But a yearlong examination of the effects of this very new technology on a very old social institution indicates that they are systemic, profound, complex and permanent. Social media, search engines, blogs, chat rooms, webinars, photo-listings and an array of other modern communications tools, all facilitated by the Internet, are transforming adoption practices, challenging current laws and policies, offering unprecedented opportunities and resources, and raising critical ethical, legal and procedural issues about which adoption professionals, legislators and the personally affected parties, by their own accounts, have little reliable information, research or experience to guide them.[40]

The report recommends Eileen Fursland's *Facing up to Facebook*[41] as the most comprehensive guide for adoptive parents, adding:

> Parents also need to understand the many ways that youth can be reached by or can reach out to original family members beyond the home computer. Many young people have smartphones or gaming systems (like Nintendo DS and Wii) that allow access to the Internet and, of course, they can and do use the phones or computers of friends, in libraries and at other public sites.[42]

The ability to make in-depth searches into ancestry and trace people through the internet at the click of a button has created significant issues for adopted and fostered children, particularly in two areas:

1. The possibility for children and young people to make unmediated contact through the internet and social networking sites indicates a need for foster carers (and social workers) and adoptive parents to initiate (at what some may perceive to be an early age) more authentic and coherent life story work with their children.

2. Social workers and other professionals may need to be proactive in mediating and facilitating indirect and direct contact before a young person reaches the age 18.

Over the last three years, Louis has experienced a surge in referrals for therapy of adopted or fostered children who have made some form of unstructured contact with their birth family. The most extreme story is of a 14-year-old boy whose adoptive placement was in difficulties. He wanted access to his files to obtain more information about his early life history. His social worker had advised him that he needed to wait until he was 18 years old. The next day, he searched for and found his birth parents via the internet. Within 36 hours, he had made telephone contact with his birth father and within 48 hours he boarded a train and went to live with the birth family again. Eight months later, he was still living with them and had been caught on two occasions by the police stealing and buying class A drugs (cocaine). Perhaps if this social worker had been open to his request for more information and offered to access his background history and make enquiries about their current circumstances, this boy would not have moved so quickly into reuniting. He would also have had the availability of a safe independent adult who could mediate and liaise with his adoptive parents about his wishes, and support him in thinking through the implications of meeting up with his birth family. If he was then stating that he wanted to meet them, accepting and working with his wishes and feelings in this way may then have led to his being able to accept the social worker contacting birth family members on his behalf and facilitating a contact meeting which focused on what he needed and wanted to know and experience.

More common examples are those of children between 10 and 15 years old who have made various clumsy attempts to discuss their interest in birth family matters. The underlying curiosity has not been picked up, or has been discounted, and has resulted in children making contact via Facebook or texting their birth family to make contact. Almost without exception, adoptive parents noticed changes (which were sometimes dramatic) in mood, character and behaviour of their children following these contacts. All of these children had used one of the many means of electronic communications which parents cannot oversee or control.

Older children in foster care may well have agreed contact with various members of their birth family including via social media, phone calls and text. Where children have been abused, prohibitions on contact with specific adults can help protect against the disruption of placements and further abuse.[43] The risk for these vulnerable youngsters is that those who have abused them in the past will find it so much easier to find ways of re-establishing contact.

Therefore, it is now imperative for foster carers and adoptive parents to initiate conversations about birth families and show *curiosity* about contact. This is markedly different from a parent trying to force a child to talk about contact. It is simply about being open and receptive to the *idea* of contact or further life story work. Children will easily pick up non-verbal cues such as furrowed brows, tightened mouths and clipped speech patterns if there is reluctance or hesitance in their parent's communication.

Of course there is also the possibility that a birth relative will search and find a child or young person, which can have a very unsettling effect. The person making the contact will not necessarily be a parent. We have heard of situations where older siblings, step-siblings or cousins have approached an adopted young person, which has then led to a flurry of communications from multiple members of the birth family.

One of the responsibilities of professionals involved with adoptive families is to support parents, children and young people in opening up discussions about the child or young person's thoughts and feelings about their birth family and their history.

## Contact in foster care

The roles and expectations of social workers who have responsibilities for children and young people placed in permanent foster care are significant, and the role is fundamentally different to that played in adoption. The local authority retains the role of 'corporate parent' and the foster carer has limited influence and power in relation to the plans that are made for contact. In any event, given the child remains looked after there remains a duty to promote contact. There is frequently an expectation and recommendation from the child's guardian and the court that direct contact *will* take place, as a minimum during each school holiday, and the local authority care plan will incorporate such expectations. This is a formulaic plan, developed to avoid disruption of school attendance and learning and to ensure that frequency is high enough to 'maintain links' with birth family. It is not based on an individual assessment of the likely impact of the child's history of maltreatment, their needs for a secure placement or how the child can be best supported in recovering from early adversity. Some children may have significantly higher levels of contact. As already highlighted, research into long-term or permanent foster care has revealed a mixed picture of the success of contact arrangements.

A more recent study into long-term and permanent foster care[44] made the following analysis relating to contact. When children were relatively comfortable with what the study termed 'dual membership', that is, able to feel part of both their birth and foster families, 'there was more likely to be contact between the foster and birth families, an acceptance that it was possible for children to be part of both families and a belief that this could be managed by a process of negotiation e.g. around contact' and 'It was not unusual for children, including those in relatively stable placements, to feel concerned about their parents and uncertain or preoccupied about their role in their birth families…but even for some children who were apparently well settled, their concerns about their birth family were often underestimated by their carers.'[45]

The report goes on to make recommendations to the children's social workers.

This is an area in which social workers, who should be familiar with both foster and birth families and can be a bridge between them, need to focus their work with children in long-term placements. It is very hard for children to be left to manage these family relationships unaided, especially if birth family contact arrangements include travel by taxi and supervision by workers who do not know both families and are not in a position to help children manage feelings about their dual family memberships.

A research study into experiences of parents of children growing up in foster care[46] commented similarly. One of the most striking findings from the study was how many parents had almost no contact at all with the foster carers who were looking after their children; they were not invited to reviews where carers were present, nor able to see them or speak to them around contact. Some parents had not talked face to face with the carers since a first meeting as many as eight years ago.

Children were left with the task of moving between the two 'parents', managing the amount of information they passed about each to the other, and somehow almost certainly managing the two sets of parents' anxiety about each other.

We have encountered a number of situations where contact plans have been determinedly followed and implemented despite situations that should have caused concern and reason for reappraisal.

## Case study: Joe

One example is a 10-year-old, Joe, whose birth mother continually harangued and interrogated him during his contact sessions, angry that he was settling with his foster carers. The boy was protesting via his foster carers about having to attend, but the professionals were questioning the motivations and validity of the foster carers' interpretations of what he was saying. This was despite the fact that the contact supervisor's reports highlighted some of the inappropriate and undermining behaviours of this angry, mentally unstable birth mother.

## Case study: Jenny

A 12-year-old girl, Jenny, had been placed in permanent foster care due to neglect. Jenny had learning difficulties and was delayed in her social and emotional development. There were concerns in placement that she would leave faeces on the floor of the bathroom or in the bath. She was also prone to making confused verbal communications and often seemed disconnected. She had been in her foster placement for over two years and her progress had reached a plateau.

Jenny had a variety of contact arrangements with various family members, who she saw every school holiday. There was direct contact with an older brother and some contact with her birth mother and grandparents. The mother, who refused to accept the need for her children to be in the care of the local authority, often turned up to the contact sessions with a 'boyfriend'. Contact with her older brother, which was supervised by his foster carer, raised concerns about sexualised behaviours between the two. Later, when this was being discussed with his foster carer, the brother disclosed sexual abuse when living with his birth mother. A younger sibling had experienced a disrupted adoption, and sexualised behaviour had been raised as one of the concerns. It had been agreed that the police would be involved and the brother agreed to being interviewed. There was also a plan to interview Jenny. However, the planned contact with the birth mother was not halted and although the man friends she brought with her were not allowed to join her in the contact, we have wondered what it meant to this vulnerable girl, knowing they were out there in the car park waiting. When the police came to interview Jenny she was not able to discuss any experiences of sexual behaviour or abuse.

Many professionals involved in adoption know that experiencing a sense of safety in adoption can lead to maltreated children needing to disclose more details about their earlier experiences of abuse. We need to be mindful of the possibility that permanently fostered children may also be burdened by intrusive memories, thoughts and feelings and that contact arrangements can inhibit the child or young person from gaining support in resolving these.

Notably, both of these children were expected to attend these stressful contact sessions without the support of their foster carers, and experienced a changing array of escorts and contact supervisors whose knowledge and understanding of the history of the relationship was extremely limited. Such contact structures undermine the potential value and benefit for the child.

Whilst we know that adopted children don't always receive the life story work, books or later life letters that could help them develop their understanding of their life experiences, it seems that children and young people who are fostered very rarely receive such information, even though their need is as legitimate as that of the adopted child. Contact needs to be reviewed meaningfully with the children and their foster carers to ensure that the experience is supporting and not undermining their recovery.

# A psychological approach to thinking about and supporting recovery

A review of research and clinical criteria for assessing contact in domestic violence was commissioned by Dame Butler-Sloss and carried out by Dr Claire Sturge and Dr Danya Glaser.[47] The focus was on the impact of domestic violence on children and the implications for contact. The report states that it would be emotionally harmful for a child if there was: 'continuation of unresolved situations, for example, where the child has a memory or belief about a negative aspect of the contact parent, for example, abuse, and where this is just left as if unimportant.'

The report goes on to point out that where abuse or neglect has been established, any denial or:

> refusal to look at apologising and other means of helping the child deal with the situation can be particularly destructive to the child both in terms of failing to validate their experience and failing to validate the child as a valid individual as a consequence and in terms of failing to recognise and help the child in his or her need to come to terms with what has happened.[48]

Whilst decisions about contact during and on conclusion of care proceedings focus on a much wider range of considerations than the impact of domestic violence upon a child (although this is often *one* of the background experiences of children), exposure to neglect and abuse are also harmful and continue to affect a child's social, emotional and cognitive development, self-perception and the way relationships with others are experienced.

Much has been written and discussed about the psychological meaning for adoptees of having been relinquished or 'given up' by their birth mothers. Often the internalised message (no matter how positively the adoption story has been relayed by their adoptive parents) is that they were not important enough, there was something wrong with them or else it was a straightforward case of having been a 'bad baby'. Children who have been exposed to neglect and abuse, whether they are adopted or in foster care, are equally likely to believe that it was something about them that caused the abuse and the resulting loss of their relationships with parents and significant others. For these children an apology from and an acceptance of responsibility by the parent(s) for what went wrong, along with a message of acceptance and permission to settle with their adoptive or other alternative carer(s), can make a significant contribution towards their developmental recovery.

Sometimes children actively seek to engage birth parents and others in discussions about the past. In the Macaskill (2002) and Neil *et al.* (2011) contact studies referred to earlier, there were children whose distress was exacerbated by the fact that a birth relative refused to acknowledge or discuss their traumatic memories.

As we have discussed, many children in the care system have troubled early life histories and the increasing number of older children, who are unlikely to be adopted but do need long-term placements, may be having regular contact where the general aim is to 'maintain links and relationships and promote identity'.

It is worth considering the question: links with what? How can a meaningful and healthy identity be promoted if it is built on a foundation of relational trauma that has never been acknowledged in a meaningful way between birth parent and child? The elephant in the room will continue to undermine the original and good intention of enabling a child to grow into a confident, emotionally literate young adult who has internalised a *coherent* understanding of the story of their life. Ian, the boy described earlier in the chapter, was a case in point.

## Case study: Ian (cont.)

Meetings with Ian's foster carers confirmed an immense anxiety on his part which was communicated through his behaviour. Prior to contact, Ian would become angry, avoidant and had taken to hoarding food beneath his bed and in his wardrobe. It was becoming increasingly common for him to soil himself and then hide his underwear. Following a contact, Ian found it difficult to settle or sleep and his self-care had deteriorated. When Louis met Ian and explored contact, he was able to acknowledge the worry and responsibility he felt for his birth mother as well as his confused and fearful feelings about his birth father. In later meetings, he described his adapted response to both parents when saying 'the only thing I could do was smile...I knew dad would be angry if I didn't look happy... the same with mum; it would shut her up...stop her from being angry or starting to cry'. The guilt Ian felt for being safe and the fear he experienced when meeting his birth father would cause him to surround himself with cushions and soft toys when he went to bed.

It was clear that Ian, his birth mother and birth father all brought many unresolved issues to their contact meetings and that both parents required significant support. In this case, it was also evident that the birth father had not been willing to engage with therapeutic intervention and was in denial about the frequency of incidences of domestic violence and his alcohol abuse. The birth mother had received a number of interventions that had not enabled her to make the kind of progress where she was able to put Ian's or her other children's needs ahead of her own. The Sturge and Glaser[47] report emphasises 'the centrality of the child's needs' in order to ensure the child's mental health where some form of trauma has been confirmed. Therefore, we can conclude that meaningful contact can be undermined by:

- a lack of structure and therapeutic planning

- an absence of purpose (what is the aim and whom is the contact really for?)

- a mutual silence or avoidance that does not acknowledge why a child is not living with their birth family

- a lack of exploration of painful issues that prohibits a child from creating a coherent narrative regarding their past, present and future.

For children who become adopted or are in long-term foster care, life story work or books can also undermine a child's ability to form a secure sense of attachment with the substitute parents, or develop a positive sense of identity and self-esteem when there is an avoidance of exploring what really happened in the past. A muddled and incoherent narrative is offered that is too often conveyed in terms of 'mum and dad loved me but they couldn't look after me'. Dan Siegel describes in the DVD, *Trauma, Brain and Relationship: Helping Children Heal,*[49] the need for children and their carers to be able to enter 'the mouth of the trauma' and work through difficult material. If this is to happen, how can contact be made more of a meaningful process, thus gaining a more coherent narrative of the trauma story; one that offers the potential for some healing?

## CHAPTER 2

# How to Facilitate Contact

## A Structured Process

Facilitated contact involves planning and structure and involves three stages:

Preparation    Facilitated contact    Debriefing

## Case study: Ian (cont.)

The contact for Ian, the boy described in Chapter 1, was assessed as being of a poor quality and his behaviour both pre- and post-contact was a cause for concern. The outcome of the care proceedings was that Ian's needs would be best met by not being returned to the care of either of his birth parents.

### Preparation

Ian's behaviours as well as his views and feelings had been taken into account by the court in coming to the decision. Ian had acknowledged in his meetings with his social worker that he was worried about both of his birth parents, as well as feeling angry, muddled and fearful at times. The court's decision on future contact was that this should be at the discretion of the local authority but with an expectation that it should occur at regular intervals. Ian's social worker and foster carer felt he was relieved when he was told he would not be returning to live with his parents. He said he wanted to know that his parents were OK and thought he would want to see them sometimes.

Some months later, and following on from some contact sessions that had been unsettling for Ian, the possibility of a facilitated contact meeting was discussed with social services.

His social worker asked him if he would be willing to be involved in a facilitated contact in which he could be supported by the social worker (and his foster carers who would be present). He was helped to prepare a list of questions and/or statements about his life with his birth family and the recent contacts.

During this exploratory phase, the possibility that Ian may have some good memories from when he lived with his birth parents was also acknowledged and there was space and permission for Ian to explore these memories.

## Preparation: working with and supporting birth parents

Key to making facilitated contact work for and benefit the child is the preparation that is done with birth parents or relatives by professionals. A recognition of the support needs of parents and other significant relatives where children have been removed from their family network and the plan is for adoption was formally recognised in The Adoption Act 2002. Research into the availability and effectiveness of the support being offered for direct contact was undertaken by Dr Elsbeth Neil and colleagues, as part of an Adoption Research initiative, the results of which were published in 2011.[1] There are two very useful summaries, numbered 8 and 9, of findings and recommendations for practice. A summary of the need for birth relative support states:

> Birth relatives' needs for support changed at different stages of the care and adoption process. After placement, they wanted information about their child's welfare and to be helped to participate constructively in contact plans.[2]

The value of such services being made available to birth parents is summed up as a key message in summary 9:

> Investment in accessible and sensitive support services for birth relatives represents an investment in service users with long-standing and multiple problems. It is also an investment in the wellbeing of adopted children and adoptive parents both in the present and in the future. As one birth mother put it:

> All I can do now is try and make the best of my life so that when my children come looking for me in the future they will find a well balanced woman rather than the mess they left behind.[3]

Sadly, the provision and quality of such services is variable and not generally extended to relatives where the plan for the children is permanency through long-term foster care or Special Guardianship.

Over many years Elsie has worked with a variety of birth relatives in a variety of settings including as a local authority social worker to help prepare and support them in managing a facilitated contact session. Most often, but not exclusively, this work has been done with birth mothers whose children have been removed and subsequently placed for adoption or in long-term foster care.

The background issues highlighted by Louis in Ian's situation are typical. Parents who have themselves experienced abuse and/or neglect in their own childhoods have mental health issues, in that their psychological development is impaired and/or they are experiencing depression, anxiety and have turned to drugs and/or alcohol as a means of trying to self-regulate and manage life. The arrival of a baby is a source of further stress for parents whose capacity to cope with stress is already compromised; babies affected by substance misuse during pregnancy can be difficult to soothe, increasing the mother's stress levels. Thus, parents are further dysregulated or distressed and may increase their use of drugs and alcohol as a means of 'self-medicating'.

Sadly, many of the birth parents of children we have worked with have not been able to make reparation as they have died prematurely due to their substance abuse or risk-laden lifestyles. It has been possible, however, to approach another relative, a grandparent, aunt or uncle and ask them to undertake a reparative facilitated contact session with the child.

A frequent response of social workers who are asked about approaching a birth parent to discuss working towards a facilitated contact is that the parent is unlikely to engage. Sometimes this is the case, but there have also been many instances where birth parents have responded positively.

## How to prepare

Preparation for a facilitated contact where the child's experience has been one of trauma caused to them through abuse and neglect can take one to several sessions. It is important to start by letting parents know that they still have a significant role to play in supporting their child's development through their role and conduct in contact. It is equally important to acknowledge the parent's own difficulties with learning or mental illness and any painful experiences, in childhood, the legacy this had on their capacity to parent, as well as the loss of their role as their child's day-to-day parent.

For those parents who have sadly abused or maltreated their children, it is common that they themselves may have experienced poor care or abuse. Therefore, changing the 'trans-generational loop' of abusive behaviour can be a motivational and therapeutic process.

Giving general information to birth parents and relatives about what supports a child's healthy development when being brought up in substitute families can help them in thinking through the positive contribution they can continue to make to their child's wellbeing. An example is being given permission to be happy with their adoptive parents or foster carers and permission not to have to feel responsible for the past or the wellbeing of the birth parent.

When working with and supporting birth parents in preparing to apologise and take responsibility for the harm they have caused their children, the reality of how difficult this will be for them to do so needs acknowledgement and empathy. A starting place could be to wonder if any of the adults who hurt them when they were children ever acknowledged the harm they did to them and what difference that might have made to them. This is their chance to do something different and positively contribute to their child's future healthy development.

Sometimes parents either deny or have buried any memory they may have of the trauma their child experienced while living with them. Parents who have been heavy substance abusers may have impaired memories or have been so 'out of it' at times that they cannot remember. Explaining the impact of substance abuse on behaviour and recall can help birth parents contextualise their own and their child's experience. Sharing details of some of the painful memories their child has shared and the questions their child may have about what and why certain things happened can help parents recall or at least understand the importance of acknowledging the child's perception of what life with them was like. Often children are also concerned to know that their parents are managing their lives, and balancing the sharing of painful information with some of the child's positive memories of living with them and the progress the child makes in placement can help support the process of enabling the birth parent to meet the challenge of a planned contact session.

Frequently, adoptive and foster parents are very grateful to birth parents/relatives who are prepared to enter into this process of facilitated contact, and conveying their appreciation can also support the birth relative in managing the task.

In some situations birth parents and adopters have not met. In these circumstances it is important to arrange for them to meet prior to the facilitated contact session taking place. Both sets of parents will need support in advance and during this pre-contact meeting.

Everyone should be prepared for the probability that at different times, different people may become tearful or upset and that is natural to the process. Birth family members can be helped to think through how they would manage or support one another if this occurred, or if undertaking the session alone, then agreeing how a facilitator may offer support.

Most facilitated contacts are structured for the birth family to leave at the end and the child to remain in the room, yet there may be exceptions depending on the needs of the child. It is also to be made clear that no gifts are brought to the contact.

Professionals also need to prepare the practical issues in terms of assessing the venue, the timings and arrival of all parties (with the child and foster carers arriving before the birth family to give the child a chance to orientate themselves). Professionals also need to make sure that the venue is comfortable, safe and as nurturing as possible. Food and drink may also be provided as a form of nurture.

On occasions, the professionals involved in the contact meet beforehand to discuss the contact and ensure that everyone is clear about the plan, its structure and who is responsible for what, including contact centre staff.

Professionals also need to ensure that there are opportunities for all three parties to debrief following on from the contact session (see John and Simon case studies in Chapter 8).

## How did facilitated contact work out for Ian?

### Preparation
Both birth parents, who had resumed their relationship, were contacted to see if they would be willing to take part in a facilitated contact, and the nature of the contact was made clear. The vital role they still had to play in Ian's life through contact was emphasised, as was the importance of their being able to acknowledge the trauma and distress Ian had experienced while in their care.

A further meeting with Ian's birth parents, fairly close in time to the facilitated contact, helped them to prepare their own responses to his questions and statements. The parents were also helped to provide their own appropriate statements and questions. In this case, the parents needed support to take responsibility for their domestic violence and respond to a particular question where Ian had asked them if they remembered an occasion on his birthday when his father hit him and broke his birthday present. At more than one point, the father said he could not manage this, yet when exploring his resistance, it emerged that he had been beaten by his father as a child. He could see history repeating itself through his actions, which was very painful to admit. However, he began to realise how important it was for Ian that he take responsibility, show remorse and say how sorry he felt about what he had done. Ian's mother was supported to acknowledge the ongoing violence, express her sorrow that she was not able to keep him safe and how scary this must have felt to him.

The foster carers were asked to be involved, and it was explained that Ian desperately needed caring, empathic adults present to support him and also be able to understand the process. The aim was also to enable the birth parents to thank the foster carers for caring for Ian and keeping him safe.

An important aspect of the facilitated contact in Ian's case was that time was made to think through and even *rehearse* with Ian what the contact would be like. This process was helped by a previous session in which Louis had shared with Ian and his foster carers some general information about our fight, flight and freeze responses. In getting ready for the contact Ian was first helped to think about his seating position in the room and where he would feel 'safe'. This *orientation* to one's environment is a feature of Peter Levine's Somatic Experiencing®, an approach that takes into account a person's physiological and *felt sense* responses (gut feelings).[4] This kind of preparation also follows the advice of Van Der Kolk and other trauma experts: in that having some control and choice over how one manages difficult situations is empowering and offers opportunities for developing a sense of mastery.

It was interesting to note that Ian's initial response was dismissive in relation to thinking about where he might sit. However, with just a little encouragement he quickly realised that he wanted the male foster carer on the side between and 'as a barrier' to his birth parents. He wanted the female foster carer next to him on the other side. He placed Louis on a mobile seat so that he 'could move quickly if things got difficult'. Ian mobilised his sensory defences in response to what he perceived as a potential threat. Ian was also helped to explore different potential outcomes such as:

- How do you want to greet your birth mum and dad?
- How do you imagine they will be during the facilitated contact?
- What do you think will be the most difficult part of the contact for you and for them?
- What shall we do if your birth mum starts to get upset?
- What shall we do if your birth dad starts to get angry?
- How shall we end the contact?
- How do you want to say goodbye?

## The facilitated contact

On the day of Ian's facilitated contact, Louis telephoned Ian at his foster carers, to offer some reassurance where needed. Louis could tell by the tone of his voice that Ian felt both anxious and excited.

The plan was for the contact to be relatively brief in order to maintain its therapeutic focus: approximately 30–45 minutes, an hour at the most depending on how the contact progressed. The social worker and Louis would be facilitating the process.

Everyone arrived on time, which was very significant for Ian as he was used to his birth mother arriving late or missing contact sessions. After a brief introduction, offering welcomes and an acknowledgement of the 'difficult feelings' that may be around, as well as an appreciation of everyone's commitment to this very different type of contact, they began.

Ian was able to read the list of questions and statements he'd prepared. For some children, a chosen adult can read them on their behalf. Each question or statement was worked through one by one, offering his birth parents the chance to reply as best they could. Sometimes, the parents require a little encouragement to focus on their 'script' or need reminding of what they want and need to say. The professional involved in helping prepare the birth parents can, for example, say 'When we talked about this earlier I remember you said you would like...to know...' Ian's mother became tearful when Ian asked her 'Why couldn't you look after me when I was a baby; did you love the drink (alcohol) more than me?' Ian's mother rose to the challenge and gave a moving and coherent account of her chaotic life. She acknowledged that it was wrong for her to neglect Ian, such as when she forgot to change his nappies, and with help, agreed that it must have felt to him as if she did indeed prefer drink to him, for which she was eternally sorry. She also apologised for all the times she had drunk herself into oblivion and neglected to feed Ian.

Ian's father was also able to take responsibility for his violent nature and express his remorse about the way he had physically hurt Ian.

A summary of the intervention was that Ian was able to express, with support, his long suppressed thoughts, fears and feelings about his birth parents and they in turn were able to offer him a far more meaningful and authentic response – something he had never heard or experienced before. The parents were supported with a reparative script that enabled them:

- to offer a truthful account of what had happened when they lived together
- to say they were sorry
- to say it was not Ian's fault that things went wrong in their family
- to say they care about him and think about him and want him to be happy in his new family
- to offer their blessing and hope that Ian will learn to trust his new family in a way he has not learnt with them.

This approach to facilitating contact could be used early in placement with children who are long-term fostered or with the slightly older adopted child. As a minimum, birth relatives who hope to embark on face-to-face contact need to be supported in telling the young child they are sorry they were not kept safe, were hurt, not well cared for, it was not their fault and that they want them to be settled and happy with their new family. These contact sessions may be a one-off, or else such a facilitated contact could help set the scene for any ongoing contact arrangements. In such situations it may be necessary to revisit the facilitated contact session as the child matures, has more memories and/or questions.

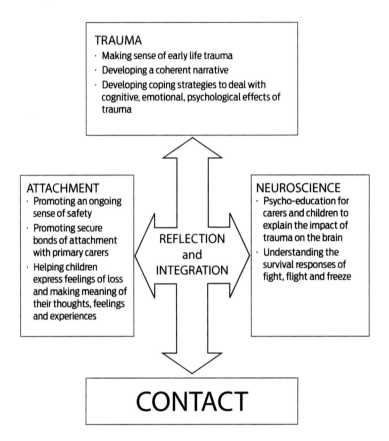

FIGURE 2.2 AN INTEGRATED APPROACH TO FACILITATING
MEANINGFUL CONTACT FOR TRAUMATISED CHILDREN

Involves focused preparation and support for all three parties, the child, the carers and the birth relative, and involves the elements above.

# Understanding the Significance of Attachment and Neuroscience for Baby and Toddler Contact

Expressed in basic terms, our thoughts and actions can be traced back to sensations that are transmitted, decoded and organised within the brain. Both internal and external stimuli are processed to enable us to regulate and organise appropriate responses. Exposure to trauma during pregnancy and early infancy alters the way the infant's brain develops and how sensory experiences are organised. There is an increasing body of research on the impact of pre-birth experience on the unborn baby.

Howerton *et al.* (2013)[1] found that maternal stress is a key risk factor for neurodevelopmental disorders, including schizophrenia and autism. Bergman *et al.* (2007)[2] found that high levels of the stress hormone cortisol during pregnancy correlated with children having a lower IQ at age 18 months than age-matched peers and that children who experienced a highly stressed and anxious pregnancy were at double the risk of hyperactivity and ADHD (attention deficit hyperactivity disorder) by age four. Therefore, if a pregnant mother has been exposed to high levels of stress, domestic violence, poor nutrition, drugs (including nicotine) and/or alcohol, we can anticipate that the foetus's developing brain and nervous system has been impacted by these chemicals.

Human beings are the most vulnerable of species at birth. The infant and young child is totally dependent on caregivers (usually their parents) to enable them to survive. They are dependent for protection, nourishment, nurture and warmth. It is argued that the multiplicity and dynamic of the interactions involved in meeting the infant's and young child's needs, and how their parents or caregivers respond in doing so, is literally shaping the child's developing brain as well as their attachment style. Exposure to relational trauma such as neglect, abuse and domestic violence have a significant impact on the vulnerable baby and toddler.

A sensitively attuned and *mindful* approach to parenting conveys to the baby, 'I think about your needs before they occur.' This contributes to the process of co-regulation for an infant, as they experience both consistency of care and repair and soothing (regulation) of dysregulatory experiences. The notion of *repair* is central to a healthy attachment. The willingness and effort to try to 'make things better' or OK in a relationship is a potential indicator of self-awareness and awareness of another's wellbeing and capacity for empathy. This enables a relationship to heal, establish trust and creates resilience. These qualities are the foundation of what Bowlby described as the secure base.

Babies and toddlers who experience repeated exposure to stress become sensitised to stress. Once sensitised, the same neural activation (the intensified response) can be elicited by decreasingly intense external stimuli. Thus, a relatively minor stressor (an echo or reminder of the trauma) can trigger a full-blown survival state response.[3] This ultimately leads to difficulties with regulation of arousal and physiological states, which in turn impact on sensory processing and the capacity for learning, self-calming and emotional responsivity.[4]

Too often we have known of or heard of babies and young children being *taken* from their foster carers (who during this period of separation from their birth parent need to provide/act as the child's secure base) and transported to and from contact sessions. Such contacts can be taking place at a frequency of as much as five times per week and a minimum of three. Journeys may involve lengthy travel time, which may feel even longer considering the way infants and children experience the passage of time. Many are likely to experience each of these separations as a further abandonment, provoking anxiety and physiological dysregulation. Such dysregulation may manifest in unhappiness and tears, or the child may learn to habituate into psychological 'flight' and appear flat, withdrawn and compliant. Arriving at contact in such a state will not help promote a positive relationship with the birth parents who in turn may be poorly equipped to respond sensitively to the baby's or young child's needs.

Often we have looked into the background records of children who have been referred for therapeutic support and have seen reports of contact sessions that have been unsettling to read. The baby or child has been in a state of distress, parents have frequently been unable to respond sensitively, have been preoccupied with their own needs and are dismissive of the child. They have argued with a partner, supervisor or social worker, or have become angry or rejecting towards the child. While supervised contact may help ensure that the child is not physically hurt, it is *failing* to protect the child from harm as these experiences constitute relational trauma. The younger the child is while these kinds of contacts are happening the more vulnerable they are to lasting effects of the impact of such repeated misattuned interactions.[5]

## Travelling to and from contact

In working with adopted and permanently fostered children one of the difficulties parents have highlighted is the distress and resistance shown by the child when travelling in a car. It could be that their early 'patterned repetitive' nature of their experiences of repeated separations when being transported to contact are triggered by the sensations and motion involved in a car journey, provoking anxiety about an impending separation from the parent. One adoptive parent had come to realise that a specific colour and make of car was causing her son particularly acute distress and realised that this was the same make and colour of car that had transported him to and from contact during his infancy (he was placed with her aged 19 months).

From the baby and young child's point of view we would argue that it is in their best interests that when travelling to and from contact, their foster carer is the escort. Some researchers and practitioners advocate foster carers being present during the contact for infants and acting as facilitators for the mother/parent and child relationship. This is a sensitive and skilled task for which foster carers need training and support and one that many with the right support could do with great satisfaction. As a minimum, however, foster carers should be present to help the infant (and older children) make the transition to and from the contact session by spending a short period (say ten minutes) with the child and parent each side of the contact session. If the frequency of contact is too high to enable this, then the value of the contact should be questioned.

When babies and children are involved in frequent contact arrangements during court proceedings the purpose is:

- to maintain family relationships

- to provide reassurance to the child and their parents

- to provide an opportunity to assess parenting capacity over time and, where appropriate, provide therapeutic support to improve the parenting.[6]

Contact needs to be thought about more creatively, drawing on practices such as Theraplay[®] (discussed later in this chapter) that could help encourage parents in developing skills and insights into their infants' and children's needs. Reviewing parent and child interactions using filmed sessions in between contact sessions could help parents to notice what contributes towards positive attachments, as well as feel connected to their child in between contact sessions. Twice or three times a week, contact could be supplemented by a feedback session for the parent using this method. Thought could also be given to creative ways of ensuring that an infant is supported in retaining a connection and felt sense of the parent in between contact sessions – for example a parent could record a familiar story or nursery rhymes which the foster carer plays to the child each day. Soft cloths with the mother's scent could be provided regularly for the child.

| When assessing or evaluating parent–infant interactions, self-reflection or supervision, the following should be considered: |
| --- |
| What stage of attachment formation is this baby/toddler in at present and at what stage did the separation from the birth mother take place? |
| Given the experience of trauma in terms of separation from the birth mother/family, what other trauma has the baby experienced in terms of sensory, emotional, physical and psychological experiences? |
| What is the attachment style of the birth parents? How might they be supported in developing their capacity for understanding and supporting their baby/toddler? |
| How may the experience of this contact with this birth mother/father impact the baby/toddler? |
| To what degree do the parents prioritise engaging the infant ahead of the supervising contact workers? |
| Who will function as the person who can assume the role of the 'secure enough' position during the contact? |

| |
|---|
| How might this person intervene to help facilitate a better sense of security when needed, e.g. might they speak for this baby/child: 'Did you hear that loud noise, that was a bit scary', 'Mum, I'm feeling full with milk right now'. Or if birth parents are too dysregulated, might this person suggest that they take a break to have a cup of tea, etc.? |
| How might we best support and prepare the birth mother/father in understanding this person's role? |
| How can this be put in place during the contact? |
| How are the transitions before and after the contact facilitated and made *attachment focused* for the child? Are the contact arrangements compatible with the child's day-to-day routines? If not, discuss. |
| How is the attachment to the primary carer able to support or hinder the contact arrangements and transitions? Is the foster carer willing/able to escort the baby/toddler to the contact session; are they willing to join the session by way of a handover? |
| How can this contact communicate to the baby that its needs are considered before they occur and that it are being held in mind? |
| How may the contact environment be shaped to be experienced as safe and containing as possible? |
| What sensory input may be distressing to the baby during the contact? |
| What sensory input may offer a sense of ease and comfort for the baby during the contact? How might we use this knowledge to assist the birth parents in understanding the need to consider a child's sensory experiences? |
| What is being communicated non-verbally to the baby during the contact? |
| Does the parent (and infant) appear to respond positively and coherently to close physical contact? |
| How is the baby being regulated? Does the parent recognise and respond to stress? |
| How does the parent appear to talk to the infant? |
| Does the parent recognise environmental hazards to the infant and provide appropriate intervention? |
| How is the baby touched or not touched by the parent(s)? Does the interaction meet the baby's needs or the birth parent's? Does the parent match the infant's rhythm? |
| How is the end of the contact managed by the infant and parent? How might the infant experience or make sense of this ending? |
| Will there be opportunities to support birth parents in developing a capacity to understand a baby's/toddler's need for co-regulation? |

Social workers and contact supervisors should have opportunities to reflect upon what is working for the baby/toddler and what birth parents are managing well enough; what, if anything, is concerning and whether there are adaptations that could help improve the quality of the experience for the baby/toddler.

## Interventions

The Mellow Babies project is an intervention designed to support mothers and babies where the mother is experiencing postnatal depression. One of the aims of the project is to increase the mother's sensitivity to the baby's needs and her enjoyment of her relationship with the baby. Puckering, McIntosh *et al.* (2010) state: 'Therapies that focus on supporting mothers have shown accelerated improvement in maternal wellbeing, but few positive effects for infants. Where interventions focus on addressing mother–infant interaction there appears greater chance of benefit to both mothers and children.'[7]

The approach adopted in the study focused both on providing support to vulnerable mothers to alleviate depression and in explicitly addressing mother–infant interaction and relationship. The group drew on approaches such as interactive coaching; baby massage; infant-focused speech; cognitive behavioural strategies previously shown to benefit both the interaction and mothers' mental state. However, mothers whose drug use was an issue were excluded from attending the intervention.

In measuring the quality of interactions between the mothers and their babies they used an observational tool which they describe briefly in their article.

Attention to these dimensions when observing contact between infants and toddlers and their parents could help inform assessments and guide interventions with parents. Interestingly, this intervention also used filmed sessions to support mothers in recognising what was working in their interactions with their babies and to reflect on misattunements.

| Dimension | Description (example) |
|---|---|
| Anticipation of child's need (infant) | Is the child given advanced preparation for a change activity? (positive, e.g. let's change your nappy now – lifts infant) |
| Responsiveness to other? | Are the parent and child responsive/reciprocal with each other? (positive, e.g. mother and infant looking in mirror, mother smiles 'beautiful baby', baby smiles looking closely) |
| Autonomy | Does the parent show awareness of the child's individuality? (positive, e.g. Do you want your bottle now? Have you had enough? negative, e.g. child fusses, parent continues dressing regardless) |
| Co-operation | Do parent and child co-operate/negotiate together? (positive, e.g. infant reaches for a pen, mother lifts it away and offers rattle, infant takes rattle) |
| Distress | Is comfort/support offered to a crying child who is upset or hurt (positive, e.g. noise startles infant who cries, mother cradles child 'did you get a fright?' negative, e.g. child cries, mother says 'Shut up' |
| Conflict and control | Does parent intervene appropriately to achieve legitimate compliance? |

Source: Puckering, McIntosh *et al.* (2001), p.33.

Another tool for assessment of and supporting contact with babies (toddlers and children) is the Theraplay® parenting domains of Structure, Nurture, Challenge and Engagement.[8] Thinking about these domains can also help inform how to encourage and direct parents in meeting the needs of the child during the contact sessions.

Taken from the therapeutic intervention that Theraplay provides so well to families, it is possible to apply these dimensions to the evaluation of contact arrangements. Let's work through these areas to see how they can inform contact planning and organisation:

**Structure:** Addresses contact in terms of the need for planning, how different parties manage boundaries, how issues of control are dealt with and any practical matters that need to be held in mind for the wellbeing of the baby/toddler and others involved. A baby's day-to-day routines need to be put to the front of plans for contact.

Consideration also needs to be given to the environment and facilities available within the contact venue, for example the sensory environment (how busy, how noisy, the visual impact of the room – is it dingy or too bright or overstimulating?). Consideration could be given to playing music that helps soothe.

Structure should also include agreements and written plans that outline the timing, purpose and responsibilities of all of those involved in the contact plans. These should include the support and advice that will be on offer to the birth parent and who will take responsibility for offering this. Mobile phones are either discouraged or closely monitored. Structure for one contact may differ for another.

**Nurture:** Ensures that all parties are provided with appropriate levels of nurture. A primary need of babies and children is that of nurture and these needs should be central to all contact sessions. Ensure that parents are prepared to meet the child's practical needs for nurture such as feeding and changing. Parents as well as children need a comfortable and accessible contact centre, which may offer decent food or drinks, appropriate facilities and resources for the baby/ young child, staff that are responsive and mindful to the constant changes of mood and emotional wellbeing primarily of the baby (and children) but also of the parent.

**Engagement:** Ensures that there are appropriate resources for stimulation and play at the contact centre, staff are able to engage with the birth parents (and know when to provide appropriate levels of space), the parents' engagement and attempts to interact with their child (and lack of) should be observed by staff members at all times. Music may be played to heighten or soothe experience during the contact session.

**Challenge:** Focuses on *developmentally appropriate* levels of challenge. Do the birth family members bring appropriate developmental games or toys? Are the parents able to use themselves as the object of play with babies or toddlers? Is the parent misreading developmental milestones, facial expressions, etc.? A common behaviour for some birth parents when having contact with their baby is to say 'Look!

She's smiling at me! And again…go on where's my smile!' It is of course an understandable response if as a parent you have not seen your child for a period of time, yet this may lead to overstimulation of an infant, meeting the parent's needs and not the child's.

Similarly, with older children parents may present inappropriate challenges by discussing subjects that are beyond the child's capacity to truly comprehend or which can unsettle or distress the child. For example, one mother told her child about the outcome of her own psychological assessment, and another talked about her recent experience of domestic abuse at the hands of a new partner whom the child had not even met. For some birth parents there may be inherent challenges in managing contact arrangements, for example keeping appointments, working co-operatively to supervisors and staying focused on the child.

Very young pre-verbal children are particularly vulnerable when carers or parents misattune to their needs and signals. Below, we have adapted the Theraplay parenting domains to offer a valuable tool for planning and evaluating contact with babies and toddlers. Practitioners can use the following grid for observation and to help plan possible interventions.

### Babies and toddlers 0–3 years: planning and evaluating contact tool

| Misattuned or low structure |
| --- |
| Parents may miss or arrive late for contact |
| Parents may leave the room |
| Parents try to take the baby/toddler out of the contact centre or to the toilet |
| Parents damage or break items 'by mistake' |
| Parents may intrude upon the baby's boundaries, e.g. any rough handling, such as being gripped too tightly or having a bottle or dummy pushed into their mouth, being picked up very suddenly, very rough play |
| Parents fixate upon food, drink, etc. |
| Parents struggle with offering any routine to the baby |
| Parents appear unpredictable and inconsistent |
| Parents struggle to leave or leave early |
| Ending is poorly managed with the infant |

| Nurture |
| --- |
| Parents may show lack of or low levels of affection |
| Physical touch may be lacking or dysregulating |
| There may be a lack of, or poor, eye contact |
| Parent may lack voice prosody (musical intonation in voice that conveys understanding or resonance with the inner world and emotional state of the infant) |
| Parents may lack practical care skills for the infant |
| Feeding the baby may be overstimulating or intrusive or understimulating and disengaged |
| Changing the nappy by the parent may appear hurried, discomforting or lacking in attunement |
| Parents may fail to anticipate the baby's needs |

| Engagement |
| --- |
| A parent may be uninterested in playing with a baby or child |
| A parent may lack an ability to engage the baby in 'motherese' (relational, vocal, facial and tactile play and soothing) |
| Parents may offer play or engagement that is developmentally too young or too old for the baby |
| Parents may give up quickly with efforts to engage their baby if not reciprocated |
| A parent may express teasing, sarcasm or inappropriate comments in relation to their baby |
| Play may present as overstimulating |
| Play may present as understimulating |
| Play may appear somewhat scary or too animated |
| Parents may seek engagement with, or from, the supervisor or other adult and exclude the infant/toddler |

| Challenge |
| --- |
| A parent may try to engage in activities that are beyond the developmental age and stage of the baby or child such as expecting a baby to smile, crawl or speak/walk |
| A parent presents as competitive with their partner for attention |
| The parent may try to relate with the baby using facial expressions and verbal expressions that are not appropriate |

| Challenge *cont.* |
|---|
| A parent may:<br>• expect too much of a baby or young child that has just woken<br>• expect a baby to take in food or drink in a way that is not possible<br>• expect a child to remain in a soiled nappy for too long<br>• admonish their child for being messy<br>• admonish their child for bringing up food after being fed. |

## The environment for contact

The sensory environment of the contact centre is an important consideration: how might children and parents be impacted visually within the environment? Is it cluttered or tatty? Is the decoration suitable? Is the level of noise acceptable or intrusive? Are there any particular smells associated with the building? What might these mean for those having contact? What tactile experiences might be involved as a result of the textiles and fabrics in a room, or is the environment sterile?

In the early stages of their development, babies' primary modes of experience are through their senses: touch, smell, taste and hearing. One can only imagine what it is like for infants who have to experience regular change to their sensory environment. For example, when being taken by an escort to a contact centre, a baby will have to navigate multiple sensory input. It will experience different touch, smells, textures and sounds. It is not uncommon for infants to have their sleep or feeding routines delayed in order to fit in with contact arrangements. The way a baby is fed (or the way its nappy is changed) will be different, as may be the quality of care and attunement to an infant's signals of distress, discomfort or bodily needs.

The baby will also need to adapt to a different rhythm in the way it is sung to, rocked, soothed, cradled and played with. It is important to note that in this area, it would be natural for family members to attempt to elicit contingent responses from their baby as attempts to activate engagement or attachment behaviour. However, the needs of the birth family members may override the needs of the baby at that particular time and be *dis-synchronous* for the baby, thus creating a need and response that are not a 'good fit'.

In terms of the trauma history (of the family) and potential further triggers, context is all important. If a birth mother is suffering from depression or presenting with manic behaviour and/or the birth father has himself suffered abuse in his childhood and been violent with the child or mother, there is a risk of cementing insecure or maladaptive patterns of relationship. Insecure behavioural patterns are internalised as 'internal working models,' which in the case of children who are abused, will tend to be maladaptive and hence, in the psychiatric sense, precursors to pathology.

## Birth parents and mentalisation

The ability of a birth parent to demonstrate mentalisation or mindsight and attune to their child is a key consideration in planning, managing and facilitating contact arrangements. Dr Dan Siegel, a psychiatrist and psychoanalyst, and prolific author and educator in mental health, describes mindsight as 'the ability to perceive the internal experience of another person and make sense of that imagined experience, enabling us to offer compassionate responses that reflect our understanding and concern'.[9] It is this fundamental ability in parenting to foster a sense of self-esteem, healthy (enough) attachment, sense of self and a child's capacity for self-regulation. To be able to 'tune in' to another's feeling state and respond in an empathic, reciprocal way is a skill that is often positively activated in healthy parenting. If on the other hand, a parent is unable to attune to a baby's signals or is unable to delay and puts their own need for gratification *ahead* of the needs of the infant, then there is a cause for concern.

Peter Fonagy and Mary Target have found correlations between a parent's capacity for reflective functioning and their ability to understand the child's state of mind.[10] Reflective functioning is essential to parenting and important in the development of attachment relationships. A parent who lacks the capacity to be reflective finds it difficult to understand the feelings and emotions of their baby and fails to see their infant as having needs, desires and intentions of its own. They may wrongly attribute behaviour – for example, by seeing a crying baby as manipulative or malevolent – and may respond harshly or inappropriately. This is an emerging area of research, but findings indicate that poor reflective functioning may put a child at increased risk of abuse or neglect. By improving parents' reflective functioning we can give children a better start in life.[11]

It is often the case that a child has been taken into care due to some form of abuse or neglect, so it is vital that planning for contact arrangements and staff involved provide the metaphorical mindsight on behalf of the child. It is the social worker or contact centre manager's supervisor's responsibility to hold the role of the mentalising adult and be able to put the infant's wellbeing and needs first and, importantly, *in context*.

If the birth parent cannot demonstrate appropriate levels of reflective function, mindsight or attunement, staff at the contact centre and social workers can be trained and provided with the skills to act as 'the adult with mindsight' during the contact. This will ensure that each infant involved with contact will have someone able to attune to them in terms of their basic emotional, cognitive, physical and developmental needs. There is also the possibility that staff could offer birth family members psycho-education where possible to enable parents to better attune and read their babies' cues, non-verbal communication and signals. This can be provided by engaging parents in *relational play*: activities, play and engagement that is child led, developmentally appropriate and attuned to each infant's particular and unique needs.

A final thought from Scott, O'Neill and Minge:

> A high level of resources is going into supervised contact but little attention has been paid to the therapeutic potential that this might represent to strengthen the parent-child relationship. A number of innovative developments are emerging and it would be helpful to have an audit of 'best practice' initiatives currently occurring in Australia. Evaluations of these models or assessment of their capacity to be introduced in other places is an important priority.[12]

## CHAPTER 4

# Contact during the Transition from Care Order to Permanency

If care proceedings conclude that a child's best interests will be served by adoption, a placement order usually terminates all contact arrangements which have been put in place in relation to birth parents (or other relatives) under the Children Act 1989.

Whilst at this stage of the proceedings there is no presumption for or against contact, all local authorities have a duty to give recommendations for contact as part of their care plan.

Most often, the care plan is to stop direct contact when the child moves into adoption and contact becomes far less frequent (although we have known of situations where fortnightly contact has continued until the beginning of adoption introductions). More typically the reduction of contact may happen in a stepwise fashion to once a month or six weekly, with a plan for a 'goodbye for now' or 'wish you well' contact. These terms have developed in recognition of the fact that once adoptees reach 18 (if not before) they may well seek a 'reunion' with their birth mother or other relatives. It may also be that by naming the session in this fashion we are being sensitive to both the child's (depending on their age and capacity to understand) and the mother's feelings. This *finale* to contact which concludes this transitional phase *(if* the birth family are able to manage them) does not happen until potential adoptive parents have been identified, from which time it may take three months to complete the stages of the matching process and to the child moving to live with the adoptive family. In some cases we have worked with, the Local Authority practice has been to wait for the final stage in which the adoption panel agrees the match. Given that the average time of placement from matching is said to be about a month, this means that the child is having to participate in this end of direct contact with a birth relative (most often their birth mother) and within weeks is then having to manage the loss of relationship with their day-to-day parent(s) (the foster carers).

## The birth parent's long goodbye

From the birth mother's perspective (or that of other significant birth relatives) this transition period is a long goodbye. If she manages to attend the contact sessions that are planned, she is doing so with some understanding (if not acceptance) that these contacts are no longer about maintaining a relationship with a view to returning the child to her care. On the surface not much may have changed; the visits are likely to happen in the same venue with the same variety of supervisory staff and yet hers and her child's lives are about to be changed forever.

Elsbeth Neil *et al.*'s (2011) research into direct contact after adoption[1] highlighted the fact that birth parents and other birth family members are often highly vulnerable individuals with complex difficulties of their own. There was a high incidence of mental health issues: 70 per cent of mothers, 59 per cent of fathers and 33 per cent of grandparents. Self-reports suggested the most common difficulties were depression, post natal depression, anxiety and stress, personality disorder and bipolar disorder; however, many people did not fit clear categories. In this research project the mental health of the birth parents was only strongly related to the need for the child to be adopted in a third to a half of cases, with other factors such as parental incapacity related to alcohol and drug misuse, learning disabilities, parental relationship difficulties, including domestic violence and social problems, also playing a role. Not surprisingly, mental health difficulties intensified around the time of the adoption. The argument for ongoing support (rather than for a limited/specific period) for birth relatives dealing with the loss of children through adoption is well made by the authors of this research, as is the need for ongoing support in managing post adoption contact.

The issues affecting birth parents of children who are to grow up in permanent foster care have been similarly commented upon:

> After the court, the parents often felt abandoned, as the attention of the professionals shifted towards putting the child's care plan into effect. This picture was supported by social workers in the focus groups, who accepted that too often in the flurry of activity to sort out placements and contact arrangements, support for the

parents about the long-term loss of their child or children was not always available.[2]

In preparation for this chapter, Joanne Alper (Director at Adoptionplus) reviewed some of the work of the Adoptionplus therapeutic counselling service offered to birth parents who were asked to give feedback on the experience and wrote the following:

## What birth parents have said about 'goodbye for now' contacts

Much discussion has taken place within the counselling about the last contact birth parents have with their children prior to them being placed for adoption. Parents talk about it being the worst and most painful thing they have ever had to do in their lives.

One birth mum said, 'It's the worst thing anyone could ever be expected to do. I don't think it's right for parents not to go to final contact…but I can understand it.'

Another mother stated: 'Don't ever say "we know how you feel"… you don't! It makes a terrible situation much worse!'

People have talked about worrying about what to say to their children, worrying about breaking down and crying and upsetting their children. The majority of parents have informed us that they have had no support or guidance. Not only will this increase the stress and pain to the birth parent, but it can contribute to this contact being even more upsetting for the child or children.

One birth mother we worked with said she had five 'goodbye for now' contacts over one week, as she had five children being placed for adoption. She explained that she had no support and no transport and had to get two buses to get to the contact centre, and two buses to get home again. She told the counsellor that the thought of it was so overwhelming she didn't think she could do it. She doubted that she could get out of bed that coming week. This was a birth mother who had never experienced positive parenting herself as a child, which in itself provides the inner resources to become a nurturing parent. Although she had not been able to parent her children, she still clearly loved them deeply and was devastated by the pain of saying goodbye to them. It's understandable that a busy social worker needing to arrange 'goodbye for now' contacts for five children may focus on the practical arrangements. However, this is so much more than a 'practical event'. Having some thought and empathy for the parent, and offering them support through this momentous experience, can not only help them now and in the future, but can also hugely improve what is a very difficult contact for the child. It can help to improve not only the child's experience of the contact itself, but also the message that it leaves the child with, about themselves, the birth parent or those involved.

While there is nothing that can be done to take away the pain of these birth mothers, they deserve recognition and support in managing this extremely distressing and challenging period of theirs and their children's lives. While some may not be able to recognise or accept the part they have played in the plan for adoption, it is also possible that this transitional phase can offer opportunities for birth parents and other relatives to make positive contributions to the child's future security. However, support in managing such an enormous and potentially overwhelming challenge involves offering a space for emotional support, which is most likely to be effective via independent confidential therapeutic counselling.

## The child's long goodbye...

We should also consider the potential impact on the children of the ongoing contact with a birth mother and father, whose capacity to attune to their children's needs (which it must be argued) was already compromised and is further eroded by the circumstances they now find themselves in.

If the child is of an age to understand that the court has been deciding where they will be living in the future then the children's guardian will usually tell the child that the court has decided they will not be returning to live with their birth parents. Contact during proceedings is aimed at encouraging the child's attachment and the parents' bonding with the child. This will have involved the parent in attending to the child's needs. They may have been expected to bring food, they will have attended to the child's personal care needs and taken them to the toilet, changed nappies and so on. The organisation and expectations for this transitional phase of contact needs to change focus and structure if it is to begin to help prepare the child for the separation. It is also the beginning of signalling the change in role of the parent, acceptance of which can be a defining issue in deciding on any future direct contact arrangements.

Less frequent, and possibly shorter, contact sessions for the child could incorporate short preparation sessions and debrief/advice sessions for the parents.

Consideration needs to be given to how the child (who is often very young) is going to be supported in managing these less frequent but potentially very emotionally charged contact sessions. During this phase the older child will also be involved in some kind of life story work by way of preparation for the move, which also has the potential for triggering strong emotional reactions.

## How can children be supported?

The child's foster carers may not have been involved in the contact sessions during the proceedings; the change in purpose and reduction in frequency affords an opportunity to include them. If the birth relative and foster carer have not had much involvement previously, could this period of transition offer an opportunity to work with the foster carer and birth parent to help form an alliance that enables them to work together in the interests of the child? This would involve professionals in offering thoughtful support and guidance to both the parent and the foster carer. If a parent was able to manage this change in role it could be a positive indication of an ability to manage some direct contact once the child is adopted; however, this should not be promised as a potential reward for co-operation, as the child's needs into the future cannot be predicted. If it is not possible for the foster carer to be present throughout contact meetings, then, as a minimum, might they be able to attend at the beginning and the end of the contact and be with the child as the parent leaves the centre? If they have not been involved in the session, how will supervisors ensure that foster carers are given feedback on the experience the child had of the contact, so that the potential for supporting the child is maximised?

Once contact frequency is significantly reduced and a clear end is in sight, rather than expecting the parent to take responsibility for managing the structure and interactions during this phase of the contact sessions, specific activities could be planned that allow for positive experiences that are less emotionally intense and could help support positive experiences and shared memories. This could include, for example, playing games that are inclusive of the child, parent, foster carer and supervisors; encouraging parents to have shared painting sessions with the child; making objects out of clay; doing hand prints, taking photographs; creating experiences, objects and written accounts of these sessions that could be part of memory boxes given to the child and parent at the conclusion of the transitional phase of contact. Parents and children could be nurtured if the professionals responsible for the contact provide snacks and refreshments.

Parents should also be prepared for the possibility that older children who are aware that they are going to be adopted (or going on to permanent foster care) may ask questions about why, and be encouraged to discuss how they could respond to their child in a way that is supportive of the child and the adjustments they are going to have to make.

## The role of the professional

Whether social worker, contact supervisor, therapist, nursery or school staff, one can feel overwhelmed by the enormity of the situation the birth parents/relatives and child now find themselves in. The decision to place a child for adoption and prohibit a parent from seeing their child brings with it a vast range of complex feelings for professionals whose focus has to be what is in the child's best interest but who nevertheless will also consider the impact of their recommendations upon the parents.

While it is sometimes the case that the social worker whose evidence has secured the plan for the child's adoption can go on to have a relationship with the parent that enables them to support the parent in managing the next phase of the journey with the child, it is not always possible. Even if caseloads would permit, and, as empathetic as the social worker might be, their very presence reminds the parent of the trauma of the care proceedings and the pain associated with the subsequent loss of their right to care for the child.

While independent *therapeutic* counselling for birth parents can make a real difference to how well they are able to manage this transition, this will nevertheless be painful. However, in terms of facilitating the transitional contact and 'goodbye for now' contacts, local authorities could also consider involving professionals who work within the department. For example, while Elsie worked as a specialist adoption and foster care social worker in a London borough, she was able to offer support to birth relatives who were coming to terms with plans for adoption and to help them begin to plan for their goodbye contact sessions. She had not been involved in, and was therefore not associated with, the trauma of the care proceedings. While some birth parents and relatives refused this offer of support, many more also wanted to get things as right as possible for their child.

Local authority children's departments seem to restructure endlessly and not all are organised in the same way. However, most do have permanency and post adoption teams and perhaps members of those teams could take on the role of supporting and helping facilitate contact sessions at this stage, which is also a prelude to developing the post adoption contact relationship. Of course, if contact has been supervised by a specific supervisor then that supervisor may remain involved. Consideration needs to be given, however, to the quality of that relationship and the role their evidence has played in the care proceedings. If the supervisor is to remain involved then they may need to be prepared to change how they interact with the parent and the child. It may also be necessary to change the supervisor, but whoever is to oversee the contact needs to understand that their role is to facilitate and support the process and not simply to watch over and take notes.

## Preparing for the time to say goodbye

When the 'goodbye for now/wish you well' contact is planned between parent and child, the aim is to provide an opportunity for the family to experience a final significant shared experience to help mark the transition. During this contact, the child's need is to receive encouragement from their birth mother and/or father (or significant relative) to move into the adoptive placement with their support. When such a meeting is understandably fuelled by high emotions such as loss, grief and rage, it can be a challenge for everyone to manage. There are times when the feelings of rage or loss are so intense that the contact may not take place or may be hurried towards an unsatisfying conclusion for all involved. Birth parents may become incapacitated by grief and freeze or collapse into a state of distress, and feel unable to participate. Some may be immersed in their anger to the extent that they continue to rage at professionals, blaming *them* for the child's removal. Therefore, parents who remain stuck in this position may be difficult to engage in the process safely. We heard of one contact recently of a birth mother who just as she was leaving the session turned and in an angry voice said to her 4- and 5-year-old children, 'Now remember you'll only ever have one mother.' These children are now struggling to settle in their adoptive placement. However, there are also many birth mothers and other relatives who do want to get it right for the sake of their children and are willing to take on this huge emotional challenge.

Parents who have attended independent counselling via Adoptionplus have told their counsellors that they have been given a list of things not to say or do during these emotive contact sessions. For example, a birth mother said, 'I know I mustn't cry and I'm worried that I might', or 'I know I mustn't say...' It could help birth parents if they were given some ideas about the kinds of things that they can say.

Managing and facilitating the 'wish you well/goodbye for now' contact requires reflection and planning on the part of the professional network to help ensure that the optimum opportunity is provided for both the children and the parents to experience a meaningful 'goodbye for now', where all feelings can be acknowledged yet contained. The guiding principle of the child being the central focus of the contact remains the same. The plan for contact should be proactive and detailed rather than passive. This is an important point, as the risk is that professionals will try to expedite the contact with the intention of avoiding (could be an attachment-related issue here for the professional!) intensity of feeling. Being proactive in the contact means being well prepared, well informed, mindful of the unique needs of the child and birth parents/relatives, with an intention of offering a contact that is meaningful, supportive and facilitative of the participants' experience, allowing for a range of feelings to be expressed. Each of these contacts could be considered as a 'bespoke' experience. Offering birth parents meaningful opportunities to prepare for this contact and practical support should be a central feature of the plan.

## Case study: Effective and enabling parent support

What follows is an example of effective and enabling parent support which was facilitated by a local authority social worker who we shall call Marie. Marie had worked with the birth mother of the child over many years and had in fact been instrumental in removing two of her three children who were placed for adoption.

Mandy, aged 7, whose underlying attachment was disorganised, frequently presented behaviours when with her birth mother Annie which were ambivalent/resistant. During the long build-up to the 'goodbye for now' contact, she had on a number of occasions said she no longer wanted to see Annie whose own behaviour during some contact sessions had been hostile and dismissive.

However, there had also been times when she and Annie had positive experiences of being together and it was thought that she should be offered the opportunity to have the final contact. Mandy's response was to say that she did want to see Annie one last time.

Annie, the birth mum, had herself been a child in care and had experienced a great deal of abuse and trauma while growing up. Annie's adult relationships seemed to repeat the patterns of her childhood attachment relationships: she was frequently abused and abandoned. As a mother, Annie's behaviour towards her children was unpredictable; she could be attentive and loving but was often hostile, dismissive, and at times neglectful and physically abusive. Annie could also be aggressive and threatening towards social workers and other professionals. However, Marie's understanding of what lay beneath Annie's behaviours had enabled her to empathise with her distress and difficulties while also managing to maintain clear boundaries. Her long-standing relationship with Annie and the level of safety Annie felt with Marie meant she was able to help Annie co-regulate. When it came to the time for Annie to say goodbye to her third child, Mandy, Marie was asked by her manager to support and help prepare Annie. Marie made time to see Annie at least three times during the build-up to the session, helping her think about how she should approach and prepare herself for the session and, importantly, what 'messages' she could convey to Mandy that would help her make the transition to adoption.

Marie knew that Annie might struggle with staying regulated and was able to talk with her about ways of calming herself, showing her some breathing exercises, suggesting sipping water and if needs be taking a break and leaving the room. One of the things Annie wanted support with was deciding on what to give Mandy as a farewell gift. She decided on a soft toy but also bought a photo frame that had a central space surrounded by smaller ones. Annie then put photographs of Mandy and herself and other relatives in the smaller spaces and left the large central space free. On the day of the contact Annie was able to give Mandy the photo frame telling her that she loved her and would always remember her and wanted her to be happy with her adoptive parents. She explained that the big space in the middle of the frame was there so she and her adoptive parents could place a photograph of the three of them. This was a highly symbolic and helpful gesture on the part of a birth mother who had considerable challenges to overcome in order to manage it.

## Conclusions

The Theraplay parenting domains of Structure, Nurture, Challenge and Engagement can be particularly useful in these circumstances as they provide a ready framework for evaluating and planning for the 'wish you well/goodbye for now' contact. They can also act as a helpful guide when preparing and planning for meetings between birth parents and prospective adopters or permanent foster carers.

**Structure:** The social worker provided structured support, and the relationship built over many years enabled Annie to accept the support and structure she offered. In all cases, involving the birth mothers in thinking about and planning how the contact would be managed will support them in adhering to the structure on the day of the contact. Issues of transport and availability of practical support before and following the contact also need addressing.

**Nurture:** From the outset, counsellors, supervisors and social workers who are engaging in this work with birth mothers and/or fathers need to model a nurturing (and structured) approach that ensures the birth parent has time to express concerns and have those concerns acknowledged with empathy. Offering nurture through refreshments and during meetings and at the final contact also helps provide a nurturing experience. Ensuring that birth parents have transport to and from such momentous life-changing events is also part of nurturing. Marie's acceptance and understanding of Annie provided her with a nurturing experience.

**Challenge:** In all cases workers need to make sure that the contact arrangements are accessible, clear and easy to negotiate. Annie was quite fragile in ways and could be seen as low to medium in terms of her capacity to manage challenging situations. The taxi booking for some birth mothers could also be seen in terms of ensuring that the 'challenge' of getting to the contact avoided self-sabotage. It was also important to work with Annie to support her in developing a simple coherent story that could be conveyed to Mandy, giving a blessing for the adoption but that was not overly challenging at this point in her journey. It is also important to ensure that any activities are low in challenge in terms of games that might be enjoyed by the children, without being competitive.

**Engagement:** All parents in this situation need engagement that is empathetic and starts by being person-centred. If the worker involved does not have a previous relationship with the parent, showing curiosity about their own childhood experiences can be a helpful starting point. Marie had previously engaged Annie in such a relationship. She also offered encouragement in respect of the significant role she had to play in her child's life and specifically at this stage of her journey into adoption. Some birth parents can be over-engaging when nervous or stressed, so a discussion about this can help normalise this tendency and open the way to exploring ways of being less excitable, which is important in the contact process. An example is the sharing of breathing techniques in order to help them calm themselves down.

**Attachment style:** Annie's attachment style appeared to be angry/dismissive when under stress.

**Trauma history:** Understanding the trauma history of birth parents is very important and reading background reports in preparation for working with them is essential. However, it is also important to encourage the birth mother/father to share their own perspective of their troubled early life history as a means of helping to make sense of behaviour and thought processes. Empathic and curious exploration of the birth parent's history can enable the mother (and/or father) to connect to a sense of purpose in terms of wanting their children's future lives to be different/happier than their own. Marie, who had known and worked with Annie over several years, knew and understood her traumatic developmental experiences very well. She had shown consistent empathy towards Annie, whom she was able to support in contextualising the impact of these experiences on her parenting.

**Neuroscience and reflective capacity:** Despite Annie's ongoing life challenges, she was robust enough to explore her own challenges and those of Mandy in a way that demonstrated she had a relatively coherent narrative. Most important was her wish to give Mandy something she felt she had too little of: compassion. She did have a tendency to become dysregulated yet Marie was able to notice this and work directly with her to enable Annie to begin to think about this process. This intervention allowed for some mindfulness on Annie's part – the ability to think about her thinking and process. Marie's capacity to be alongside Annie enabled her to think and plan for the contact with Mandy. With Marie's support, Annie was able to reflect on the kind of messages she could convey to Mandy that would tell her she was loved and held in mind by her birth mother, *and* had her full permission to attach to and settle with her adoptive parents.

# Preparing birth parents for 'goodbye for now' contact

The following is a summary of points to consider in preparing to support birth parents in managing the 'goodbye for now' contact.

- To think about how she (or he) might prepare herself on the day (and even the day before the contact) in order to try to enable her to be more self-regulated.

- To think about arrival at the venue and to explore what thoughts, feelings and behaviours might be likely for her.

- To think about any strategies to deal with the above.

- To prepare for how she will begin the session and what support she might require at this point.

- To rehearse and prepare a 'coherent narrative' (a basic story) of what she needed to say to the child and to explore what behaviour would support this process.

- Once this basic story has been agreed on, suggest directly supporting the birth mother staying on message, if necessary, by prompting with, for example, 'I know earlier you told me…'

- To explore what small and meaningful gift she might want to give the child and what would be an appropriate message to put in any card.

- To consider what interaction, games and activities might be appropriate for the occasion.

- To think together about the different responses of the child or children and how she might respond.

- To create a subtle signal that could communicate that the birth mother needs 'time out' or help.

- To think about how to end the contact meeting and what level of support would be useful.

- Explore with the birth mother her family/social network and whether any one of them could be trusted and relied upon to offer her practical support and assistance on the day of the 'wish you well/goodbye for now' contact.

- To consider how the birth mother will manage the rest of the day, week and month after the goodbye contact and review support network.

- To plan a follow-up telephone call and home visit, ideally within the first week after the goodbye contact.

## Other good practice ideas

We have heard of a number of innovative practices being employed by social workers around the country in managing these 'wish you well/ goodbye for now' contacts. For example, one local authority films the sessions with the agreement of the birth relative so that the recording is available to the child in the future. This could be particularly important to very young children whose capacity to hold in mind the event will be limited. Knowing that the relatives cared enough to attend such a contact can mean a great deal to the adoptee. Other supportive practice has included having the foster carer present. If foster carers could be involved in the transitional contact sessions, their presence will be incredibly supportive for the child and may also be of some comfort to the birth parent. Allowing the birth parent (be it mother or father) to be accompanied by a trustworthy member of the family known to the child can also be supportive. It is not unusual for a grandparent to present in these situations or perhaps an aunt. Sometimes for the older child who has taken on a caring or 'parentified' role in relation to the parent(s), seeing that the parent is being supported and cared for can help redress the child's sense of responsibility.

Parents with learning disabilities may need specific support from professionals who are skilled in offering advice and support to this client group. Involving these professionals in the preparation, planning and direct support of the parents can help ensure that the potential benefits of the experience for the parents and children is maximised.

Mental health and substance abuse professionals known to parents could also be invited to be involved in a similar way.

It is also a good idea to write up the contact session in some detail as a record for the child. If birth parents or other relatives have been off-message, the professional who is facilitating and writes up the session should record this fact in a way that shows empathy for the child, contextualises the birth parents' difficulty in doing so and suggests the message the child deserves to receive.

If a birth parent or significant relative has not been able to attend such a meeting then consideration could be given to a videoed message (see Chapter 7).

Whether or not a birth parent or other significant relative has managed this final stage of the journey with the child who is moving into adoption, encouraging and supporting them in writing a letter for later life detailing the circumstances and reasons they needed adoption, along with positive memories of the child as they were growing up could be added to the child's sense of their earlier history and convey the message that they are important. When parents are not able to, or are no longer alive, grandparents, aunts and uncles could help fill the void that the birth parents' inability or absence leaves in the child's life. This could also be an experience which is valued and supportive to the birth parents' relatives who are likely to have experienced pain in relation to the birth parents' behaviours and distress, as well as being impacted themselves by the loss of the child to adoption.

## Contact between birth and adoptive parents

The details of reports outlining the behaviours of birth parents and the experiences of maltreated children make difficult reading, particularly for the prospective adoptive parent. Knowing the impact of the parents' neglect and abuse will understandably have an impact on how the adoptive parents view them.

While social workers are encouraged to record details of the parents' personality and think about their positive attributes when writing the Child Permanence Report, the quality of this is variable and in any event parents may be confused or reluctant about engaging in the process. While social workers endeavour to discuss and convey the positives about birth parents to prospective adopters, an actual meeting with a child's birth parents can help humanise them. It can also convey a more rounded understanding and help form a psychological connection that can benefit the child, the adopters and the birth parent. This form of experience can help adoptive parents begin to claim the child and is the start of supporting their capacity for 'communicative openness' with their adopted child. Even when no direct contact is planned while the child is growing up, knowing that their adoptive parents met their birth parents helps give the child permission to be curious and ask questions. This meeting could also help support the development of the kind of relationship that is necessary for any future contacts that might take place, as well as enabling ongoing letterbox exchanges.

Once again, such meetings need professionals to work together to plan and prepare both the birth parent (most usually the mother) and the adoptive parents. These meetings need a clear structure and both sets of parents should have the support of a social worker. Sometimes a birth mother or father might also bring along a partner or other relative for support.

Adoptive parents need to think about what messages they want to convey to the birth parent:

- I want to give her the best start I can.

- She will always know she has a birth mum and dad.

- When she is old enough and asks to meet you I will support her.

- We will do our best to explain why you couldn't look after her in a sensitive and caring way.

- She will be able to look at photos of you when she wants to.

- We will think about the talents, interests and physical features she has that come from you and be sure to let her know about these.

## Case study: Effective and enabling parent support (cont.)

Birth parents need preparation too! In the case of Annie, Marie again supported her in meeting Mandy's adoptive parents. Annie's current partner was also included in this meeting as he was an important source of support and would also be able to help her remember and process the meeting over time. The adoptive parents knew and understood a lot about Annie as Marie had attended Mandy's life appreciation day. Life appreciation days are held with the aim of enhancing the adoptive parents' understanding of the child's life story through bringing them together with foster carers, social workers and other professionals who have known the child and their birth family. Maria's contribution had been important and moving as she was able to talk with care, compassion and realism about Annie's life and personality. For all of her difficulties, Annie had a recognition that she would not be able to parent Mandy in the way she needed and wanted to give a gift to the prospective adoptive parents that could convey gratitude and in some way connect her to them. Mandy had wondered about a tree for their garden. Marie had liaised with the adopters and their link worker, who thought this a wonderful symbol and suggested a fruit tree.

During the meeting Annie showed both her vulnerability and her volatility as well as her sense of humour. She was able to talk about her interests. The actual meeting was very emotional and intense with both Annie and the adoptive parents in tears at different times. The adoptive parents let Annie know that they understood why Mandy needed to be adopted and that they also knew that as her birth mum Annie would always be important to Mandy. They would plant the tree in the family garden and Mandy would know it came from her and that as the seasons changed they would be able to reflect with Mandy about how life and changing seasons were also happening for Annie.

## CHAPTER 5

# Contact with Foster Carers

## Moving from Foster Care into Adoption

While reflecting on the issues relating to children who are moved into adoption from foster care, Elsie recalled the following memory:

## Case study: Johnny

Many years ago I was involved in helping facilitate some contact sessions for 3½-year-old Johnny with Ann, his maternal grandmother and her sister Joan, his great aunt.

Johnny had regular contact with them while he was with his foster carer Kathleen and was now newly placed for adoption. He had been placed with Kathleen at 11 months of age following the traumatic death of his mother, which Johnny had witnessed. No one in the birth family was in a position to bring Johnny up but they were committed to supporting him through contact. An expert assessment presented to the court recommended that direct contact with Johnny's grandmother three times a year would benefit Johnny's long-term emotional and psychological development. Ann, who had had bouts of depression throughout her adult life, experienced a further deterioration following the loss of her daughter. Joan, Johnny's great aunt, had been instrumental in offering Ann both emotional and practical support. This included managing contact sessions; and so it was agreed that she too would remain involved, which would help provide consistency and continuity for Johnny.

There was quite a large extended family network, many of whom wanted to maintain links with Johnny, and it had been a painful process for Ann and Joan to move to a position of accepting the plan for adoption and their limited role while Johnny was growing up. However, they were prepared to work with the plan, accept guidance and they were able to manage the first and second facilitated contact sessions with Johnny and his adoptive parents very well.

His adoptive parents understood the long-term significance of the contact for Johnny and were committed to maintaining what seemed to be a meaningful connection. They decided to bring Johnny back to the area where the birth family lived for the third contact session. This involved them in a lengthy trip and they were arranging to stay overnight in a local hotel. Part of the reason they decided to do this was so that Johnny could also see Kathleen, his ex-foster carer. Once she and Ann had some time to digest this information and discuss it with the family, Joan phoned Elsie. She wanted to express her own and the rest of the family's feelings about being treated unfairly in relation to having contact with Johnny. Why was Kathleen who was not even related to Johnny being allowed to see him when so many of his actual birth family were not?

Elsie understood Joan to be a caring and thoughtful woman who wanted to do the best by everyone. Elsie listened while Joan talked about how she and the rest of the family were feeling and then explained that the contact was arranged in recognition of what Johnny needed and not to meet the needs of Kathleen, who would nonetheless be very pleased to see him. The fact that Kathleen was not a blood relative was not something that was a concern for Johnny. He had lived with her for almost two and a half years (more than two-thirds of his young life) before going to live with his adoptive family. He was grieving and missing Kathleen. His adoptive parents were aware of and able to accept Johnny's attachment to Kathleen, were listening to, and tuning in to, him and were responding to what they felt he needed by arranging for him to see Kathleen. Joan listened carefully and then said, 'I really had not thought of it that way; I was thinking of it from our point of view and not understanding it from Johnny's.'

## Dealing with separation and loss

We have frequently heard social workers express a view that a child who has developed an attachment to their foster carers will be able to 'transfer' that attachment to adopters and that the introduction period helps facilitate the process. Sometimes introductory periods are quite short, especially when the children are as young as Johnny. The degree of follow-up 'face-to-face' contact with ex-foster carers is variable and often very limited. Sometimes this is about agency policy and established practices. Sometimes foster carers and adopters are reluctant, as either or both may feel that having contact with the ex-foster carers will unsettle the child and negatively impact settling and 'transferring' their attachment. The views about the child's attachment experiences that inform these practices differ significantly from those that have framed and dictated practice in relation to a child's relationship and attachment to their birth parents. Court proceedings are no longer part of the picture, during which thought, planning and resources are focused on trying to ensure children have frequent and regular contact with birth parents and, where possible, there is a planned stepwise reduction of contact once adoption is the plan.

While we have worked with local authority teams that have at the placement planning meeting made developing detailed plans for a stepwise reduction of contact with foster carers which takes place in the child's adoptive home, just as often the recognition and focus on the significance of the child's attachment is viewed very differently when the child is moving from foster care into adoption. While it can be expedient for a variety of reasons to have very limited if any face-to-face contact sessions with foster carers, once a child is placed for adoption and has said their 'goodbyes' such an approach is not always in the child's interest.

Sometimes what evolves in relation to planning contact with the child's foster carer depends on how the adopters and carers' relationship has developed during the very demanding and emotionally intense period of introductions. Facilitating the understanding of both foster carers and adopters about the meaning of attachment relationships for the child offers potential and opportunities for helping meet the child's needs. At the same time the child is meeting the challenges inherent in leaving one family and joining another.

Sometimes adoptive parents have expressed a worry that if they maintain contact with the foster carer the child will not be able to settle with them and want to return to who/what they know. This is an understandable perspective when people are just starting out on the journey of becoming parents to a child; however, with support such anxieties can be worked through and contained and the potential benefits of contact for the child can be maximised. While timing and frequency of follow-up contact needs to be considered on a case-by-case basis, providing foster carers are able to give the child the right messages, then such contact can be very beneficial. It can let the child know that significant people do not just suddenly disappear from their lives and that they were lovable and valued by people from their past. Such contact can be particularly helpful for children who are not able to maintain other links with significant people from their birth families.

Vera Fahlberg states:

Children respond to being separated from their parents in many different ways. Responses vary from severe depression in children who are well attached to their carers and then abruptly separated from them to almost no reactions in children who have been emotionally neglected and have little connection to their parents. The reactions of most children entering the child care system fall between those two extremes. The two primary factors that influence an individual's reactions to loss are the strength of the relationship being broken and the abruptness of the separation.[1]

This is one of the reasons why it is accepted good practice that child care services and social workers first try interventions which support families in ways that avoid the need to separate children from their parents/carers. They try to establish a placement with family members or friends known to the child, or alternatively plan for the separation so that the child has an opportunity to be introduced to the new placement and the parent/carer can be available to support the child in making the transition. Fahlberg goes on to highlight the three stages of grief that 'well-attached' children go through when separated from their primary caregivers. These stages are most evident in children aged from 6 months to 4 years.

1. Initially the child protests and makes attempts to recover or bring back their parent/carer. The child may go to the door or try to find them.

2. The child begins to despair about the return of the carer but continues to be watchful. The child appears to be preoccupied or depressed. In response to sounds of someone approaching, a car or a noise at the door, the child becomes alert, hoping their parent/carer is returning.

3. The child becomes emotionally detached and appears to lose interest in carers in general.[2]

Fahlberg also suggests using Elizabeth Kübler-Ross's model of the stages of grieving to help inform how we think about the experiences of children and their parents/caregivers when experiencing loss through separation. The stages are: shock, denial, anger, bargaining, sadness/despair and acceptance. The grieving process is fluid, and we move in and out of different feelings over time.

Supporting the child (and the parent/caregiver) in adjusting to separation and loss is also one of the primary reasons for arranging regular contact sessions.

## Building on the child's developing sense of safety

We have worked with many children who have been placed in foster care at a relatively young age due to experiences of neglect and abuse.

It is an expectation that foster carers offer children a safe haven which includes having their emotional as well as their practical needs met. Emotionally responsive foster carers have been available and accepting of the child's initial grief reactions and supported them throughout the stages of adjustment necessary as care proceedings progress and final decisions are made. Over time, children whose earliest experiences have resulted in the development of an insecure attachment style and 'an internal working model' of parents/caregivers as unpredictable, frightened or frightening begin to internalise another 'internal working model', one of parents/carers as more predictable, responsive and benign. For the majority of maltreated children who go on to adoption, the foster home will be the first caretaking environment in which they have begun to experience a sense of safety. Social workers and foster carers can often track and reflect on positive changes the child has been able to achieve whilst being looked after, such as changes in self-esteem, skills, behaviour and insight. As social workers and foster carers begin to prepare children for moving on to a new family and discussions ensue about new mummies and daddies, it is not unusual to hear that children have either begun to ask or tell foster carers that they want to call them mummy or to say 'I want you to be my mummy'. Of course this needs sensitive handling and it is important not to mislead children. However, it is also understandable that all children in this situation will feel anxious about the as yet unknown 'mummy and/or daddy', and most would not choose to leave a home and carer where they have found a measure of safety and begun to recover from early trauma.

## Preparing for adoption

Preparing children for the move to adoption also means that they are having to make sense of why they will not be returning to live with their first mummy and daddy. While some young children may have some specific memories of frightening things that happened while they lived with their birth family and need permission to express these, generally it is unlikely to be helpful to give very young children a lot of detail at this stage. However, they will need to understand that they will not be returning to live with a mummy/daddy who are not able to care safely for children. The child may well have both implicit and explicit recall of the earlier neglect and abuse associated with a mother and/or father that surfaces during the process of being prepared for a 'new mummy and daddy'. Indeed, there have been cases where children being prepared to move on to a new 'mummy and daddy' have been triggered into 'remembering' and disclosing very serious abuse, including sexual abuse which had previously been unknown to either social workers or foster carers. Similarly, children who have moved to adoptive parents have begun to disclose memories of abusive experiences that they have not previously been able to articulate or share.

Professionals will, of course, usually prepare prospective adoptive parents for a possible regression in the child's behaviour during the early stages of placement. Foster carers may be asked to help by sharing details of how the child presented during the early stages of placement with them. We might hypothesise that this regression is a response to the stress inherent for the child in dealing with this life-changing event and see the child as reverting to their old coping mechanisms and defences. These are, perhaps, based on their earliest associations of what to expect from a mummy and daddy with the correlating negative self-beliefs about why they were neglected and abused once again taking centre stage.

While children do survive the process of moving placement and can go on to thrive, they nevertheless have to manage the impact of the losses of their relationships with the foster family while building new attachments with their adoptive parent(s). In some situations their sense of abandonment by, and loss of their primary attachment relationship with, the foster carer can be so overwhelming that their capacity to begin to build an attachment to their adoptive parents is compromised. In Johnny's case he had already experienced the sudden and tragic loss of his relationship with his birth mother. To cut him off so quickly from any contact and sense of connectedness with Kathleen was extremely anxiety-provoking for him: he was clingy, controlling and constantly hypervigilant to any perceived abandonment by his adoptive mother. These feelings and behaviours were interfering with his capacity to develop a more secure sense of attachment to his adoptive parents. Kathleen was an experienced foster carer who had a proven track record of managing the positive handover of babies and young children to adoptive parents. Kathleen both sought and accepted advice and guidance on what to do and how to interact and talk with Johnny and his adoptive parents during the introduction period. She was able to convey to Johnny that she continued to care about and hold him in her mind, while ensuring he knew she was pleased he was with his adoptive family and that he had her permission to settle. She supported the development of trust in his adoptive parents and encouraged the deepening of his attachment to them.

## Case study: Therapeutically facilitated contact

Mary Jane, who was placed with Carol and Peter for adoption, was referred to Adoptionplus when she was about 4 years 9 months old. She had been in her adoptive family for 15 months at this point. Mary Jane had appeared to settle early in the placement but after a few months she had become increasingly anxious, and was easily triggered into dysregulation and tantrums. She was also clingy and very hard to soothe or reassure when distressed. Mary Jane experienced reoccurring bad dreams and described being hurt and frightened by people (in her dreams) and spoke about her fear of being hurt within her adoptive family.

To help the team at Adoptionplus understand Mary Jane's history and the effect this had on her, details of events and the likely impact of these on the developing child were mapped out and highlighted.

The records showed that Mary Jane was 20 months old when she was removed from her mother's care and placed in foster care with Helen. She was the youngest of seven children; the next youngest was six years older. The other children had also been removed from their mother's care and placed elsewhere. The birth mother was primarily a lone parent although she had intermittent relationships with various men. She was diagnosed as having a personality disorder with an avoidant and dismissive attachment style. She was viewed as forceful, showing little emotional responsiveness and employing an angry, critical and punitive parenting style. Professionals had become increasingly concerned about the older children's wellbeing and the nature and distortion of the sibling relationships. This included violence and sexualised behaviour, and the fact that the siblings were inappropriately caring for Mary Jane. There had also been concerns about Mary Jane in relation to how she was fed and to neglect, for example severe nappy rash. It was also reported that her mother not only shouted at her but also hit her.

Mary Jane was anxious and wary on placement with Helen. She was also seen as trying to be self-reliant and prone to dysregulation. Helen also noticed that Mary Jane had absences which resulted in her being tested, but not treated, for epilepsy. Gradually, Mary Jane had begun to settle. She caught up on meeting her milestones and, while still showing signs of needing to control her environment, Mary Jane had developed a strong attachment to Helen. Care proceedings concluded that Mary Jane's best interests lay in adoption. Helen recognised how attached Mary Jane (who had begun to call her mummy) was to her and worried about how she would cope with having to move.

Mary Jane was introduced to her adoptive parents when she was 3 years 5 months old. The introductions took place over three weeks.

In her adoptive home, Mary Jane was resistant to going to bed and going to sleep and once asleep she would frequently awake due to a bad dream. She could not play age-appropriately and was difficult and controlling at mealtimes.

The adoptive parents became concerned about what had happened to Mary Jane in the past, and what could be prompting her to relay fragmented and confused stories of being hurt and frightened. They were also concerned about the fact that Mary Jane was talking about not feeling safe within their family and that she would be hurt by them. One of the issues that concerned Mary Jane's adoptive mother, Carol, was that she seemed confused not only about her past but also about her relationship with her ex-foster carer. Mary Jane frequently wanted to see photos of Helen, her ex-foster carer, and seemed to idealise her, for example by saying she had always been kind and let her do as she wished. Carol also reflected on the fact that Mary Jane was very sensitive to having her behaviour corrected and, in response, had on more than one occasion said she did not like having Carol as her mummy and wanted to go back and live with Helen.

Carol and Peter had been advised at the time of Mary Jane's placement that maintaining a level of contact with Helen would be beneficial for her. However, Carol and Peter had an older child, a busy life and somehow, despite their best intentions, they had not managed to instigate any contact meetings.

It was agreed with Carol and Peter that an approach would be made to Helen's supervising social worker to discuss the possibility of a visit to Helen by a member of the team. The aim of this was to gather a more detailed picture of Mary Jane's development and experiences while she was living with Helen.

Julia Davis, who was working with Louis and Elsie as part of the team, went to meet Helen with her supervising social worker. Helen was pleased to have the opportunity to talk about Mary Jane. She was also worried about her and wondered what could be so troubling and unsettling for her. The discussion with Helen enabled the sharing of a much more detailed picture of Mary Jane, her earlier experiences in placement, her reactions to contact with her birth family and her development while in foster care. Helen described how sad and cut off Mary Jane had seemed on placement, how she had been difficult around feeding and how she fought to avoid being placed in her pushchair. Gradually Mary Jane had settled and Helen felt they shared a strong attachment bond. Helen had wondered about keeping Mary Jane as a long-term foster child but understood that adoption would better meet her needs. Helen had liked Carol and Peter and saw that Mary Jane was responding well to them during the introductory period. Helen, who instinctively understood the meaning of Mary Jane's attachment to her and the significance of losing the relationship, said she had felt guilty and very sad about saying goodbye. It had been difficult to help such a young child make cognitive sense of the move while also trying to avoid giving her the feeling that she was being rejected. Helen felt that when Mary Jane had left her home for the final time that she had not truly understood that this was goodbye and that she would not be returning.

Once Mary Jane had managed the transition from nursery to primary school and her adoptive parents began to feel more able to manage her anxious, controlling behaviour, it was agreed that some therapeutic life story work involving her adoptive parents could help Mary Jane begin to understand and integrate her earlier experiences. During this phase of the work the Adoptionplus team developed a puppet show that told the story of Mary Jane's earliest experiences of living in a chaotic, neglectful and frightening family. The story cumulated in Mary Jane being taken by a social worker to meet and live with Helen; the information shared by Helen helped shape this part of the story. The significance of Mary Jane's relationship with Helen was discussed as part of the show, with the narrator describing how in Helen's care Mary Jane began to be looked after, played with, fed and kept safe, and how in turn Mary Jane had grown to feel safer and happier. The narrator described how Helen talked to the social worker about how pleased she was to be looking after Mary Jane. Mary Jane sat with Carol throughout, watched intently and asked some very pertinent questions. On conclusion of this part of the show, she went to the doll's house at the other side of the room and enlisted Carol's help to play out various family scenes.

In the next session we did a short review of the previous week using the puppets to get Mary Jane to comment on what she remembered. Mary Jane wanted to take control of the show and it was agreed that she and Carol would do the next part of the show. This would tell the story of how Mary Jane came to meet her adoptive parents and subsequently move to live with them. The therapy team were able to use puppets to help explain some of the feelings Mary Jane and Helen might have had. For example, the social worker puppet said that although she knew that Mary Jane would feel sad at leaving Helen and Helen was sad to say goodbye, Helen was also happy because Mary Jane was going to have her very own adoptive parents.

In between sessions Carol kept in touch with the team by telephone and reported how much more settled Mary Jane seemed and how she was beginning to make connections with how she was feeling and why.

The next session was to involve a facilitated contact with Helen. Carol was briefed beforehand on preparing Mary Jane for this contact. Carol told Mary Jane two days in advance that the next time she came to Adoptionplus Helen would be coming to visit. Carol understood how much Mary Jane had missed Helen when she left and thought it would be a good thing for her to see Helen again, and that once she had seen Helen, she and Carol would be going home together. Carol wondered if Mary Jane had questions she wanted to ask Helen, things she would like to say to or tell Helen. Carol also told Mary Jane how much she was looking forward to seeing Helen and telling her how well Mary Jane was growing. Carol was also prepared for the possible range of responses Mary Jane might have on actually seeing Helen again. Carol also thought about how, in talking in front of Mary Jane to Helen, she would convey the message that she understood how important Helen had been to Mary Jane, how she was pleased that she had come to see her, whilst also claiming her as her daughter to ensure that Mary Jane understood with whom she now belonged.

Meanwhile, the team had been in touch with Helen's supervising social worker who was going to attend the contact to support Helen. They discussed with her the preparation of Helen for the contact. Helen, like other ex-foster carers, needed to be helped to prepare for the possible range of reactions a child might have. At one extreme of the continuum a child could seem withdrawn and stay close to the adoptive parent(s), and at the other the child might run to the foster carer, want to sit with them and hug them and seem to exclude the adoptive parent(s). If Mary Jane was withdrawn, then the team would guide the session reflecting on how

Mary Jane might be feeling, ask Helen to say a little about how she remembers Mary Jane when she first came to live with her and some of the changes that took place. These should include some of the positives, for example favourite toys and games, as well as some of the difficulties from both of their points of view, including saying goodbye. Helen needed to be prepared for acknowledging this sadness but at the same time giving permission for Mary Jane to be settled and happy with her adoptive family. However, should Mary Jane go and sit with and want to snuggle up to Helen, we asked that Helen return the hug, tell her how good it was to see her and her mummy, how pleased she was that Mary Jane was now with this mummy and how she would like to see her sitting with and cuddling this mummy, as this would be a lovely picture for her to remember.

On the day of the contact Mary Jane and Carol were scheduled to arrive half an hour before Helen to prevent meeting in the car park and to give time for Mary Jane to settle. When Helen and her supervising social worker arrived they were shown into a separate room where Julia had a short meeting and gave Helen and her supervising social worker a chance to ask any questions they might have.

Mary Jane was prepared for the fact that Helen was coming with her social worker and that she may not know until she actually saw Helen how she would feel or whether she would like to say hello to Helen. She was also told that whatever she felt or did would be OK and that mummy would look after her and would be taking her home.

When Helen entered the room Mary Jane was clearly pleased to see her, smiled and looked at her. However, she went and sat on Carol's lap. Helen was clearly pleased to see Mary Jane and made very positive comments about how she'd grown and how lovely she looked. Mary Jane relaxed and began showing Helen some of the things she liked to play with when at Adoptionplus and Carol supported her in doing this. The team guided the session by light touch, referencing to some of the issues that had been explored during the life story work in terms of how scared Mary Jane had been as a baby when she first came to live with Helen and how important Helen had been to her. Helen said that Mary Jane had been important to her too and how pleased she was to see her feeling safe and close to Carol. Meanwhile, Mary Jane went over to Helen and leaned into her. Helen responded by putting her arm around Mary Jane for a short hug. Mary Jane then returned to Carol and sat on her lap. This returning to Carol and sitting on her lap for a brief period continued throughout the session. Carol was invited to tell Helen that she and Mary Jane had been thinking about seeing her and that Mary Jane had thought of some things she would like to say. Carol then encouraged Mary Jane to talk to Helen. Mary Jane who was standing beside Carol then whispered in her ear. Carol asked her if she wanted to say that herself or wanted her to tell Helen. Mary Jane whispered again and Carol looked to Helen and told her that Mary Jane wanted her to know that she loved her. Everyone in the room was very touched both by Mary Jane's expression of feeling and Carol's willingness and ability to support her in doing so. The session ended with Carol giving Helen a picture Mary Jane had drawn for her and the team taking photographs of Mary Jane with Carol and Helen.

This facilitated contact was not a magic wand, but it did help Mary Jane make sense of her move from Helen and help confirm both for her and for

Carol how her attachment to her adoptive mother had grown and developed. Throughout the session Mary Jane continually returned to Carol, using her as her secure base and then being able to spend a short time connecting with Helen, who in turn was able to convey her permission for Mary Jane to settle and deepen her attachment to Carol.

Sometimes, particularly if families live long distances apart, it may not be possible to arrange face-to-face contact between the foster carers and the adoptive family. Other ways of helping children know that their ex-foster carers continue to care about them and want them to be happy with their adoptive parents can be considered.

It is not unusual, for example, for the older child to have telephone contact with their foster carers and while this can work well, sometimes the exclusive nature of the telephone call can be unsettling for the child and/or the adoptive parents, who are unsure of what is being talked about. One child would ask her foster carer when she was coming back to live at her house, and the foster carer was unable to give a clear message that she now lived with her adoptive parents and there was no need for her to return to live with her. This same child had, after living with her adoptive parents for a week, asked them if she was good for a further two weeks could she then go back and live with her foster carers (bargaining stage!). In these situations arranging brief whole family Skype sessions could be helpful, in that the message is conveyed to the child that not only they but also their adoptive parents retain a connection with the foster carers. It also enables the adoptive parent(s) to pick up on and correct any misunderstandings that might occur. However, all of the adults involved need clear guidance about the purpose of the contact and how they will respond to any testing questions the child may have.

Other possibilities are helping foster carers to write letters that give clear messages to the child about deserving to have a family of their own and the foster carers' wish for them to settle and be happy with their adoptive family. Such a letter could be helpful to the child even where some ongoing face-to-face contact is planned. Undertaking a videoed interview with the foster carer(s) where they are prepared and supported in giving the child the kinds of messages that will help them know they will be held in mind and that they have permission to settle, deserve to be happy and grow to love their adoptive parents can then be shared with the child and their adoptive parent(s).

It might also be helpful if, during the introduction period, a short film is made when both sets of parents are together with the child while at the foster home, just as it is now common practice for adopters to receive a short film of the child before they have met them and for adopters to make a short film of themselves and their home by way of reassurance and introduction. The child would be able to watch this along with the foster carers, being able to recall, see and hear that foster carers and adoptive parents were together in wanting the child to be happy. This could help reassure the child while they settle in to the adoptive family. Such a film could be particularly reassuring for the younger child such as Mary Jane whose age and developmental stage made understanding her move from her foster carer difficult. Of course, adoptive parents may need support in thinking through how to use such a film and how to accept and empathise with their child's inevitable feelings of loss and/or the ambivalence they may express.

## Reflections for professionals, foster carers and adoptive parents

The aim of post placement contacts is to help minimise the trauma of loss and separation for the child through:

- helping prevent denial/avoidance of meaningful experience
- revisiting emotions about separation at manageable levels
- providing opportunities for support for the full range of feelings
- providing opportunities to review reasons for the separation
- decreasing 'magical thinking' and fantasies
- decreasing loyalty issues and proactively working with 'splits' and conflicting thoughts and feelings
- continuing transference of attachment/empowerment of the adoptive parents.[3]

The availability and quality of support from the foster carer during and following the introduction period for a child of whatever age is pivotal to the process of helping the child manage the anxiety that is inherent in such a huge life-changing event.

## The foster carer's change in role

A good foster placement has offered the maltreated child a period of respite and caregiving that has begun to set them on the road to recovering from their experiences of relational trauma. The foster carer(s) have supported the child through the many transitions and challenges that are part and parcel of being a child whose future is being decided.

For the child, the idea of a 'new mummy and daddy' may not only signal the loss of the foster carer and the familiar environment but can also remind the child of earlier neglectful and abusive experiences *their* mummies and/or daddies may have exposed them to, bringing past experiences back into the present. Sometimes children may be able to find words to describe their fears (one child wrote her fears down and put them in a worry box, and what became apparent was that this little girl had experienced serious physical and sexual abuse that was hitherto unknown). Some children may only be able to express their fears through their behaviour. It is essential that current carers and social workers can empathise with the child's anxieties, accept ambivalence and reassure the child that they will be helping them and their new parents get to know each other.

Introductions are about handing over the child's practical care and routines as well as the intimate knowledge the foster carers have developed about this individual child's preferences, needs and wants, what soothes and reassures, what might trouble or worry them, what gives them pleasure and what excites them. The explicit and implicit messages being conveyed to the child are that the foster carer(s) trust the prospective adopters to meet this child's needs.

The introduction also offers opportunities to help reduce the child's fears and worries about the unknown, help initiate the grieving process, as well as supporting the child and prospective adoptive parents in making a commitment to sharing a future.

Just as it is crucial for birth parents to be able to accept their change in role if they are to maintain a direct link with their child in adoption, foster carers also have to understand and accept their change in role and therefore *act* differently when they have post placement contact with the child. For example, while it may seem natural to pull out a tissue to wipe the child's nose, respond to behaviours that seem to indicate the child needs to visit the toilet, encourage the child to finish up the food on their plate, or correct their behaviour, interacting in these ways (which are essentially parenting activities) can be unsettling for the child who may experience these caretaking behaviours as a signal that preparations are under way for *another* move and set up conflicts of loyalty. Similar considerations need to be given to how the contact meetings are structured. For example, the adoptive parents should stay alongside the child while the foster carer is visiting, as withdrawing to give them time alone could also be reminiscent of the introductory period during which the foster carer withdrew to allow the child and adoptive parents time and space to develop their relationship.

Introductions that may have seemed to go smoothly without any protest, anger or sadness from the child may be an indication that the child is in the denial phase of grieving prior to moving. Even when foster carers and adoptive parents follow the kind of structure outlined above during post placement visits, the child may nevertheless protest as the foster carer is leaving, and show anger and distress during or following the visits. Such reactions are part of the grieving process which may not have surfaced previously.

Adoptive parents may need advance preparation and ongoing support in making sense of these reactions, and if they can meet their child's angry and sad feelings with acceptance and empathy, they are supporting their child in achieving a sense of resolution and facilitating the deepening of their attachment. However, the child's social worker may also offer the child support by using some of the many books and tools available to help children express and contextualise their feelings of anger and loss. Foster carers also need advice and support in managing the child's and their own grieving both during the introduction period and at subsequent post placement contact.

The purpose of these post placement visits is to support the transition of the child to their adoptive family. The timing and frequency needs to be agreed by the adopters, foster carers and professionals. The age of the child should guide frequency and spacing. However, they should not be at an intense frequency, first starting, say, within days then spreading to weeks after placement and should be reduced stepwise. If a long-term link can be maintained through the exchange of cards, telephone calls and even the occasional get-together, such a link can help support the child's self-esteem and integration and acceptance of the past.

Adoptive parents are cautioned against facilitating contact with ex-foster carers at the child's request when they are experiencing discord within the parent–child relationship. It is important to ensure that they and their child have effected a repair in the relationship before arranging the contact.

## CHAPTER 6

# Letterbox Contact

## Rachel Staff

The preceding chapters within this book have addressed some of the numerous complexities and considerations in relation to thinking about the needs of children within contact arrangements. Another essential area of contact to consider when we are thinking about contact for children in permanency is the practice of 'indirect' or (as it is most commonly referred to) 'letterbox' contact arrangements for those children who are adopted. This chapter will explore some of the complexities and considerations that are present in meeting children's needs within this form of contact. They mirror many of those highlighted within the areas already discussed by Elsie and Louis and, I hope, illustrate the parallels in the considerations that must be made when thinking about the needs of children within all forms of contact arrangements.

Letterbox contact is the most common form of contact within post adoption contact arrangements. Often agreed before children are placed with their adoptive families and often within the court arena towards the close of proceedings, letterbox contact has become such an integral part of adoption plans for children that the majority of children who are adopted will carry with them a plan for this type of contact.

The plans for letterbox contact are often made within the context of the emotionally charged period when the final decisions are made regarding the plan for adoption for the child. Social workers and all those involved in the court processes are usually understandably moved by the desperate loss for the birth family members that this decision represents. Anxious to lessen the impact of this loss and with the hope that the potential benefits of contact will help both the child and the birth family to manage this loss, a plan for letterbox contact is made. Often the plan is made without a more detailed consideration of the factors that will need to be in place in order that it can be both possible and meaningful for all parties involved. Unfortunately, often a plan is made because letterbox contact is considered simply to be 'the norm' in adoption practice to which local authorities and the courts automatically adhere.

Letterbox contact usually involves the exchange of letters (and often photographs) between the child and their adoptive family and birth family members. The exchange of these letters can range in frequency and complexity from an annual exchange of letters with one birth family member (most commonly the birth mother) to up to four exchanges within a year with a number of family members (sometimes being inclusive of birth parents, grandparents, aunts and uncles and siblings). Some local authorities will encourage the exchange of photographs and birthday and Christmas cards within these arrangements; others are more cautious of these exchanges, for reasons I will discuss below. Whilst all exchanges of letters will pass through local authority post adoption teams, local authorities will vary hugely in how they facilitate these arrangements. For some local authorities the exchange will be managed primarily as an administration task, although usually with at least a checking of the information contained within the birth family member's letters to ensure that the letters are appropriate. Other local authorities will provide a fuller service including active support for birth family members, as well as the children and adoptive parents, in thinking about the impact of the contact arrangements for the child. The volume of letterbox contact arrangements within different local authorities will also vary hugely. I have spoken to social workers who are responsible for managing over 500 arrangements single-handedly, whilst other teams have a number of workers allocated specifically to a smaller volume of arrangements in order to manage these effectively.

My professional experience in the last 11 years has been as a social worker and team manager within the field of post adoption support. This experience has included working within local authorities and specialist adoption agencies. I have been responsible for managing contact services as well as providing therapeutic support for adoptive families and training for other professionals involved in adoption support. Prior to this, I worked as a social worker within the earlier stages of the adoption process and, prior to that, as a social worker in both child protection and for looked after children. The scope of my experience within the field of children and families work has been an important factor in the way in which I view and approach the issue of post adoption contact for children with their birth family members.

Like many social workers who began their careers within child protection I have witnessed first-hand the trauma that children can experience within their birth families and the chaos and pain experienced by both them and their birth family members once they have been removed from their families. It is impossible to forget the experiences of children who have often experienced great distress and trauma at the most vulnerable times in their lives. Nor indeed is it possible to forget the confusion, pain and vulnerability of the birth family members who are (as Elsbeth Neil's research highlights[1]) often the most vulnerable people in society. I have witnessed both birth family members and the adopted children struggle to make sense of, and come to terms with, the traumatic experiences and loss that lie at the heart of the beginning of the adoption journey. The emotional context of the beginning of the adoption process for the vast majority of children begins within the context of child protection. When children have been or are at risk of being significantly harmed the emotional impact of this for both the families and children involved is profound. Loss, grief and anger are just some of the emotions that both the children and their families experience both at the beginning, but also throughout, the adoption journey.

The enormity of the experiences and events that preclude the adoption of the majority of children who have been adopted in society are acknowledged within the rigorous and extensive processes that the birth family and the child move through before a final decision to recommend a plan for adoption is reached. Social services files, police files, numerous forums and meetings involving a range of professionals record the extent of concerns that social care systems will hold and attempt to address before a plan for adoption is even considered for a child. Ultimately of course it is only within the court processes that plans for permanent care outside of the child's birth family are considered. Indeed, adoption as an outcome of those court processes would not be an option in the court's decision making unless the circumstances of the child's life had warranted such concern and need for society's intervention that no other decision could be reached (such is the gravity of the decision to end the legal relationship between a child and their birth family).

Once a child has been adopted the consequences of those early experiences do not disappear. The ongoing needs of adopted children and their families are acknowledged and recognised within the provision of post adoption support from local authorities, from CAMHS (child and adolescent mental health services), from specialist support agencies, and have recently been further highlighted by the government's agreement for provision of additional funding for post adoption support services. Adoptive families live with the very real consequences of children's experiences within their birth families throughout their child's lifetime. The reality and gravity of the impact of the past on the present seems finally to be increasingly accepted. We cannot underestimate the impact of children's early experiences on their current wellbeing. The past is always present in children's ongoing development; it is present for their adoptive parents in the parenting and care their children need.

How then should we approach our thinking about letterbox contact whilst holding in mind the complexity and emotionally profound journey that precedes the placement of the adopted child with their family? How should we approach our thinking about the needs of the child within the exchange of letterbox contact whilst holding in mind the reality and implications of the very nature of their early relationships with the birth family members with whom we are expecting them to continue to communicate throughout their childhoods within their adoptive families? I will argue within this chapter that we must do so with a great deal more thought and understanding of children's emotional needs than much of our practice has often done so to date.

Despite everything we now understand about the enormity and gravity of children's experiences within their adoption journey, it has often struck me as slightly nonsensical that the form of contact given the least thought in planning is the one used most frequently. Letterbox contact is quite literally a communication between the past and the present. It brings the links with the child's past into their present lives and indeed into their home and their adoptive family. This past is, as we have considered above, often one which has been characterised by rupture, loss and chaos. For a long time there has been a general acceptance that despite the often-traumatised nature of the past it is still in the child's interests to receive this contact. Furthermore, there has been a general acceptance that letterbox contact (in not being a face-to-face contact) is a form of contact which is less intense in its emotional effect and automatically 'safe' for the child in its implementation.

My experience of managing a post adoption contact service in a local authority and working with birth and adoptive families post adoption is that there are indeed potentially positive gains for all involved in the adoption triangle in undertaking letterbox contact. However, my experience has also reinforced my understanding that letterbox contact, without appropriate planning and support, can have a detrimental effect on the child's emotional wellbeing. My experience is that, far from being a benign and inconsequential event for children, their adoptive families and indeed their birth families, letterbox contact can be highly emotive and profound in its effect for all involved. It is not sufficient to assume that letterbox contact should be planned automatically for the adopted child. On the contrary, it is essential to ask the questions:

- What purpose should the sharing of letterbox contact hold for all parties involved in the adoption?

- What meaning can the child make of the contact?

- How can this form of contact be helpful for the child and when is there a risk of it being harmful?

If we do not attend to these questions when considering every plan for letterbox contact for every individual adopted child we risk putting in place contact plans which lack meaning or purpose and which are potentially risky, unrealistic and untenable in their original intent (both Loxtercamp (2009)[2] and Selwyn, Frazer and Wrighton (2006)[3] provide useful discussions about the potential for letterbox contact to create difficulties for children's emotional health). Furthermore, it is not enough to ask these questions only at the beginning of a child's preparation for moving to an adoptive family. As I will explore below, they must be asked at regular intervals and certainly at key developmental stages throughout the child's life. Children's development is not static; if we only consider these questions once how can we possibly be meeting children's needs as they grow within their adoptive families?

When considering the purpose of contact we should essentially be considering the potential positive benefits of letterbox contact for adopted children. In the introduction to this chapter I referred to the fact that often contact plans are made within the emotionally charged context of the decision-making conclusion that the plan for the child is adoption. I would in no way want to devalue social workers' capacity to feel empathy for birth family members and to want to lessen the pain that those family members experience at that time. In my experience, it is one of the many qualities and skills that many social workers have which make the profession so uniquely valuable. We do, though, have to hold in mind the fact that the child's emotional wellbeing is paramount within any contact arrangements.

There are a number of possible benefits that social workers will often have in mind when making plans for letterbox contact when they are considering the child's wellbeing. In exploring these below I would like to suggest that whilst all of them are entirely valid, we cannot assume that by following the process in itself we automatically ensure these benefits for the child.

The following exploration of the potential benefits of letterbox contact for adopted children uses case studies to highlight the considerations and dilemmas that can arise for children and their adoptive and birth parents. Each section addresses the different potential benefits of letterbox contact that social services often have in mind when making contact plans for children. The sections contain discussions and case examples of situations when it has been possible to use contact as a way of helping children with their emotional development, when it has been felt appropriate to find a compromise within arrangements, and when it simply isn't safe to proceed with contact arrangements at all. The case studies and discussions that accompany them are by no means exhaustive but it is hoped that they illustrate some of the key considerations we must hold in mind when both planning and facilitating letterbox contact arrangements for our children (the names of children as well as any identifying details have been changed in order to protect families' confidentiality). The case examples also highlight the need for social workers to take a fluid and often-creative approach to letterbox contact, whilst holding in mind the emotional experience and needs of the children and young people involved.

## The potential for letterbox contact to support the child's understanding of their birth or 'genetic' identity

Often there is an assumption that this can be achieved purely through the process of exchanging letters alone. In my experience, this is not often the case within letters, which usually give a general overview of what the birth family member has been doing since the last contact exchange. It is possible to support this area if there is an active dialogue between the adoptive parents and child as to the child's experience of the information they have received, which enables them to ask questions to help them make sense of the contact exchange. This may be simply a case of the adoptive parent 'wondering about' what impression, feelings or questions the letter raises for the child. An example of this would be the adoptive parent wondering aloud about how the birth parent's life is and how they are getting on, placing this within the context of the information received within the letter. This can open up a dialogue between the parent and child, which helps the child to make sense of the birth parent as a whole beyond the scope of the letter. Sometimes, an attuned adoptive parent can use their observation of the way in which their child responds to letterbox contact to increase their understanding of their birth parent further.

## Case study: Steven

A lovely example of this occurred within a letterbox exchange I managed for a 12-year-old boy, Steven, who had been adopted by his foster carers. Steven had twice-yearly letterbox contact with his birth mother. Steven had been removed from his birth mother at the age of 7 years because she was unable to care for him safely as a result of her drug and alcohol abuse. Steven's memories of his life with his birth mother were of a chaotic existence in which he was sometimes left alone, often did not have enough to eat and was sometimes on the receiving end of explosive temper tantrums from his mother. Steven's birth mother had apologised to Steven for her lack of care and had shown genuine remorse that she had frightened him and neglected him in the past. She had accepted the plan for Steven to be adopted as her own health deteriorated, and had been reassured that he was to be adopted by his foster carers. She had had some direct contact with Steven with his foster carers in the early stages of his placement but this had not been a positive experience for Steven as her addiction problems had meant that she was inconsistent in her attendance. Social services had subsequently recommended that the plan for contact should be via the letterbox system only and she had eventually accepted this with the support of her drugs and alcohol worker who had been an independent counsellor for her for some time. She was able to be consistent in her letterbox letters, showed pride in Steven's achievements and clearly missed him.

Steven looked forward to her letters but often showed a great deal of angry behaviour after receiving them. Steven's adoptive mother was sensitive enough to note that Steven had conflicting feelings in relation to the contact, and after sharing one contact with him talked with him about this. She explained to Steven that she had noticed he both liked receiving these letters, but that they also made him angry and she suspected more than a little bit sad. She wondered with him about whether there was anything she could do to help figure out how to help him with these feelings. Steven was able to articulate his feeling that it made him angry that his birth mother could write nice letters to him, but that she didn't love him enough to look after him properly when he lived with her. He wondered if she was 'pretending' in the letters, or whether she had changed enough to be able to look after him but didn't want him back. Steven could explain that he sometimes thought his birth mother was a 'bad' person and that it didn't make sense to him that she could write nice letters but couldn't look after him.

Steven's adoptive mother contacted me to see if there was anything she could do to help Steven with these understandably confused feelings. I had met Steven's birth mother on a number of occasions and knew that, despite her difficulties, she genuinely cared for Steven and would like to help. I decided that it would be worth talking to her to see if, with support, she could help Steven to make more sense of her as a person and to provide some explanation herself as to what had happened in her own life to create the difficulties that had led to her neglect of, and abusive behaviour towards, Steven.

During the meeting with Steven's birth mother I explained to her that I did not know much about her own life, that I knew things had gone badly wrong but not why. I asked her to talk to me about her own experiences as a child and if there was anything that she felt could help Steven to understand her better. What Steven's birth mother was able to explain was very moving and proved to be very beneficial for Steven. She explained that she felt her early childhood had been OK. She had grown up with her mother and sister until her mother had remarried when she was 11 years old. Her step-father had been an extremely abusive man. She had witnessed her mother being badly physically assaulted on numerous occasions and she and her sister had been regularly beaten. By the time she was 13 years old she was escaping the nightmare at home by staying away as much as possible. She began drinking, slept wherever she could (often with risky adults) and began taking harder drugs in her later teens. She had naively believed when she became pregnant with Steven that she would be able to change and give him the kind of childhood she had wished for herself. She had not, though, been able to overcome her addictions; her lifestyle remained chaotic and she had found the demands of caring for Steven completely overwhelming. Her own health continued to be poor, her life expectancy was limited and she expressed a huge degree of shame and guilt that she had failed Steven so badly. When I asked her what she would like me to tell Steven about herself her words were, 'that I haven't always been like this, I wasn't born such a mess'. I asked her if she could tell me something about her earlier, happier childhood. What had she been like? What did she enjoy doing? She explained that she always asked Steven in her letters how his swimming was progressing. This was because she felt very proud of his clear talent and achievements in his competitive swimming, but also because she herself had competed in swimming competitions and had been very talented. She had loved swimming and gained a lot of self-esteem from competing and winning. She felt great that Steven had this too and was very proud of him.

I left the meeting with Steven's birth mother with a much better understanding of her as a person. Her story was moving and I had a clear sense of the girl that she once was before her life descended into chaos. I made an appointment to visit Steven and his adoptive parents. We agreed that I would talk with Steven (with his adoptive parents present) about my meeting with his birth mother. I would try to help him understand why things had gone wrong and to give him a fuller sense of his birth mother beyond his memories and his experience of her as a mother who had got things so terribly wrong.

A few days before my meeting date with Steven a package arrived through the post from his birth mother. Inside was a card as well as a bundle of swimming certificates and swimming medals. After our meeting she had visited her own mother and asked if she had kept any of her old swimming awards. She had sent these to Steven with a message relaying her own love of swimming and her pride in his achievements. She expressed her wish that Steven keep her own medals and a hope that he would understand that this represented a positive part of who she had once been and perhaps a positive part of their identity that they could share. I discussed the package with Steven's adoptive parents and they agreed that they felt it would be beneficial for him to receive it.

Talking to Steven about my meeting with his birth mother and passing on the package she had sent for him was a highly emotive experience. Steven was incredibly sad when thinking about his birth mother's early life; sadness for his birth mother but also for himself. His anger towards her did not magically evaporate; these were complex feelings that would take a lifetime to come to terms with. His increased understanding of his birth mother as an individual whose life had changed so drastically over time helped him to begin to think about her in a more rounded sense. His surprise and joy that they shared a positive connection was clear to see. Steven understood the value of the gift that she had given to him in wanting him to 'hold on to' the more positive sense of identity that she had once had in the child that she had once been.

This is one example of how letterbox contact can help adopted children to make sense of their birth family member's identity, who they are, in a much wider sense. Sometimes children ask much more simple questions: what TV programmes do they like to watch, do they live in a nice place, what is their favourite food? In my experience, even these more day-to-day enquiries help the child, as time goes by, to build an understanding of their birth parent or other birth relative which is more widely defined than just the account of 'what went wrong'. It is a difficult balance for children, and indeed us as adults, to hold in mind the fact that as human beings we are much more complex than 'good' or 'bad', particularly when an individual's actions have caused so much harm. Yet, I do believe that using letterbox contact as an opportunity to begin to understand the fuller and more complex picture of the birth family member's identity and background is valuable for children. I have often worked with teenagers who begin to consider much more complex and abstract questions in relation to their own identity and what their 'birth identity' means in relation to this. Many of these young people hold fantasies about the inevitability of 'becoming like' their birth parents. This sense of an almost inevitable destiny is often based on the young person's understanding that their birth family members were simply 'bad'. Often, adopted teenagers themselves may have a rocky adolescence during which their behaviour becomes difficult. These difficulties can leave them with a sense that they are hurtling towards a destiny in which they will repeat the mistakes made by their birth parents. The young person will often believe that they are driven by a genetic template, which determines their emerging identity. Helping teenagers to understand the complex interplay of nurture and nature in who we are as human beings is an essential part of life story work at this age. If they are able to understand the complexity of their birth family's own story they are far better placed to begin to make sense of their own story and emerging identity and to feel more empowered in determining their own future path. Using their experience of letterbox communication and their understanding of their birth family member can be extremely helpful.

These are just some of the ways in which letterbox contact can be used to help the child develop a sense of their birth family members and consequently their own 'genetic identity'. There are, of course, also the possibilities of birth family members providing information about the child's physical/medical history. They can also provide information in relation to positive memories of the child's early years if this is possible. It is, though, highly unlikely that the exchange of this kind of valuable information will emerge without support from the exchange of letters alone. This requires the child's adoptive parents to be alert to the questions, feelings and fantasies that children are likely to hold in relation to the contact exchange and to be able to provide a voice in order to begin to articulate the exploration of these. Professionals need to be ready to support adoptive parents in making sense of their child's feelings that come to the fore as a result of the letterbox contact, and to be able to support birth parents in providing a response to the child's questions. In my experience, many birth parents will be able to do this when the request for information is coming as a direct result of the child's expressed needs. Finally, professionals will need to be ready to support the adoptive parents and the child in 'making sense' of the wider communication that results from these initial explorations.

## The potential for letterbox contact to reassure children about the birth family's wellbeing

Receiving regular letters from birth family members can play an important part in reassuring children that they are safe and well. Many children worry about their birth family's ongoing wellbeing after they have been removed from them; this is often particularly the case for children who have experienced domestic violence or other experiences which have posed a very real threat to their birth family members' safety. If this is possible, it can alleviate anxiety for children who may be preoccupied with their birth family members' safety and happiness.

The process of planning and agreeing the exchange of letterbox contact does not, however, guarantee that this benefit will be possible for the adopted child. Many birth parents have, and continue to lead, particularly risky and chaotic lifestyles. The very nature of their daily lives often means that they will struggle to maintain letterbox contact after the child has been adopted. In my experience, as a letterbox coordinator, these birth family members often require the most support in being able to take part in contact arrangements. Trying to locate and enable these birth family members to communicate about their wellbeing for a child often requires a flexible and proactive response from the local authority contact service.

## Case study: Lucy

Whilst managing the contact service for a local authority in the Midlands, I worked with Lucy, an 8-year-old girl who had been adopted after being removed from her birth mother's care at the age of 5 years because of her mother's involvement in a relationship which was characterised by domestic violence. Lucy had received intermittent contact from her birth mother in the following years, which was of a reasonable quality but inconsistent. As she approached mid-childhood her adoptive parents were becoming increasingly concerned that Lucy seemed to be becoming more and more anxious about her birth mother's safety, reporting preoccupations and anxieties that she may be dead or still 'being hurt' by her previous partner. I agreed that I would see if I could find out any information in relation to the birth mother's whereabouts.

As a part of supporting birth family members with contact arrangements I had previously visited a number of organisations within the local area to talk with the teams about post adoption contact and the letterbox service. These teams were the support services that I felt were most likely to come into contact with birth parents in the intermediate and long term. These organisations included: drug and alcohol support teams, housing support teams, domestic violence services, local authority social services teams and health teams. In letting the services know about post adoption contact and the support available for birth family members, I hoped that they would be able to direct to our service those birth family members who spoke about the fact that they had children who were adopted. The teams within these organisations had been receptive to this idea, as a number of them had supported clients who had spoken about their children but they hadn't been aware that the potential for contact existed.

I contacted the housing support teams in the area initially as I was aware that the birth mother in question had had to use domestic violence hostels on a number of occasions and was often homeless as a result of fleeing domestic violence. Whilst the support workers were not able to advise me whether the birth mother had or was using the service, they agreed that if they were in contact with her they would pass on my request for contact and let me know if she agreed to meeting with me. Fortunately, this was the case. A housing support worker within a local hostel who was currently working with the birth mother contacted me. Lucy's birth mother had agreed to meet with me as long as her support worker could be present.

Meeting with Lucy's birth mother was very useful. She was actually in a very different position to the one in which she had been in the intervening years following Lucy's adoption. Within the last year she had found stability within supported housing and was attending college. Lucy's birth mother explained that she had thought that Lucy and her adoptive parents no longer wanted to have contact with her. She felt ashamed about her failure to protect Lucy in the past and that she had been so inconsistent with her contact to date. Sometimes she felt that Lucy would be better off if she just 'disappeared' so that she could enjoy her new life with her adoptive family. When I explained that Lucy still very much thought about her and worried about her, she was very surprised. She explained that she thought about Lucy every day and had really valued the letters she had received from the adoptive parents. She was delighted that she could still write to the adoptive parents but explained that she was barely literate (something else she felt deeply ashamed about). We agreed that her housing support officer would help her to write the letters and that she could eventually use the support of the post adoption team for help with this, should she need it. (Contact with social services was something that Lucy's mother was still very reticent about, following her own childhood experiences of being in care, but also because of the adversarial nature of her relationship with the children and family teams following the removal of her own children.)

Lucy's birth mother was able to write a reassuring letter for Lucy and her adoptive parents apologising for the fact that she had been inconsistent in her contact and explaining that she was in a much better place and wanted Lucy to be happy with her adoptive family. She was able to express her genuine thanks to Lucy's adoptive parents for making such efforts to maintain the contact. This was a very important message for Lucy to hear. Both her birth mother and adoptive parents were working together to look after her emotional needs.

In other families I have worked with it hasn't been possible for birth parents to engage in consistent contact with their child. This has been despite efforts to help and support them to engage in the contact through a variety of support services. Some birth parents simply do not have the ability to do so; they may have extended periods of homelessness, experience mental ill health or continue to have addiction problems that mean they lead very chaotic lives. Contact with the local authority is intermittent and it is often difficult to locate them. In these circumstances, adoptive parents need support in thinking through what their decisions may be in relation to continuing the contact. Some children will express a need to know when their birth parent does make contact; others may find the uncertainty unbearable. In my experience, adoptive parents will make a decision about ongoing contact according to what they feel is best for their child. This may mean that they decide to continue to send their own letters to the local authority regardless of the birth parent's inconsistency. In doing so, they are often sending a clear message to the child that they will continue to honour their contact agreement even if the birth parent isn't able to. They will share contact from the birth parent with the child when it is possible but be clear with their child about the inconsistency and help them in validating any feelings their child may have about this.

In other circumstances, adoptive parents may feel that it is too upsetting for their child to manage the inconsistency and uncertainty of contact and decide to end the contact until the birth parent is in a position to maintain it. The adoptive parents may need help in explaining to their child that they feel it is just too hard for the child. Often these decisions are made when there is a history of very poor contact, and knowledge about the parents indicates that this is unlikely to change. These are not easy decisions to make and often the parents will need support in balancing the potential implications for the child in not just the immediate but also the longer-term future. Additional work may also be required with the child from professionals within the post adoption team to explain the decision made by the adoptive parents. If the child is given the message that this is a decision that professionals also think is best for the child, it can help to prevent the child 'blaming' the adoptive parents and focusing all of the responsibility for the decision with them.

In some situations it simply won't be possible to reassure the child about their birth family member's welfare, because the birth family member is not OK. The effects of long-term drug and alcohol abuse, violence or just poor health in itself can mean that birth family members die. This may be a reality that many adopted children have to come to terms with, which can be incredibly challenging and distressing for adoptive families to manage. In these situations, families will often require additional support to help their child cope with yet further loss.

## Contact from birth family members can reassure the child that the family still thinks about them and cares for them

Lucy's case also illustrates this point and, indeed, I have worked with many birth parents who, with support, have managed to provide this message via letterbox contact in an appropriate and sensitive way. It is important because many children will worry that their birth parent or other birth relatives no longer cares for them or thinks about them once they have been adopted. Many adopted children will struggle with feelings of rejection and abandonment because of their past experiences. Appropriate messages to the effect that birth family members still think about them, care for them and want them to be happy can help to alleviate the sense of rejection and abandonment that many adopted children carry with them. It is important to consider, however, the nature of the messages we are communicating to children from birth family members. Sometimes birth parents will be able to do this but when they are not, it is sometimes possible to find this message communicated from another birth family member.

## Case study: Two sisters

I once worked with two sisters who had experienced an early childhood characterised by neglect, domestic violence and their birth mother's mental health difficulties. Their birth mother was incapable of engaging in letterbox contact. Her lifestyle was chaotic, she did not accept that the girls should have been adopted and she exhibited violent behaviour towards social workers and other professionals. This meant that she was unable to access support to help her shift in her understanding or views. The letters that she sent to the service for the children were full of statements about how much she missed them and thought about them. The contexts of these statements were, unfortunately however, submerged within expressions of her own feelings of injustice and her belief that her parenting had been good, that the girls should never have been removed from her care and would return to her one day.

The letters were not appropriate to pass on to the girls. Such a profound level of denial of the reality of the girls' experiences would be distressing for them and could impact on their ability to form secure attachments to their new family.

The birth mother's emotional expression was entirely focused on her own needs and didn't take any account of what the girls' emotional needs may be. Receiving letters, which expressed such a lack of ability to hold the girls' needs in mind and indeed to put their needs first, would retrigger many of the distressing feelings that the girls had experienced within her care.

In managing this particular situation I agreed with the girls' adoptive parents that I would meet with the girls (and their parents together) to talk about the nature of the letters and birth mum's ongoing struggle to understand or accept what had gone so wrong in their early lives with her. Within the sessions with the girls we focused on helping them to understand their birth mother's difficulties and the particular nature of her mental health difficulties. We explained that her difficulties were unlikely to change and that for this reason it was highly unlikely that she would be able to write letters that we could send to them (as had been the initial plan when letterbox contact was agreed). We were clear with the girls that their birth mother still thought about them. This was important to the older sister in particular because she was 6 years old when she left her birth mother's care. We also tried to help the girls understand that in her own way, the birth mother cared for them. Our emphasis, however, in explaining to the girls why we wouldn't want to pass the letter on to them was in talking about their 'emotional safety'. We acknowledged that their birth mother's behaviour in the past had been very upsetting for them and that we would not wish to keep on exposing them to this feeling. We did, however, agree that we would let the girls' adoptive parents know when we had received letters from the birth mother so that the girls would know that she was OK (as much as she could be). The adoptive parents who were able to hold a great deal of empathy for the birth mother would still send an annual update of the girls' progress to her.

The girls were able to accept the decision not to pass on the birth mother's letters directly to them. Their grief in the loss of their birth mother (a loss that was present not just within their removal and subsequent adoption but also in the loss of what their birth mother had never been able to provide) was still an ongoing struggle for them. They did, however, understand that her letters were likely to be upsetting for them. During the sessions the older sister explained that her maternal birth aunt, who had provided some care for her and her sister when they lived within their birth family, had tried to help her understand that her birth mother wasn't well. She had not shared this memory with her adoptive parents or her previous social worker but it became evident that the maternal aunt had played an important part in trying to help the girls emotionally during their tumultuous times with their birth mother. This information was very new for both the adoptive parents and myself. There had been no record of plans to include the maternal aunt in the contact plans and the older girl had no idea of why this was the case.

After the sessions with the girls I searched their historical files to try to find out more about the maternal aunt and her role in the girls' history. Earlier records did state that she had provided respite for the girls. Records also indicated that she had been approached by the local authority as a potential carer for the girls but she had not felt that she could do this. At ten years younger than her sister, only 21 years of age and still studying, it was clear that this wouldn't have been appropriate. What was also clear, however, was that she had not been considered in longer-term contact plans for the girls. With the adoptive parents' permission I decided to write to the maternal aunt at the address we had for her. Our hope was that it may potentially be possible to maintain a relationship through contact with the girls, as it had been positive in the past, and to provide a source of contact that could potentially provide the supportive messages for the girls, which the birth mother wasn't able to do.

The aunt did contact the department; previous social workers had not approached her about the possibility of having post adoption contact with the girls. She described her relationship with the girls in their younger years as a positive one but explained that this relationship had been intermittent in nature both because she was away at university and because the girls' birth mother had often prevented her from having contact with the girls when she had been in periods of more acute mental illness. The aunt had a good understanding of her sister's mental health difficulties, which had developed whilst she was in her late adolescence. She explained that her sister's chronic drug use had begun in an attempt to self-medicate when she was experiencing episodes of severe mental ill health and that eventually the combination of drug use and the recurring mental health difficulties had spiralled out of control. She felt sure that, when well, her sister had genuinely loved the girls but didn't feel that her sister would ever be well again. She had extremely limited contact with her sister who experienced a great deal of paranoia and didn't trust her family members.

The aunt was both surprised but also delighted that she may be able to have letterbox contact with her nieces. She was keen to be able to explain to them that she often thought of them, missed them and wanted them to be happy but also to help them understand that their birth mother's illness was very much beyond her control. She was very moved to hear that her oldest niece had remembered her and some of the conversations they had had together.

The girls and their adoptive parents were pleased to hear about the aunt and her willingness to provide this very useful contact for the girls. The contact aided the girls' understanding of their birth mother but also helped to ease the sense of a slightly fractured history that they both held in having been removed from the birth family. The adoptive parents were rightly confused as to why the potentially positive relationship with the aunt hadn't been promoted by the department, whilst the difficult and unrealistic contact with the birth mother had been so prioritised without any realistic assessment of how she would be able to manage this. Their feelings were valid; looking back over the previous case records it was clear that the girls had a number of changes of social workers in the latter stages of the process of moving towards adoption. The existence of the aunt and her role in the earlier stage of the girls' lives had simply been lost without a consistent worker who could hold the girls' whole story in mind. The aunt, as is common with many birth relatives, had assumed that adoption meant the end of contact with birth family members.

Again, sometimes it is simply not possible for children to receive this message from any birth family member. For some children who have experienced traumatic and extensive abuse within their birth families there aren't any family members who can provide a message that can be received safely by the child. Children who have been sexually abused within their birth families, for example, and where abusive behaviour was carried out by multiple family members, or where other family members were collusive in the abuse, are at risk of feeling highly unsafe because of the risk of hidden messages or trauma triggers contained within statements within letterbox contact. When birth families are highly risky and will remain highly risky for children (be it because of sexual abuse, extreme violence or other reasons) it may be preferable to state very clearly from the beginning of the child's adoption that contact can never be safe for them. This is a very 'final' decision but children will sometimes need to understand that their birth family is very unsafe. Work to help them process this and come to terms with it over time will, of course, be important.

Many children will remember and understand themselves how unsafe they felt whilst with their birth family. In some of these situations it would be highly inappropriate for the child to receive letterbox contact from their birth family members within their new adoptive home. It is essential that the adoptive family and home feels safe and secure for children; contact with some birth family members could seriously undermine that very basic sense of safety for some adoptive children.

## Taking responsibility and apologising

If a birth parent is able to provide the message within contact that they take responsibility for not being able to care for the child and apologise for this, it can be of enormous benefit for the child.

Whilst it can be very valuable for a child to have the reassurance that the birth family member thinks about them and continues to care about them, there is an additional aim of letterbox contact, which is very important. Contact is at risk of being meaningless if the reasons for the break in relationship with the birth family are not acknowledged or indeed denied. Children need the birth parents to be able to acknowledge what went wrong if they are to make sense of their experiences. Of even more value is the possibility of a birth parent providing an apology and acceptance of responsibility for the events that led to the child's removal from their care. This can be an important part of repair for the child. Many children are left feeling that they are responsible for the events that led to their removal from their birth family. Sometimes birth family members have explicitly expressed this belief; sometimes it may simply be that the child (as children do) believes that they must have been responsible. Elsie and Louis highlight this important need within Chapter 2 on facilitated contact; it should also be an important aim within letterbox contact.

Some birth parents are able to do this with support within letterbox contact. I have worked with both birth mothers and birth fathers who, in understanding this need for their child, have written very moving letters in which they both accept responsibility for and apologise for events of the past.

In other circumstances, a parent may want to do what is best for their child but may need significant support in being able to do so.

## Case study: Sarah

I worked with a 10-year-old girl, Sarah, who had been removed from her birth father's care when she was 2 years old because of concerns about neglect. Her birth mother had abandoned her soon after birth. Her birth father had gone on to marry and have further children, all of whom remained in his care. He had maintained letterbox contact with Sarah's adoptive parents and this had seemed to proceed smoothly. He was consistent and reliable with his contact, was complimentary towards the adoptive parents in his letters and gave Sarah the message that he was glad she was happy and doing well with her family. He provided information about her half-siblings and reassured her that he was well and happy. He shared Sarah's letterbox contact with her siblings and spoke of her with them. When Sarah was 10 years old her behaviour at school began to deteriorate and she became very oppositional at home. Her adoptive parents approached the local authority for support.

After some exploration with Sarah it emerged that she had recently had a letterbox contact in which her father had included a family photograph of himself and his wife and children on holiday. Although Sarah had not reacted to this at the time when her parents shared it with her, it had, in fact, upset her greatly. Coinciding with a key stage of development in which she had begun to think in much more complex terms about the meaning of her history and the reason that she had been removed from her father, Sarah became preoccupied with thoughts that it must have been her fault that she was removed from her father's care. There in her father's photograph was clear evidence that he was a good father with a happy family; the only explanation as to why he hadn't been able to look after her must have been that she was a bad child who was too difficult to look after.

Whilst Sarah's father had always written supportive and considerate letters to her and her adoptive parents he had never explicitly addressed the difficulties that had occurred in his parenting when Sarah was so small. Sarah's adoptive parents had not thought to ask about this. Why would they? They had felt that the contact was a very positive thing for Sarah as she had progressed through her childhood.

I decided with the adoptive parents that it would be useful to discuss Sarah's feelings directly with her birth father. We felt that whilst Sarah's parents may be able to provide an explanation of what had been so different in her father's life back then, this would be far less powerful than if her father were able to do it himself.

Sarah's birth father found this extremely difficult. The time at which Sarah had been removed from his care had been a terrible one for him. He was deeply ashamed of his behaviour in the past and found it extremely difficult even to think about. He was upset that Sarah felt it was her fault that things had gone so wrong but struggled himself to understand why he had behaved so badly. Despite his ability to acknowledge that things had gone wrong and to be clear that what had happened was not Sarah's fault, his deep sense of shame and avoidance of the memories of what had happened prevented him from being able to make sense of this for Sarah. It was agreed that a letter to Sarah acknowledging the elements that he was able to articulate (i.e. that it was his responsibility that things had gone wrong and that he was sorry about what had happened) would be helpful for her, but we were disappointed that he was not able to move past this point.

In time, Sarah's father approached us again; this time he was requesting more support. His children who were still within his care had begun to ask similar questions to Sarah about what had happened to lead to Sarah being adopted. Again, he had struggled to provide them with an explanation. He agreed that he would like to take up a previous offer of birth parent counselling. Eventually, Sarah's father was able to begin to face the trauma of his own past and therefore help Sarah and her siblings to understand Sarah's adoption. His ability to meet Sarah's needs was gradual and took a great deal of time. His willingness to try, however, was a clear indicator of the ongoing positive impact that his contact could have for Sarah and was, we all felt, worth pursuing.

Of course sometimes it is not possible for birth parents to take responsibility or say sorry for what went wrong in their parenting in the child's early years. Most social workers will be familiar with the particularly tragic stories of those children who are scapegoated by their birth family and given a very strong message that they are indeed 'bad' and the cause of everything that went wrong in their lives. Such powerful messages are incredibly damaging for children. In situations like these, where birth family members clearly focus the blame within the child, or within others when birth family members refuse to acknowledge any responsibility, we do really have to question whether the contact is too damaging for the child to experience and whether it should continue.

## Supporting adoptive parents

Contact can potentially provide an essential message of support for the adoptive parents and 'permission' for the child to be happy within their new family.

The process of participating in letterbox contact arrangements can provide for the child a message of acceptance from birth family members of the child's adopted status and place in their new family. Some of the cases above highlight when this is possible. However, this does not automatically follow unless some basic ground rules are adhered to which help the child understand this message. One of these ground rules is that birth family members should address the beginning of their letters to the adoptive parents and the child together, rather than to the child directly. This provides a very direct message that communication is open and accepting of the child's adopted status. Where possible, birth family members should also provide messages of support for the parenting that the adoptive parents are providing for the child. Both birth and adoptive parents have reported that meeting together prior to, or soon after, the child's placement with the adoptive parents can help in setting this kind of tone for the letterbox contact. These meetings can help both adoptive and birth parents allay fears or fantasies they may have about each other and help them in directing their contact to one another.

A friendly tone from adoptive parents, which the child understands to be positive in intent, is also beneficial for the child. The majority of birth parents involved in ongoing contact with birth children are also able to make positive statements about their child's achievements and happy times.

These kinds of messages can be helpful to children in minimising the sense of divided loyalty that children can feel in relation to their adoptive and birth families (particularly during the exploration of their identity in their teenage years).

If birth family members refuse to acknowledge the presence of the adoptive parents and choose only to address their child within letters, this can be difficult for the child. An approach to contact from birth family members, which gives a strong message of a lack of acceptance of the adoption and the adoptive parents' presence, is inappropriate and should not be allowed to continue. Unfortunately this does occur and is sometimes due to a lack of challenge to, or support afforded to, birth parents by the local authority facilitating the contact. It is one of the key responsibilities for those facilitating the letterbox contact arrangements to ensure that these expectations are clear and adhered to.

## Helping to process birth family history

Contact can also provide a trigger for discussing and processing the experience and meaning of birth family history for adopted children.

All of the above case discussions highlight the way in which letterbox contact can aid a child's understanding of their birth family's narrative and help them to make sense of their own adoption journey. Receiving letterbox contact can provide a natural trigger for this. Children do not often have the words to ask the questions that can help them to make sense of their experiences, nor indeed be aware of the questions they may have. Most adoptive parents will be aware of their child's need to have a life story book or life story work which helps them to make sense of their experiences and this is usually available from the time of the child's placement with their adoptive parents. Unfortunately, these tend to be time focused and static documents or pieces of work. Letterbox contact affords the opportunity for these narratives to become a more fluid and ongoing part of the child's development which change over time along with the child's cognitive and emotional development.

Maintaining contact in the early years can help to prevent some of the more worrying outcomes that can present themselves during adolescence when some teenagers will seek out contact with birth family members of their own accord.

It is common for teenagers to start seeking 'unregulated' contact with birth family members outside of the constraints of the letterbox arrangements once they move into adolescence. The adolescent's drive towards developing their own adult identity, their disinhibited impulsivity and need to begin to individuate are a combination of factors which in some ways makes their curiosity about and drive towards additional contact with birth family members almost inevitable. Making this contact is often only a click of a button away on Facebook, and at this stage of the young person's development many adoptive parents feel powerless to stop them. Whilst parents' influence on their children's decisions can feel diminished, the impact of earlier stages of positive letterbox contact can help to impact positively on the outcomes of teenagers' 'unregulated contact' in their adolescent years.

## Case study: Charlotte

I worked with a teenage girl, Charlotte, who at 14 years of age had made contact with birth family members via Facebook. Fortunately, her adoptive parents had been having regular letterbox contact with Charlotte's birth mother and grandmother from the time of Charlotte's placement with them. The relationship between the adults had developed in time and there was a sense of trust and understanding between both the birth and adoptive family that Charlotte's wellbeing mattered to each of them. Their conversation about Charlotte had been an ongoing one for 11 years.

Although Charlotte's adoptive parents felt that it was too soon for Charlotte to be having direct contact with her birth family, they knew that Charlotte did not share this view. They worried that she would travel to her birth family without them unless they were proactive in thinking about managing Charlotte's need for direct contact at that stage. Consequently, they arranged a meeting with Charlotte's birth mother and grandmother and suggested that they all meet together with Charlotte to give her the opportunity to see her mother and grandmother, but with a strong message that they and the birth family members were thinking together about her needs.

The meeting went well and they agreed that they would meet regularly together in the future. Charlotte, however, was entering a period of her life in which she was struggling with her identity and, indeed, in individuating in a secure way. She struggled with school and her peer relationships and began to rebel, staying away from home and expressing a high degree of rejection towards her adoptive parents. Inevitably, one day she 'ran away' and arrived unannounced at her birth mother's home address. In a panic and not knowing what to do for Charlotte, her birth mother phoned her adoptive mother and let her know that she was there. This was a very powerful message for Charlotte; her birth mother was working with her adoptive mother in trying to respond appropriately to her. The nature of the relationship between the adoptive and birth families had to adjust yet again in meeting Charlotte's needs.

There followed a period of time in which the contact between the birth and adoptive family took on a completely new shape. Charlotte herself was given the opportunity to undertake some therapeutic work and eventually she began to feel more 'at ease' with her identity and unresolved feelings of anger and loss. This was not a path that either the adoptive or birth families would ever have imagined when they began letterbox contact when she was 3 years of age. I have no doubt that without their shared history of letterbox contact they would not have been able to adapt together to Charlotte's changing needs in the way they did. Their ability to be flexible and pragmatic in their approach was very much to Charlotte's benefit during that difficult period of her life.

## Providing positive messages of acceptance

When adoptive parents are able to facilitate contact in an open and reflective way for their children they are providing positive messages of acceptance and ability to 'hold' and process difficult feelings for their child.

Acknowledgement of the child's complex identity needs, acceptance of their different genetic inheritance, ability to help the child think and feel about their past within the context of the different developmental stages are key tasks for adoptive parents. Helping the child to engage in contact and providing a clear message that the adoptive parent is alongside them in supporting them with this is a very powerful way of communicating the above. It is very important that the adoptive parent supports their child in sharing the information contained within birth family communication and being reflective about this for them. If they effectively 'opt out' of the process by leaving the child to receive communication from their birth family, they are risking leaving their child with overwhelming feelings, which he or she will have to manage on their own. They are also maintaining a sense of the past and present as being unintegrated for the child. This is not positive for the child, and can lead to an ongoing fragmented sense of identity and, sometimes, divided loyalty, particularly as the young person gets older.

## Birth siblings and the role of letterbox contact

Much of the above has focused on letterbox contact with birth parents. For the majority of adopted children, this will be the most common form of contact via letterbox arrangements. For adopted children with birth siblings there is often a strong preference for contact to take place through direct contact arrangements. Elsie and Louis have discussed the particularly complex issues that can arise within direct contact for siblings in Chapter 8 (including the potential benefits of these ongoing relationships), so I will not repeat these here. However, it is important to remember that when a decision has been taken that sibling contact arrangements should take place via the letterbox process it should not be assumed that this is a simple process.

It is important to acknowledge that letterbox contact between birth siblings can work very well. In my experience, it works best when birth siblings are placed in different adoptive families, either as a supplement to direct contact or in place of it when this is felt to be more appropriate. In these circumstances, respective adoptive parents often have a shared understanding of the birth siblings' histories and a shared intent in wanting to promote a sibling relationship via contact.

For adopted children whose contact is with birth siblings who have remained within the birth family (whether this is with birth parents or extended family members) receiving or sending contact letters can be more complex and evoke very powerful feelings. Sarah's story is one example of this but additional complexities can also arise. Adopted children can often feel anxious and confused about their birth siblings' welfare: 'if it wasn't safe for me how can it be safe for them?' Careful life story work is required with children if they are to begin to understand the subtle nuances of change within their birth parents' lives that enable them to care for siblings after they themselves had to be removed from their care. It is also sometimes incredibly difficult for children to accept the finality of adoption if they understand that their birth parent/s are in a much better place and therefore able to care safely for subsequent children born into the family. I have worked with children who have struggled with very painful feelings about why they cannot return if their parents are now safe to care for them. This can be equally painful for adoptive parents, of course, who can feel very rejected by the part of their child who in some ways feels that they would like to return to their birth parent. In these circumstances, both birth and adoptive families are likely to need support to find the words to explain why the child will remain with their adoptive family, even though circumstances have changed within their birth family. It is very important to be honest with children about the reality of the finality of adoption while also accepting their feelings of injustice that they could not remain with their birth family when their siblings could. Often, when working with children who are experiencing this particular difficulty, further exploration reveals a more complex position than that of simply wanting to return to their birth family. These children often do not really want to leave their adoptive family and the parents they love. Rather, they are expressing their pain at the earlier ruptures and losses in their life and an understandable sense of grief that they carry because they could not remain in the family to which they were born.

In these circumstances it can be incredibly helpful if a birth parent is able to reinforce the explanations and messages that the adoptive parents provide for the child within their own letters. Most birth parents will need significant support with this. Usually they wish that their child could return to them. Helping them to understand why the child needs them to reinforce the messages the adoptive parents are providing can be challenging.

It is also the case that adopted children may also feel jealous of their birth siblings who have been able to remain within their birth family. Conversely, birth siblings can feel jealous that their adopted sibling is with a family who perhaps seems to be in a much better position than themselves, who remains in a family that continue to struggle in many ways.

## Case study: Mia

I once worked with a teenage girl who, after having had regular letterbox contact with her birth sister (who had remained with paternal grandparents) throughout her childhood, made direct contact with her birth sister via Facebook at the age of 14 years. After the initial excitement of meeting together, a number of issues arose between the sisters that caused difficulties within their relationship. Mia began to express feelings of resentment that the birth family had been able to care for her sister whilst her birth sister felt resentful about the more materially comfortable and less chaotic upbringing that Mia had experienced within her adoptive family. Additionally, both sisters struggled with the different narratives each had about their respective histories. The birth sibling who had remained in the birth family, perhaps unsurprisingly, had a slightly different version of the events that had led to her sister's removal. A great deal of work was required with both families, as well as with the girls together, to give them a shared narrative of the past events, which helped them to make sense together of their experiences. Their feelings about the different paths their respective lives had taken, as well as the implications of those early decisions taken about their future, would take longer for each of the girls to accept and come to terms with.

If this work had taken place with each of the girls as they were growing up, they may have experienced less difficulty in 'coming together' in their early adolescence. I do believe that work to support those in parenting siblings who are separated is very important. Developing a shared narrative, even for those siblings who are involved in letterbox contact only, must be considered supportive of the future sibling relationship, even if those issues don't seem pertinent to the content of the actual letterbox contact at the time.

These same principles of openness and shared understanding of their shared histories for siblings also apply when birth siblings are placed within long-term foster care. Support around letterbox contact for them is very important. Foster carers need to receive support from their social workers and possibly the post adoption team to help the children with the emotions that contact will evoke and, indeed, to understand what is appropriate content for the letters themselves.

Direct contact between adopted siblings and siblings in foster care carries potential risks of information being passed to other birth family members. Letterbox contact can also carry these risks. Siblings may want to share the letters they receive (and perhaps photographs) with other birth family members. Clear risk assessments and support for helping siblings to manage letterbox contact should be in place at the time that contact is planned and reviewed regularly.

It is also important, of course, to remember that sometimes sibling relationships within birth families have been abusive. Growing up within the context of parental abuse can mean that older siblings are abusive and exhibit frightening behaviour towards younger siblings. When this has been present within the sibling dynamic it is important to hold in mind the possibility that letterbox communication from those very siblings can undermine the adopted child's sense of safety within their own home. We must be careful that we don't ignore the potentially harmful aspects of some of these sibling relationships. We must be clear about any potential risks within this contact in the same way that we must in contact with birth parents and other family members.

## Potential risks in the exchange of photographs

The above highlight some of the potential difficulties that can arise for children emotionally if letterbox contact does not fulfil certain key functions. There are also, however, potential risks within letterbox contact that social workers must be aware of when both planning and also facilitating letterbox contact arrangements.

The exchange of photographs is important to consider. Often local authorities pay attention to the possibility that photographs can inadvertently provide clues as to the location of the adoptive family's home, or school that the child attends, therefore compromising the confidentiality of the adoptive family. Whilst it is certainly wise to be mindful of photographs in which the child is wearing a school badge or standing in front of a street sign, I would also ask the question why adoptive parents are being asked to send photographs of the children if local authorities fear that sending any inadvertent clues to identification could place the child at risk. On occasions I have heard local authorities suggest that it would be preferable if adoptive parents didn't send photographs in which the child's face was clearly visible. This is a very confusing message for adoptive parents. If birth family members are so unsafe that sending photographs could undermine the child's safety then photographs should not be sent to the birth family.

Additionally, adoptive parents need to be made aware of the fact that once photographs have been sent to birth family members the adoptive parents do lose control over the way in which their recipients may share these photographs. I once worked with a birth mother who would put the photographs she received of the children on her social networking site. Whilst she didn't intend any harm in doing so this is not what the adoptive parents would have wanted. Nor would this be a positive experience for the children should they, in later years, have found such an extensive collection of their own childhood photographs on the social networking site. Social workers need to be clear about the birth family member's ability to be boundaried about how they may use the photographs they receive. Many birth family members are very respectful of this and use the photographs they receive appropriately, but social workers need to be mindful of the fact that some may not.

Social workers also need to bear in mind that birth family members' situations may change. I once worked with a birth mother who had a long history of relationships with men who were sexually abusive. At the time of her children's adoption she had ended her most recent relationship and so the social worker decided that it was therefore safe for the adoptive parents to send photographs of the children as part of the letterbox exchange. This decision seemed to ignore the historical context of the mother's relationship choices. Indeed, she did subsequently enter into another relationship with a risky male and the adoptive parents were later horrified to discover that he had had access to their children's photographs.

In another note about the development of technology, I would add that we have seen an incredible advance in social media and the sharing of information online in the last ten years. We do not yet know how this technology will develop further. If there is any doubt as to the way in which birth family members may use photographs online either to identify or share images of the children, we need to consider carefully the way in which photographs should be shared.

# Practice guidance

When planning and reviewing contact arrangements/assessing potential benefits and risks for children within contact arrangements, consider the following:

## Who should be involved in planning for the post adoption contact arrangements?

It is important that sufficient information is gathered in order to make an informed decision about the likely impact of continuing contact on the child. Information should be gathered from:

- Previous contact notes/contact co-ordinator: The quality of previous contact and the child's experience of contact with birth family members is important to consider in assessing the likely emotional impact for the child in having ongoing letterbox contact with birth family members.

- Looked after children's social worker: The looked after team will have valuable information about their contact with birth family members and knowledge of the nature of the relationship between the child and their birth family members throughout the child's journey through the care system.

- Social worker for any siblings to be included with contact arrangements: It is important to have a realistic assessment of the needs of any birth siblings who are to be involved in contact plans. This should include a clear plan for what they may require in terms of their own support in order that the contact can be meaningful for them.

- Previous foster carers: Again, foster carers will hold important information about the impact of previous contact on the child and the child's experience of this over time.

- Professionals who have provided support for the birth family member/s: These can be a valuable source of information for planning, understanding the position of the birth family member, judging their capability to access support, take part in contact arrangements and meet the requirements to enable the contact to be beneficial for the child.

- Adoption and post adoption team social workers: These teams are essential in providing information about what the adoptive parents are likely to be able to manage in regard to contact arrangements and what support is likely to be available from the adoption support team in facilitating the various demands of contact.

- Adoptive parents: It is important that the views and wishes of the adoptive parents are considered, even if this happens later in the process. The success of contact arrangements is dependent on the openness and ability of the adoptive parents to maintain contact arrangements in a way that is meaningful for the child.

- Birth family member: It is important to be realistic and clear about both the expectations and responsibilities that ongoing letterbox contact entails for birth family members. They are likely to need support with this and early open and honest discussions are important in our duty of care to those birth family members who will be involved in contact.

- Child: Assessing contact needs to take place within the context of the child's previous experiences of contact but also with the knowledge of what the child may need as they move through their different developmental stages. Children may, of course, verbalise their wishes and feelings about contact and these must be listened to and understood within the context of their current developmental stage and emotional needs.

## Frequency of contact arrangements

The majority of contact arrangements will occur on an annual or twice-yearly timetable. When planning arrangements it is important to consider that contact can be unsettling for children and requires a great deal of professional and parent support in ensuring that it is successful. Contact levels should be at frequencies that aren't overwhelming for the child, beyond what the agency is realistically able to support and should also be set at a level that is realistic for the birth family members to manage. Letterbox, as well as direct contact, can be very stressful for birth family members and they will often require significant support in order to manage it for themselves. It is important that birth family members can be consistent and reliable in providing contact for the child. Expectations must be realistic about their ability to do so and at what frequency this will be possible.

## The timing of contact arrangements

Consideration needs to be given to the amount of time that passes between a child's final (goodbye for now or wish you well) direct contact with the birth family member and the first post adoption contact letter exchange. Social workers need to bear in mind the child's experience of the timing of the contact. Sometimes a final contact can take place a significant amount of time before the first post adoption exchange is ready to happen. This may be because of delays in the child moving to an adoptive placement, or because of delays in cases being passed to the post adoption team, which is responsible for facilitating the contact arrangements. It is appropriate to have a gap in contact but I have known cases where a year or more has passed between these contacts. Such a long gap is often confusing for the child.

## Birthdays and Christmas contacts

Many adoptive children struggle with managing birthdays and Christmas, as they find it difficult to deal with their excitement and anxiety, and, generally, the dysregulated feelings that these occasions evoke. Throwing letterbox contact into this potent mix is on the whole inadvisable, as the feelings that contact generates can also be overwhelming at times for children. In my experience, it is usually best not to have contact at these times.

## Content of letters

All parties should receive written guidance about what is appropriate content within letter exchanges and specifically the way in which birth family members address the letter and refer to themselves within the letter. It is important to note that sometimes a simple exchange of information is entirely appropriate in meeting children's needs. At other times (such as those detailed in the cases above), letterbox contact will need to address children's questions and developing emotional needs and, therefore, significant work will be required around the content and function of a particular contact exchange. Elsie and Louis highlight a number of ways of providing effective contact for children including facilitated and video contact. I would like to emphasise the need for a fluid approach to thinking about contact, even if the primary form of contact is letterbox. Moving between a videoed contact and letterbox contact may be entirely appropriate for some children, as may be moving from letterbox to a direct facilitated contact.

## Assessing the level of support required for all parties

It is likely that all parties will require some support in managing contact arrangements at some point throughout the contact process. The adoption and post adoption team are responsible for the ongoing support for contact arrangements and it is therefore essential that they are a part of the planning process. Support may be required for the different parties at different stages of the process and the following will need to be considered:

> **Birth family members:** Birth family members are likely to need practical and emotional support in managing all forms of contact arrangements. It is advisable that a named worker from the post adoption team is allocated to their case as early as possible in order to provide the support required and clarity about expectations and requirements within the contact process. Referral to birth family counselling services is also advisable as early as possible. Some birth family members may struggle to engage with social services directly because of their history with the department. It may be beneficial for the post adoption social worker to liaise with a professional who is able to provide the birth family member with support in order to begin to build a relationship with the birth family member. Therefore if the Post Adoption Social Worker can establish a relationship with other services that are likely to come into contact with birth family members (such as housing support, drug and alcohol support, etc.) it can be beneficial generally in ensuring that birth family members are aware of the services provided by the post adoption team in relation to contact through other professional contacts.
>
> Siblings involved in contact arrangements will also need significant emotional and practical support in order to engage in the

contact. Foster parents, respective adoptive parents and social workers will need to have a clear understanding of the contact arrangements, an understanding of the emotional challenges these may pose for siblings and access to support services in order to meet the siblings' needs. Life story work is likely to be needed in order to help the siblings make sense of their history and the context of the contact arrangements with their adopted sibling.

**Adoptive parents:** Adoptive parents will need support in understanding the requirements of the contact process and the potential benefits and risks for the child within the contact. They may also need practical and emotional support in managing the contact arrangements and will therefore benefit from having a named worker who will manage their contact arrangements over time. Continuing contact arrangements can feel very challenging for adoptive parents at times. Whilst the majority of adoptive parents are able to place their child's needs first and indeed retain empathy for the birth family member, they too will experience strong emotional responses within the contact process. I have heard many adoptive parents describe their feelings of anger towards their child's birth family as they try to support their child with the many difficulties they can experience as a result of their early abuse within those birth families. These are not easy emotions to contain and adoptive parents will understandably need support with them at times.

Adoptive parents will also need support in understanding the potential emotional impact of contact on the child, to understand the emotional and behavioural signals that may indicate that their child is struggling with contact; and to be able to use contact as a tool for helping their child understand and reflect upon their life story generally.

Training for adoptive parents in relation to contact is important and many local authorities do provide this on an annual basis.

**The child:** The child will need the support of their adoptive parents in order to make sense of contact arrangements and understand them within the context of their birth history. It is important to understand that children will have different needs in relation to contact depending on their developmental stage. Children will experience contact in different ways as they move through different developmental stages. Cognitive development and the consequent changes in the child's understanding of their history will inevitably impact on their emotional experience of the contact. As children approach 5 years of age, then 8 years (mid childhood), then 11 years (adolescence) and then later adolescence, they will need support in processing and making sense of the meaning of contact anew. It is preferable if post adoption teams managing contact arrangements both advise adoptive parents of this in their guidance material and also, perhaps, identify these key points as good times to 'check in' with adoptive parents to review the contact arrangements. It is quite possible that children will require life story work at key stages within their developmental pathway (please see the developmental chart in the Appendix). Professionals will need to be able to support adoptive parents in recognising behaviours that may indicate their child is struggling with contact, such as re-enactment, exploration of identity and regressive behaviours.

## The monitoring of changes within the birth family or adoptive family

Successful contact arrangements require both the adoptive and birth family members to be committed to, engaged with, and mindful of the child's emotional needs. Workers within the post adoption team need to be aware of any significant changes within either the birth or adoptive families and to be able to support family members in helping them to consider the impact of those changes on their own role within contact, as well as the potential emotional impact on the child. Traumas within adoptive and birth families such as deaths, divorce or serious illness can impact on an individual's ability to manage contact effectively. Additional support will often be required at these times.

## Resourcing letterbox contact

Managing letterbox contact well requires significant resources. Whilst it is unlikely that every contact will require ongoing intensive input it is the case that local authorities need to provide a proactive and flexible service if we are truly to meet children's needs within the contact process. Many local authorities do provide an excellent service and feel that the active management of letterbox contact also serves to maintain a positive relationship with adoptive parents. This ongoing relationship in itself can have many benefits for adopted children; it is more likely that therapeutic needs can be identified at an early stage and appropriate resources provided, for example. Adoptive parents also benefit from the feeling that they are well supported and are more likely to engage in training and other services themselves. Benefits can also extend to birth family members who, as a result of active support in contact arrangements, can sometimes engage in their own process of reflecting on the past and making changes that are ultimately beneficial for them. We mustn't forget that many adopted teenagers and adults will need to explore their birth family histories and relationships in a fuller sense as they mature. Letterbox contact can provide a safer 'grounding' for this stage and leave all of those in the adoption triangle better equipped to manage the complexities of this process.

## Options in decision making

Contact arrangements rarely proceed without changes in the circumstances of those involved with them, or without variations in the quality and benefit to the child at different times. Reviewing the purpose and impact of the contact on the child should take place within conversations with adoptive parents at the time of each letter exchange or annually if this is possible. If this is not possible, it will be beneficial to review the needs within the contact arrangements at the child's key developmental stages (approximately: 5 years, mid childhood and early and mid adolescence).

There will be circumstances in which contact arrangements will need to end, either because the contact is not safe or too distressing for the child, or because birth family members or adoptive parents withdraw from the contact. It is very difficult to be prescriptive about decision making in contact arrangements. Generally, if contact is felt to be risky or there is no possibility of it meeting the child's emotional needs, my view is that serious consideration should be given to it ending. The above cases do, though, highlight the complexity of contact arrangements for all those involved in them. I would always advocate that, where possible, a fluid and creative approach should be sought in meeting children's needs within contact before final decisions are made or possibilities closed down. Maintaining a message of openness and the possibility of change is a good starting place for those involved in managing letterbox contact. It can, after all, provide the basis for a therapeutic process and the preparation for the lifelong journey that adopted young people and their adoptive and birth parents make.

## CHAPTER 7

# Contact Using Video Messages

There are occasions when, for different reasons, it may be decided that contact can be best enabled through the use of a filmed interview or 'video messaging'. For example, it may be the case that a birth parent is living with health and/or mental health problems or is simply considered as too unstable to manage either the practical or emotional demands of the facilitated contact.

There have also been occasions when we have been able to use 'video messaging' with children in adoptive placements where there has been no face-to-face or letterbox contact with any member of their birth family for many years. Children in this situation sometimes struggle within their permanent foster or adoptive placement and using a video message that helps to address their anxieties and questions about birth family can help them settle.

Some birth parents may have found maintaining direct contact during care proceedings, and subsequently, too difficult. Sometimes the state of a parent's mental health or issues of addiction means meeting the challenge of maintaining contact is impossible. Some have not managed even 'goodbye for now' or 'wish you well contact' or any kind of communication to the child that helps them make sense of the fact that they will not be growing up in the care of their birth mother or father. Sometimes, birth parents have managed to attend a final contact meeting but have communicated in a way that has left the child feeling that they do not have permission to settle elsewhere and/or that the child is somehow responsible for this devastating outcome. However, some years down the line these same birth parents may, if approached, be in a mental and emotional state that will enable them, with the right support, to be willing and able to give the gift of showing the child they have survived, put the reasons they are not parenting the child in context and give the child permission to settle. Such work of course is dependent on the willingness of the local authority in which the birth parent lives to approach them or forward communications from the agency that is working with the child and their adoptive family.

There are other situations when contact through the use of video can be useful:

- if it is considered that a child is too unstable/emotionally vulnerable to manage face-to-face contact

- if a child has accessed unmediated contact through social networking or Facebook. Video contact can be used as a therapeutic intervention to manage the process and to facilitate 'contact at a distance', which may address any thoughts, feelings and experiences of the child

- if a birth family member is ill, without mobility or in prison

- if a birth family member lives in another country.

The application of filmed contact interviews allows for a more controlled experience and exploration of contact, yet still carries the same need for preparation, facilitation and debriefing. The process is somewhat less intense than face-to-face contact and creates a sense of being 'one step removed' from the potential intensity of feelings aroused by contact. The use of filmed contact allows for a more sensory experience and feeling of connection than does letterbox contact.

## Case study: Jodie

Jodie (aged 13) had been adopted since she was 4 years old. She now had twice-yearly contact with her birth mother, yet was struggling in her relationships with her adoptive parents. At home, she was becoming increasingly aggressive with her birth mother and at school was finding it hard to keep friends. Jodie had also begun to shout 'You are not my mother! I'm going to leave you when I'm older!'

When Jodie had contact with her birth mother, the adoptive parents took an approach of spending time together as a group and at some point they encouraged Jodie to 'have some time alone' with her birth mother. Their reasoning behind this was to 'let Jodie know that she could have some special time with her birth mother'. The adoptive parents noticed that for the last three contacts, Jodie's behaviour worsened for up to a month before and after contact and sleep had become a problem.

Worryingly, Jodie's birth mother Janet had experienced a recent relapse in terms of her use of alcohol. There were other social factors that were challenging such as moving home and the illness of her mother. Jodie's adoptive parents received a phone call from Janet's social worker to say that her birth mother needed to cancel the imminent contact. Jodie's behaviour worsened and culminated in a huge family argument during which she disclosed that Janet often told her in their recent contacts when alone that 'Jodie could always come home (to Janet) if she needed to'. Jodie had then run out of the home and for the first time took a bottle of alcohol with her.

When Elsie and Louis met the family, it was clear that Jodie was suffering terribly and feeling muddled and conflicted over her loyalties to her adoptive family and birth mother. Elsie described to Jodie how her behaviour was understandable given the depth of her feelings and wondered with Jodie if there were things she had not yet dared to ask her birth mother or if there were things she would like to ask her birth mother or always hoped her birth mother might say?

After a couple of superficial questions, Jodie described how she had always wondered why she had not been able to live with Janet if she was no longer drinking alcohol. At this point Jodie shared that Janet had told her that she could always return home if she needed to when she was older. The recent events had shocked Jodie who had perceived Janet's encouragement of a reunion in the future as a definite sign of her newly found health.

Jodie also wanted to know more about Janet's housing situation and her grandmother's illness. Jodie was interested in what her grandmother looked like. Louis observed Jodie's protective attitude towards her birth mother and asked her if she worried about Janet. Jodie's response was a fine testimony to the power of non-verbal communication when she replied 'Oh yeah, I can always tell if she's having a good or a bad day...she hardly looks at me, never asks me anything about me and her hands go like this.' Jodie showed with her hands a nervy, wringing motion.

It was agreed with the adoptive parents and social services that an approach to Janet would be made to explore the idea of her making a video message to Jodie. The aim of this was also to explore whether this process could be used therapeutically to help Jodie:

- make greater sense of the questions she had about her early life history
- be able to check that Janet is OK and about her move of home (a part of Jodie feared that Janet may move far away)
- find out a little more about Janet's mother, Jodie's maternal birth grandmother
- understand that Jodie would never return to live with her birth mother as she could not look after her (or more accurately was not able to manage being a parent to *any* child)
- to have permission from Janet to settle and be happy with her adoptive parents.

Elsie and Louis made contact with the post adoption team responsible for the administration of contact arrangements with Janet. A post adoption social worker who knew Janet accompanied her to an initial meeting to discuss the idea of a video contact. Janet had almost cancelled coming to the meeting saying she could not afford to travel. The social worker gently encouraged and supported her and used a taxi for the journey to the contact centre. Elsie helped Janet to feel more settled and expressed her gratitude to Janet for coming.

As discussion progressed, Elsie shared the purpose of the meeting: to ask Janet to be involved in a video message to Jodie in order to help Jodie settle with her adoptive family. Elsie acknowledged how important Janet still is in Jodie's life and that she believed that Janet wanted Jodie to be happy in her life. Elsie also acknowledged that Janet herself had experienced a very tough start and that she imagined Janet wanted Jodie to have a better life than her own. This moved Janet to tears and there followed a conversation that addressed the struggles she had suffered as a result of her abusive childhood. Elsie moved this discussion with Janet into the role of addiction to alcohol and drugs in people who have such early experiences, the impact of such addictions or attempts at 'self-medication' on the individual and their capacity to cope with life and parenting. Janet was then able to acknowledge the role her use of alcohol had played in social services intervening in her care of Jodie, and the challenges she had faced in working towards recovery and her subsequent relapse. Janet was also able to reflect on how wonderful and yet stressful her experience of becoming a parent had been, not at all the way she had imagined it would be before having a baby. She had felt overwhelmed and isolated and this had, in turn, led to her increased use of alcohol.

Note: This line of exploration of Janet's own attachment history and difficult start to life can be helpful for birth parents. The vast majority of birth parents want the very best for their children and when acknowledging their own early life setbacks or trauma (their own abusive childhoods) this can be used as motivation for them to offer their child something different. In other words, it may sometimes be difficult for some birth parents to want their children to attach and love new parents, yet it is easier to want to ensure that the child does not suffer in the same way that they have in the past.

Louis said that Jodie had a number of questions about her childhood as well as things she hoped to find out about her wider birth family. It was important to make clear to Janet that:

- she would be fully prepared and supported through the process
- she could even access birth parent counselling to help her manage the thoughts, feelings and anxiety that might arise
- she had control to 'pause' the video-making process if she became distressed
- what she was offering was very important to Jodie's wellbeing and need to have a safe, caring family into adulthood
- she was welcome to bring a friend to support her through the video making, yet this friend would not be part of the filming
- while the main focus of this therapeutic work was Jodie, birth parents can also find their involvement and contribution to the process therapeutic

Janet was committed yet nervous about making the video, as she wanted to 'look OK' for Jodie. As there was a positive momentum, Elsie and Louis booked an appointment to make the video message in the near future.

Jodie was excited to be creating questions on a sheet of paper for her birth mother and needed a little guidance to be able to reflect on what she really wanted to ask and how to phrase each question. All of this preparation included her adoptive parents and Elsie and Louis. Her questions focused on her early life history, Janet's mother, whether Janet was having a 'good or bad' day and (as suggested by Louis) 'Are you OK for me to be happy with my adoptive mum and dad?'

The last question, although it was not initiated by Jodie, elicited a very animated response from her: 'Yes...put that one in!' It addressed one of the fundamental needs for Jodie to have her birth mother's blessing to be happy with another family and essentially be claimed by her adoptive parents. Janet's recent suggestions that Jodie might return home when older also needed to be explored.

When Elsie and Louis met Janet, she was visibly nervous yet was able to settle. She was reassured to hear that Jodie had also felt nervous yet excited to be able to ask her birth mother questions. Elsie suggested that she read the questions one by one and that we all take time to reflect on each question.

Janet was visibly struck by the idea that Jodie had asked whether she was having a good or bad day. 'Did she really ask that?' she said.

Elsie explained how common it was for children to notice a lot about their parents and now that she was able to use the medium (and safety) of a written message, she could ask Janet the kind of questions that she might not feel able to ask in person. To help Janet provide a more 'coherent narrative', she was supported to share that it would be helpful to say that she 'was having a good day, yet sometimes she did still struggle and have not so good days'.

It was clear that Janet did indeed want to do the right thing for her birth daughter. With this in mind, Louis opened up the subject of Jodie's disclosure that Janet had suggested that Jodie could always return home in the future. Janet looked worried, yet when Louis wondered if a part of her had never fully given up hope (that Jodie would return home), she became tearful. Janet shared how desperate she was for Jodie to know that she loved her and that it was 'all I could do to make up for what has happened'. Elsie shared how muddled this had made Jodie feel, particularly when she knew her birth mother still had good and bad days. Although the intention was good, it served to make matters worse in Jodie's mind. Conversation explored whether Janet really believed she could look after and be a parent to Jodie.

How would she manage if she had another relapse? How would that be for Jodie to see this happen all over again? Louis suggested that a part of Jodie desperately needed to hear Janet say that she could not look after her and that Jodie needed to let her adoptive parents love her and look after her in the way that she (Janet) could not. This was naturally very moving for Janet, yet it also allowed what had become 'unspeakable' to be expressed. In ways, it was a relief for Janet to acknowledge this.

Louis and Elsie suggested that they write down (script) Janet's answers to Jodie's questions and then have a rehearsal (practice) before making the video message. Elsie started the film by thanking Janet for agreeing to make the filmed interview for Jodie and then read Jodie's questions for Janet to answer. Janet became a little tearful when it came to make a statement about not being able to look after Jodie, yet she was able to make a spontaneous expression of 'how I want you to make a go of it with Andy and Sally (the adoptive parents)...no-one taught me to be a mummy (a comment made by Elsie earlier with Janet)... and I hope you might be a mummy when you grow up...Andy and Sally can help you with that, not me...they can give you the childhood you never had and teach you to be the person you dream of'. It was a terribly moving and meaningful statement by Janet and one that can sometimes come from birth parents.

In our experience, it is the structured approach and containing process of the preparation that ironically allows for a creative, heartfelt authentic expression of what needs to be said. It can be helpful as it was in this case, that Louis had suggested that they film the 'rehearsal' as practice for the video message. Everyone agreed that the practice was perfect as it was and as it had been filmed, there was no need for a further recording.

Jodie watched the video message with her adoptive parents and Elsie and Louis present. A time was chosen to watch the video message when Jodie could relax and did not have any distractions. Louis ensured that she sat between her adoptive parents and Elsie introduced the video by simply telling Jodie what she was about to see and hear and how long it would last as a way of orienting Jodie. Jodie was also told that there would be time afterwards to think and talk about what she had seen and heard and she could say 'pause' if she needed to stop the video for any reason. Jodie decided that she did not want to hold the remote control herself and would ask Louis to press the pause button for her. Jodie then huddled up to Andy and Sally.

When the video had finished, Jodie was still cuddling her parents. She had looked pleased and visibly moved when Janet had made clear that she could not and would not be looking after Jodie in the future. This was the thing that she said she remembered most about the message.

In this case, Jodie 'randomly' discussed the video with Andy and Sally over the next two weeks. It was as if she was processing different aspects of what was said and the implications over time. Andy and Sally were encouraged to be open and curious about everything that Jodie explored in order to convey that they welcomed Jodie's inner wonderings.

Two months later, Jodie asked Sally if she liked being her mum and whether sometimes when Jodie was 'bad', she wanted to send her back to Janet. Unsurprisingly, Sally made clear to Jodie that she loved being her mother and had never wanted Jodie to leave the family with anyone else! The day after, Jodie asked if she could pause contact with Janet for a while. When asked by Sally how long a while was, Jodie replied 'Maybe a year?'

Jodie was invited by Elsie and Louis to make a video message back to her birth mother; however, in this instance she did not want to do so. Janet was informed by the post adoption social worker that contact was being paused for a year to enable Jodie to practise (maybe for the first time) living wholeheartedly with her adoptive parents. Andy and Sally wrote a letter to Janet thanking her for the video message that had given Jodie permission to attach to them more fully. They also made clear that they had no intention of blocking contact in the future with Janet.

Elsie met Janet with the social worker to process this news. Janet was sad in ways yet acknowledged the significance of and Jodie's legitimate need to attempt to bond with her adoptive parents without an underlying worry about betraying her birth mother.

# Case study: Shay

Shay was almost 9 years old and had been with his adoptive parents, Tim and Jack, for one year when he started some therapeutic life story work with Louis and Elsie. His adoptive parents were concerned because he was struggling to settle, was prone to angry outbursts and perceiving rejection and criticism where none was intended. At other times, Shay behaved as if he were an adult and tried to take on the role of looking after his adoptive parents. Shay was also ambivalent about having his adoption finalised and was clearly confused and very angry about what had happened when he had been living within his birth family.

Shay's birth mother Amanda had left the family home when he was nearly 2 years old and his sister was 9 years old, leaving both children in the care of her husband John. Some months later she had taken Shay's older sister to live with her and her new partner. Initially after leaving the family, Amanda had managed to make arrangements to see Shay and had also taken his older sister to these contacts. Shay remained in the care of John, Amanda's ex-husband until he was almost 6 years old and the local authority initiated care proceedings.

Over time, Amanda's contacts became very sporadic. By the time the care proceedings were initiated, Amanda had given birth to another daughter, was pregnant with another and did not feel able to resume the parenting of Shay. Amanda struggled with maintaining contact during and after the proceedings and only managed to attend two sessions during this period. At the first contact she came with her new partner and their first daughter, Shay's older sister, was also present. By the time she was able to manage the second contact, Amanda had another baby daughter who was also included in the contact session. Arrangements were made for contact post the care hearing but Amanda did not attend and Shay was left feeling let down. Amanda said she found travelling to contact sessions too much of a challenge. The local authority had tried to set up letterbox contact for Shay with his mother as part of the adoption plan; however, Amanda had not responded. It was during the care proceedings that Amanda had shared the fact that her ex-husband was in fact not Shay's biological father.

During the therapeutic exploration of Shay's life story it became clear that Shay believed his mother had left him behind because there was something wrong with and bad about him. Shay also expressed a great deal of anger towards his 'stupid idiot' of a mother. Shay had expressed a wish to see Amanda so he could tell and show her how angry he felt, something he thought would help him 'get his anger out'. It seemed that underlying this wish was a fear that his angry outbursts were contaminating his relationships with his adoptive parents. On the other hand, Shay idolised John, the man who he had believed was his 'father' and who had in fact been neglectful and emotionally dependent upon Shay.

With agreement, the local authority continued to try to make contact with Amanda and to help her engage in some kind of letterbox exchange that could help give Shay the message that she did not feel that he was worthless. Finally, a response came, when she and his older sister sent cards at Christmas, but unfortunately the written messages were felt to be inappropriate and misleading. A social worker from the post adoption team was able to arrange a home visit (Amanda was struggling to manage life and was fearful about going out of the home and travelling). The social worker talked with Amanda about Shay and how he was struggling to make sense of his current situation and asked her if she would be willing to meet with Elsie to discuss helping Shay. Amanda agreed to this and Elsie went with the social worker on a home visit.

Given the history of Amanda's vulnerable mental health and unpredictability there was no certainty that she would keep the appointment, therefore Shay was not told about the visit. He did know, however, that the social worker was trying to find his birth mother. Shay had (with support from his adoptive parents) been able to convey his questions and feelings about Amanda during his life story sessions, so Elsie had a good idea about the sorts of things he would like her to ask Amanda.

One of the issues Shay's adoptive dads told Elsie was on his mind was the fact that he was placed with two men. It was a testament to their openness and Shay's developing sense of equality (also helped by his school's approach to diversity) that Shay had opened a conversation with Jack on one occasion, saying 'Daddy I don't mean to be racist, but do you know if Amanda knows that I have two dads now?' Shay did already know that John, who he had believed was his birth father until the care proceedings, knew he had two dads and had seen for himself during a facilitated contact session that John not only knew but had also given his 'permission' for Shay to settle and be happy with Tim and Jack.

Tim and Jack had thought through the fact they were a same sex couple prior to becoming adoptive parents, and had been proactive in involving their mothers and female friends in Shay's life. Jack's mother and father lived locally and Shay saw them very regularly and went on family holidays. When talking about Shay's experience of living with a same sex couple Tim and Jack conveyed a concern for Shay, wondering if deep down he may believe that he did not deserve to have a mum. Jack (who is a very nurturing man) also said that Shay had told him that in some ways he saw him as his replacement mum, as he tended to do many of the things for him a mum might do. This also meant that Shay was more likely to direct his hurt, angry and rejecting feelings towards Jack.

While it was possible that Amanda would not agree to take part in a filmed interview, Elsie took along the camera 'just in case'. She was hoping that if Amanda would not agree to a filmed interview that she would at least agree to being photographed with Elsie, as a photograph would offer Shay some concrete evidence that his birth mother had been willing to meet with Elsie and talk about his needs and confusion. Amanda's own childhood story was a very sad one. A neglected and abused child, Amanda had become a vulnerable and emotionally dependent adult who also had some learning difficulties. Her first meeting with the social worker had helped her begin to understand why Shay needed her help to come to terms with his past and why, as she said, 'he had questions and needed some answers'. It was agreed that what Shay needed to hear from Amanda was:

· that he had done nothing wrong and that the reasons she left the family home were about her own emotional state and unhappiness in her marriage with John

· a simple explanation about the circumstances of Shay's conception

· that she could accept and understand how and why he felt angry with her

· that Shay deserved to be happy with his adoptive parents

· that Amanda knew Shay had two dads and wanted him to settle and find happiness.

Amanda was able to talk about how unhappy she had been in her marriage and had come to have a relationship with the man who was Shay's biological father. He was someone she felt had for a time been sympathetic and supportive of her in a way that John had not. Amanda said she could understand why Shay was angry with her and was emphatic that Shay had been a very lovely baby and her reasons for leaving were nothing to do with him. She had been very unhappy and in a confused emotional state and, although she did not make it explicit, there was a sense that the man she went to live with when she left Shay and his sister had not wanted her to bring the children. When asked, Amanda was willing to be filmed being interviewed by Elsie. The interview took barely ten minutes to complete. During this interview Amanda was able, and supported, to convey answers and explanations for all of the above points. She let Shay know that he had done nothing wrong and was a lovely baby; the reasons she had left were due to *her* own unhappiness and confusion. Amanda also said that she thought about Shay every day and was sorry for what had happened. With guidance from Elsie, she was able to hear and accept how angry Shay felt towards her and say she understood why, and could imagine feeling that way herself if she were in Shay's position. As illustrated in a previous case study, the nature of the work involving a compassionate exploration of Amanda's own life history and its impact on Shay's upbringing generated a soulful expression of Amanda's feelings. She also spontaneously said that she wanted Shay to know that 'despite the circumstances of his birth he was *never* a mistake and how loveable he was'.

Elsie talked about what a fine boy Shay had grown into and how well he was doing at school and how proud Tim and Jack were of him and how much love they felt for Shay. Amanda expressed how pleased she was that Shay was with loving adoptive parents, explaining he deserved to be looked after and loved in a way that she was unable to manage. Amanda had clearly meant what she was saying and had at times cried and had to wipe away tears. However, the focus of what was being conveyed was an age-appropriate explanation for Shay of his early life history and Amanda's non-verbal communication was coherent in terms of what she was trying to convey.

Elsie showed the interview to Shay's adoptive parents, Tim and Jack who were moved to tears. They agreed that Amanda had done well and felt that the filmed message would be helpful to Shay. When they came in for their next session, Shay was aware that Elsie and Louis had something important to share. He was asked if he had any ideas of what it might be and, seeing the TV in the therapy room, he guessed it might be a film and something to do with his 'stupid idiot' of a mum. He looked both nervous and excited when told that Elsie had been to see Amanda and had recorded a video message for him to see. Shay sat very still (unusually for him!) between Jack and Tim and decided he would hold the DVD remote controls. He watched intently, stopping the film only once to re-hear what Amanda said about him being a lovely baby whom she enjoyed cuddling. Both Tim and Jack were moved once again to tears and although Shay's lip trembled, he did not express any other emotion. While Louis was supporting Shay in exploring what he now thought and felt about his birth mum, Shay was able to say he no longer wanted to call her 'a stupid idiot' and wanted to refer to her as his birth mum instead. Tim and Jack cuddled Shay and shared how happy it made them feel that his birth mum had been able to answer some of his questions in this way.

Shay's adoptive parents told Louis and Elsie that Shay had over the following few days spoken about the filmed interview and some of the things Amanda had said. He had also been calmer, more relaxed and very affectionate towards them. He had continued to be demanding of their time, seeking their engagement, but did seem more able to feel reassured by having his attachment behaviours met and then being able to move into exploratory behaviours, becoming absorbed in a book or a game. Interestingly, Shay did not ask to see the film again which he was aware he could do.

Given Shay's tendency to feel responsible for the adults in his life, it was decided that he should not be asked to film a response for Amanda or be asked to write a letter or card, unless of course he asked to do so. Shay made no such request; however, Elsie wrote a letter to Amanda thanking her for being willing to undertake the interview and letting her know how helpful it had been for Shay.

There have been occasions when the details shared by a birth parent have been judged too distressing to share and it has been necessary to edit. In such situations it is important to explain to the birth parent that not all of the film may be shown at this stage. In these circumstances, parents have agreed to this process. In showing an edited film to a child they may ask why. The value of the edited film is in allowing the child to see that the birth parent is alive, and thinks enough of them to have made the film. As a minimum, usually parents can be supported in relaying a hope for the child's future happiness. In such situations it is important to give an honest answer, for example by explaining that some of the things the birth parent had talked about were difficult things that had happened in their lives and not things that should be shared with children. In one of these situations one girl said, 'Well I bet I know it anyway, she always used to tell me about the things that upset and worried her.' This allowed her to open up and talk with her therapist and adoptive mother about some of her own harrowing memories of being five and six years old, and of trying to support and care for a distressed birth mother who had shared her experiences of partner violence and of being raped.

## Key aspects of video contact

- Video contact can be used when there are concerns about face-to-face contact.

- Video contact can be a relatively safe way to reintroduce contact with a birth relative who has not had or been willing to maintain contact previously but where a focused filmed interview could be beneficial for the child and help them feel more settled in their placement. If possible, visit the birth family member to assess whether they are able and willing to take part in the contact (ideally this visit explores *the idea* of video contact).

- Prepare the child for the video contact by exploring questions, statements and be direct enough to wonder about questions that may as yet be 'unspoken' by the child. (This dynamic approach can also be used in exploring a child's perception of their life story and in preparing a child for face-to-face contact sessions.)

- Prepare the birth family member with the above questions and statements and prepare and support them in developing appropriate answers.

- Is there a fundamental issue or issues that can also be addressed with the birth family member and made clear in the video?

- Record the video message; it is possible to pause the message if the birth family member is becoming overwhelmed, off-message or too emotional, although some expression of feeling helps convey that what is being said is authentic.

- Structure the playing of the video to the child: prepare the adoptive/foster parents. Showing adoptive/foster parents the interview in advance of sharing it with their child helps them process their feelings and encourages reflection on how they will manage the session and support the child. Ensure the child sits with, or at least close, to the adoptive parents and that there is a debriefing afterwards. Offer the child some control while watching the videoed message; they could hold the control ready to pause or else the facilitator could offer to do this whenever the child asks for this.

- Debrief: What part of the video did the child remember most of all? Why? What did he or she like most about the video? Was there anything they did not like about the video? Was there anything that surprised them?

- Ensure that the foster carers or adoptive parents keep communication lines open with the child and try to avoid moving too quickly into reassurance.

- Agree who will follow up with the birth relative and offer them feedback.

## Safety

We are aware that a great deal is being asked of birth relatives involved in being asked to undertake this kind of interview. For example, if a parent can say 'I'm sorry I was not a good parent and let you down', or 'I know I used to shout at you a lot and I'm really sorry', or reveal as Amanda did in Shay's videoed message the circumstances of his conception, they are making themselves very vulnerable. In these circumstances, along with the power to share via websites such as YouTube, any one of us might worry how widely such information could be shared. The process can be helped to feel safer for the relative if they are given a copy of a written agreement that specifies what the purpose of the interview is. It includes a reassurance that the agency will retain the only copies of the filmed interview, which children and young people can revisit as and when they and their adoptive and foster carers feel it would be helpful to do so.

## CHAPTER 8

# Sibling Relationships and Facilitating Sibling Contact

## The significance of sibling relationships

Brothers and sisters may offer each other one of life's longest intimate relationships, surviving that of the parent–child relationship by some 20 years or more. Siblings can provide one another with emotional support, a sense of belonging and continuity, serve as confidants and allies and play a crucial role in the development of self-esteem and sense of identity.

Prior to the 1989 Children Act, research into fostered children showed that children who were placed with siblings settled better and were more likely to return to live with their birth parents. The researchers Rowe et al. (1984)[1] also reported that children who were in longer-term placements often found the presence of a sibling reassuring and supportive.

While it remains the case that many children could benefit from being placed with siblings, finding and maintaining placements for siblings can prove challenging. For example, finding placements with enough accommodation for a group of children can be difficult, and therefore children may be separated from their brothers and sisters by default.

However, post the 1989 Children Act, more attention has also been given to the disruptive impact of maltreated siblings on placement stability and the potential for recovery of the individual children. Professional observation and comment has hypothesised that the emphasis on using reception into care as a last resort[2] means that sibling groups may have experienced prolonged exposure to dysfunctional parental care and maltreatment and that these experiences have shaped not only the parent–child relationship but also those of the siblings.

Julie Selwyn (2004) has written that:

Each child will have a different experience of relationships within the birth family; they will have different roles, be of different levels of maturity, and have different experiences of abuse. Contact plans need to take account of this and ensure that damaging and abusive patterns of behaviour are not repeated during contact visits.[3]

While this observation was made in relation to planning for contact with birth parents it is also relevant to thinking about how separated siblings can be supported in maintaining relationships, and in developing a shared understanding and narrative account of the events that led to removal from the care of birth parents. Siblings supported in developing a shared understanding may find it difficult to validate and accept one another's experiences. Reviewing each child's understanding of their history using an age and developmentally sensitive approach will offer ongoing opportunities to help children and young people begin to integrate and make sense of their early experiences.

The focus of research into the nature of sibling relationships within the larger population has changed during the last 15 years or so revealing a much higher prevalence of sibling disharmony and sibling on sibling abuse (which includes physical, sexual, emotional and psychological abuse) than had previously been recognised.[4]

Dr John Caffaro, one of the authors of *Sibling Abuse Trauma: Assessment and Intervention Strategies for Children, Families, and Adults*,[5] in commenting on the research by Dr C.J. Tucker *et al.* (2013) stated that sibling violence is by far the most common form of family violence, occurring four to five times as frequently as spousal or parental child abuse.

In exploring the family environments in which sibling on sibling abuse occurs, John Caffaro states:

Certain systemic risk factors characterize both sibling assault and sibling incest. For example, parental unavailability and lack of supervision are frequently implicated in both types of abuse. Parental caregivers themselves may be emotionally overwhelmed...may work long hours, misuse drugs, suffer from mental illness, or lack the parenting skills needed.[6]

The authors also comment on what they term the 'Sibling Offender':

For example, often maintain thinking errors that minimize or distort abusive behaviour... Many sibling offenders themselves are victimized by parents, older siblings, or others outside of the family. Therefore it may be that the offender recreates learned behaviour associated with his or her own trauma through the abuse of a vulnerable sibling.[7]

While it remains true that *some* sibling relationships will have been a protective factor for children growing up with parents who have been neglectful or maltreating, it is important given the 'systemic risk factors' identified above and the prevalence of these within the family backgrounds of the children in need of alternative family placements that professionals and carers keep open minds about what may be perceived as 'sibling rivalry' or 'an understandable need by an older sibling to control the younger' sibling.

## Supporting and facilitating contact between siblings

Whether a child is living in foster care or in an adoptive family, it is common for there to be contact arrangements involving siblings. This may occur once or twice yearly and in some circumstances more often. We have experienced contact taking place within a wide variety of structures:

- children meeting in a venue mutually agreed and supervised by the carers

- children meeting at a foster carers' or adoptive parents' home, sometimes with the support of professionals

- children meeting in a therapeutic setting where they and their adoptive parents and/or foster carers receive therapeutic support

- children/young people meeting at a contact centre, where they are supervised by contact centre staff but are without the support of their adoptive parents or foster carers

- children/young people meeting through social networking or through the use of Facebook (this will be explored more fully later on)

- children/young people meeting in secret without carers' knowledge/consent.

For siblings who share a history of trauma and troubled experiences, some of the venues chosen are likely to trigger the child's nervous system into flight or fight response. For example, soft play areas or other kinds of activity centres can activate the ambivalent or disorganised child into acting in unsafe ways. Both the kinds of activity and the number of other children and adults in such places can lead to children feeling overwhelmed and subsequently undermine the value and aims of contact.

An example of the kinds of activities that can help young children enjoy one another's companionship could be meeting in a park with tricycles or pedal cars (the effort involved in pedalling can help organise and regulate the children). Some children might manage parks where there are climbing frames and safe places to hang from, as these kinds of activities can also be regulating. For more ideas on these types of regulating activities see Éadaoin Bhreathnach's children's books *The Scared Gang*[8] which are aimed at helping children recognise the kind of activities and foods that can help them feel more regulated.

Whatever the structure for contact, we have rarely encountered sibling contact arrangements which have had a purpose or focus that is aimed at helping the children:

- develop a shared understanding of why they no longer live with their birth parents

- begin to make sense of their shared trauma and the reasons they needed to live in separate adoptive or foster families

- address any of the individual behavioural or emotional responses the contact generates.

When evaluating contact arrangements, it is always useful to know if there is any particular person 'driving' the contact. Aside from contact arrangements agreed in court, sometimes a child or adult may be identified as the person for whom contact is more important. The needs and wishes for contact amongst sibling groups are likely to change over their life course, particularly in the context of how each sibling's attachment constellates within their adoptive or foster family. In other words, as one sibling forms stronger attachments to their primary carers, there may be an impact upon their need or wish to connect with their birth siblings. The same can be said if a child has suffered a disruption or rupture to their adoptive or foster carers.

If it is the child pushing for contact, discussion to explore what is behind the wish for contact can be revealing.

## Case study: Annie's contact with her siblings

One 10-year-old child we worked with, Annie, was identified as the 'parentified' child in a sibling group. Annie was the eldest of three siblings born to her birth mother; her younger sister who was 8 and her brother who was 6 years old had been placed together with the same adoptive parents. The decision to place Annie separately from her younger siblings had been based upon an assessment that highlighted the need for her to be the youngest child within a family. There were no other young children in Annie's adoptive home. Annie had taken on the role of being the carer when the children lived with their birth mother who was often emotionally and practically unavailable due to her poor emotional health and use of drugs and/or alcohol. Even though Annie had been adopted for over four years, she still identified with the role of 'holding the family together'. This adapted response could be seen as being caring and an act of loving kindness, yet it was clear to her adoptive parents that she found it hard to relinquish control in many other areas of her life. Annie also struggled to conceive that she was equally entitled to as much love, care and affection as the youngest of the sibling group. Careful exploration with Annie revealed her ongoing fear that without her imagined 'holding together' of her siblings, they would struggle to remain adopted. Annie's behaviour at home had swung from expressing anger with a two-year-old cousin 'for not being able to sit properly' to wanting to be given a baby's bottle at bedtime. When Annie lived with her birth mother, it was common to be hit at the table for not 'sitting nicely'.

Annie had been referred for psychotherapy or therapeutic intervention because of her increasingly challenging behaviour. However, an appraisal of her wider life issues revealed the fact that these emergent issues formed an increased pattern of behavioural concerns before contact with her siblings. Annie also had begun to ask 'random' questions about her life story and had berated her adoptive mother for 'being weak'. Annie appeared to be defending against allowing the 'weak' or vulnerable side of herself, preferring instead to project and attack this feared feeling onto her adoptive mother. In this case, Annie was able to engage with a more robust exploration of her life history and it was clear that a significant part of her desperately wanted (and feared) greater closeness with her adoptive parents, who were, with their social worker, supported to reframe Annie's wish for contact.

Therapeutically, Annie was enabled to reflect on the idea that her need to care for her siblings was born from a very natural desire to maintain their safety, and to some degree it was the only way she could gain some approval from her birth mother. She agreed that she no longer needed to do this and that the greater challenge was for her to allow herself to be cared for and parented and to relinquish some control.

Strategies were created to help Annie for the next contact:

- She was given a 'secret code' of communication to let her adoptive parents know that she was feeling worried about being in less control.

- The structure of the contact was changed to a shorter contact (thus making it more manageable) and in an environment that allowed her adoptive parents to be more physically available.

- Annie was also helped to think through situations when she might want to be 'a parent' to her siblings and what she could do differently.

- Through a simple guided visualisation of imagining the contact, Annie was helped to begin to recognise her bodily responses as indicators of worry or distress and how she could regulate these feelings. Annie was given 'crunchy food' (a sensory motor intervention to help self-regulation) to assist the process.

- Annie was helped to think ahead and plan in advance where she might sit, stand and move. She realised that she would always sit near the youngest sibling as she felt protective and would put food on his plate. On this occasion, she was going to sit with her adoptive parents... between them!

A member of the post adoption team also met with the adoptive parents of the younger children in advance of the contact session. The adoptive parents of Annie's siblings were briefed on the aim of the therapeutically facilitated contact for Annie, and their views on the benefits or otherwise of the contact sessions for their children were explored. They were committed to ensuring that the children were enabled to maintain contact and grow up knowing each other. The adoptive parents of the siblings had noticed Annie's tendency to want to look after her siblings during the contact sessions and had allowed this, as they had an understanding of why she did this and had not wanted to upset Annie or her adoptive parents. Annie's siblings were doing well, although there were still some signs of insecurity and the eldest child still had difficulty believing that there would always be enough food and had a tendency to overeat. There were also times when she had shared memories about her experiences of living with Annie and her birth mother. She could remember a time when their birth mother had been slumped over on the settee and Annie had tried to wake her up because their baby brother was crying and there was no food or milk. The adoptive mother of Annie's siblings decided that she would bake some cup cakes to share during the contact session and that she would encourage Annie's sister and little brother to help decorate them.

The contact went well and Annie's adoptive parents were delighted at how she allowed them to care for her. Annie had 'noticed' that she could see how much her siblings were loved and cared for by their adoptive parents. When she got home, she had become angry about what seemed an incidental situation, yet Annie and her adoptive parents had been well prepared and this had been foreseen as a possibility following a successful contact. Therefore, Annie was not allowed to sabotage the experience and thus reduce it to being a 'one-off'.

It is a wise process to evaluate sibling contact as the children become older and just because it appears to be 'working' may not mean that it is always the right thing to do in its current form.

## Case study: Facilitating contact and supporting siblings who share a history of abuse and neglect

John and Simon were aged 12 and 8 ½ years old when they and their foster families were referred for therapeutic support. They had been in care for two years and had lived in the same foster family for the first year. Apart from a younger sister who had been placed for adoption, they had grown up as the youngest of a large sibling group, all of who were now young adults.

Their mother had experienced a very troubled childhood and presented with complex issues and needs, and had both physical and mental health issues. She had difficulty sustaining her partner relationships and the children had a number of different fathers. Periodically her capacity to cope physically seemed so compromised that she could barely walk and her children were seen to be looking after her. At other times, she seemed to be well and was out and about enjoying a social life while the older children were left in charge of the youngsters. Social services had been intermittently involved due to child protection concerns around neglect, behavioural issues and school absences. Support was put in place in the home with the aim of relieving the pressure the children were experiencing; however, the situation continued to deteriorate and the children were taken into care. A psychiatric assessment of the mother showed her to have a borderline personality disorder with limited insight into the emotional needs of her children. At times, the mother could be very angry and hostile towards the children, including hitting them with belts, and at others she portrayed a neediness, and expected the children to be able to respond to her needs for emotional and psychological support. A file search revealed that there had also been concerns about the number of inappropriate adults that the mother had been involved with.

When they had been in foster care together, John was observed to be very aggressive and controlling towards Simon whose ability to feel safe and develop his capacity for regulation was being continually undermined by the threat of John's close proximity. After a year, John was therefore moved to another foster placement and regular contact was arranged between the two boys.

Simon, who also had some learning difficulties, was the first child referred for therapeutic support. In working with him and his foster carers, it soon became apparent that while in many ways Simon had made good progress in the care of his experienced, sensitive and committed foster carers, he remained developmentally traumatised and confused about his early life experiences. Sometimes his foster carers reported being concerned and confused themselves by what Simon said to others. For example, while out with his foster mother he had told a shop assistant that his foster mother had hit him. She had not hit Simon and tried to reason with him about this but he had remained adamant that she had. Another major concern was Simon's seemingly unpredictable periods of severe tantrums when he appeared out of reach and unable to respond to the nurturing care on offer. With support to the foster carers to think about Simon's difficulties within the context of his developmental experiences and with attachment-focused parenting approaches aimed at meeting the needs of a much younger child, Simon's capacity for self-regulation began to increase. Given opportunities to revisit his life story, Simon also began to talk with his foster carers about some of his frightening experiences while living with his birth family.

His foster carers were committed to maintaining contact between Simon and John, but did notice that Simon's behaviour regressed leading up to, and following, each of the contact visits, which both sets of foster carers worked hard to ensure were fun.

John and his foster family were referred subsequently for therapeutic support. While John had made progress and was a very likeable boy there were some very concerning behaviours. For example, John had been stealing, absconding from school, frequently wet the bed and most concerning had been found trying to engage the foster carers' 3-year-old granddaughter into interacting with him sexually. His foster carers remained committed to caring for John and worked with professionals to develop a home care plan aimed at ensuring that everyone in the family was kept safe. This involved John in discussing and drawing up the plans. An aspect of the plan was that John and the foster carers would have access to some therapeutic support.

Meanwhile, contact between Simon and John continued, and Simon's behaviour continued to regress. Simon's foster carers had witnessed some of the physical aggression and bullying behaviours John had perpetrated upon Simon, and they had tried to reassure Simon that they would make sure he was safe and able to have some fun time with his brother when they all met up. Following some life story work, Simon told his foster carers that he had bad memories of when he and John had lived with their birth family that John had not only picked on him and punched him but had also done some 'rude things' and hurt his bottom.

John, who had begun to explore his own painful history within the birth family, did not deny what Simon was saying when he was asked why he thought Simon was saying these things; and spoke of how he had also been abused in a similar way by an older brother. While there had been no formal arrangements for contact with this brother who was currently 20 years old, he frequently turned up at the school playground to 'check in' and say hello to John.

While John had a range of feelings, one of which was relief in acknowledging his abusive experiences with his foster carers and social worker, he did not want to talk about these experiences with the police. He did, however, agree that his older brother should be approached by social services and told that John did not want to have any contact with him and that he should not keep turning up at his school. It was agreed that the current contact plans between John and Simon would be suspended.

With the support of their foster carers, John and Simon were separately prepared for a facilitated contact.

Louis and Elsie had both worked with Simon and his foster carers previously and both were party to helping Simon and his foster carers, who came 45 minutes before John and his foster mother, to prepare for the facilitated contact.

## Working with Simon

Simon, together with his foster carers, worked in a room that was familiar to him and where he felt safe. Simon had been prepared by his foster carers for coming to the facilitated contact, and they had explained that they would be with him throughout both to support him and keep him safe. The fact that contact with his brother had been put on hold had been explained to Simon when the decision was first made and the news had come as a great relief. He had wanted to know if following this meeting he would be expected to start seeing John again and was reassured that contact arrangements would only be made if that was what Simon felt he wanted.

Simon was encouraged to think about what memories he would like to ask John about and whether he had any specific questions for him. Simon found it difficult to write and it was agreed that Louis would write the questions for him. In exploring his life history Simon had shared some very sad and frightening memories. For example, he had come to believe that the ghost of a child lived in a cupboard under the stairs. He also remembered fights between adults and teenagers and hiding for what seemed like hours under the bed. He recalled being very hungry sometimes and worrying about his baby sister and trying to stop her crying because she and he might get into trouble. He wondered if John could remember any of these things.

Simon's foster carers had already told him they were very sad to hear how much he had been hurt by John and were sorry that they had not realised all that had happened to him sooner. With their support Simon wanted to ask John why he had hurt him and done those rude things to him. Simon also wanted to ask John if he knew that it was wrong to do those things to other people, even if they were your brother.

Elsie then explained that she was now going to meet with John and his foster carer to help them get ready for the facilitated contact. It is important to empower children who have been victimised, and preparation for meeting with someone who has hurt the child in the past is essential.

So Louis worked with Simon, who knew the room where he and John along with their foster carer and the facilitators would meet, and was able to discuss and plan where he would like everyone to sit. He was also able to choose whether he or John would enter the room first. Simon was also encouraged to think about how he could get support from his foster carers, should he feel the need, and he said he would hold his foster mother's hand. He also knew that he could let her know he had something he needed to say by squeezing her hand. If the situation was too difficult and Simon needed a break he said he would tell his foster mother he needed to visit the bathroom, knowing that she would go with him.

## Working with John

John's social worker (who was also Simon's social worker) had, along with his foster carers, begun to prepare him for a facilitated contact with Simon. John had already begun the processes of exploring his life history and had begun to make connections about his earlier experiences and some of his behaviours and reactions in the past and the present. He had received support in beginning to explore his own experiences of abuse, first and foremost in working out what could help him feel safer. This had included telling his adult brother, Gary, to stay away from him and having a designated staff member for support and a safe place at school should he need it. John did not want to think or talk in detail about his past abuse and this was respected. However, he was able to communicate some of how he had felt, which included scared, angry and confused. John was also aware of feeling shame about what had happened to him and what he had done to others. His social worker and foster carers had been able to empathise with him and had offered him emotional support. Given the work that had already been done around the safety of the foster carers' grandchild, John was very aware of what was appropriate and inappropriate behaviour.

In preparing for the facilitated contact with Simon, Elsie, who already knew John, met with him and his foster mother. John's courage in being willing to come and meet with his younger brother in order to talk together about what had previously been kept a secret was acknowledged, as was the hard work he had been doing in learning how to keep himself and others safe.

The fact that thinking and talking about the past could be upsetting was acknowledged and John was encouraged to explore ways he could be supported. For example, he was asked where in the room he would feel most comfortable and where he would like his foster mother and Elsie to sit. John decided he would like his foster mother to sit beside him and that Elsie could sit off to the other side. Elsie then explained how the meeting with Simon and his foster carers (who John knew very well) would be structured and explained the role of Louis (who John and his foster carer also knew) in supporting Simon.

John was asked to consider Simon's questions. He understood how Simon could have come to believe that there was a ghost in the cupboard under the stairs, as that was one of the stories that some of the older siblings and their friends had sometimes told the younger children, and John had also been afraid. John could also remember the fights and going hungry. He was also able to confirm that he and Simon had been expected to keep their baby sister quiet when their mum had a hangover. Sometimes when their older siblings were out, John had been expected to look after Simon before their sister had been born.

With this shared understanding of some of their history established, John was then asked to consider Simon's questions about his physical and sexual abuse. John was probably being truthful when he said he did not really know why he did those things to his little brother but that sometimes he had felt very angry with him. He had also not liked hearing him cry, partly because he might get it from their mum if she heard the crying. Because of his learning difficulty and speech delay other kids in the neighbourhood had made fun of Simon, and John had felt ashamed and angry with Simon about this also.

Elsie wondered if John felt that in some ways Simon was to blame for the way their relationship had turned out. John thought about this for a moment or two and, looking at his foster carer, he said, 'No not really, I guess it's like you said about what Gary did to me that was not my fault, was it?' His foster mother nodded and said, 'That's right, that wasn't your fault.' John's eyes began to fill with tears; it was important that Elsie accepted that this was a conversation that could allow John's grief to emerge. Elsie then wondered if John had thought it was his fault, to which he answered yes he had. She then wondered if he thought Simon might think what John had done to him was his own fault. John said he thought he might. Elsie then suggested that it could be helpful to Simon to hear John say that it was not his fault. John's face looked worried, yet he nodded.

'We can help you with this, John, you've been carrying these worries for so long and it can be hard to say sorry to someone you care for,' said Elsie.

When asked if he knew it was wrong to do those things to other people even if they were your brother, John cried and nodded. His foster mother gently put her hand on his and John turned into her so he could receive the hug she was ready to offer.

Elsie acknowledged how painful it was having to think about how his behaviour had hurt Simon, and his foster carer told him she was proud of him for being able to take responsibility and come and see Simon in this way.

Elsie then asked John how he thought Simon would have felt when John had behaved in those ways towards him. With tears still running down his face, John said he was scared.

Elsie then asked John if he thought he would be able to say something to Simon in answer to his last question. John nodded and said he wanted to say sorry for hurting him. John also said that he wanted Simon to know that he would try to be a better brother to him in the future. Elsie could see how important it was for John to try to say this to his brother and said 'You want things to be different between you now.' 'Yes please,' said John. He sounded as if he were 4 years old.

Elsie went on to explain that their social worker, their foster carers and the team (Louis and Elsie) had decided that this kind of contact meeting could be helpful for both John and Simon. However, this did not mean that the pattern of regular contact would restart, as everyone would need to think about what would be best for both boys after this meeting, because Simon was still not sure about how he was going to feel.

Louis then joined the session briefly and Elsie was able to tell Louis how hard John had been willing to work and his foster mother said how proud she was of him. Louis then explained how the session with Simon would be organised. Simon and his foster carers were already in the room so all that was required now was for us to join them.

## The session

Simon sat between his foster carers on one side of the room; there were three seats circled out at a right angle and Elsie took the one nearest Simon's male foster carer. John sat next to her, then his foster mother sat next to him. Louis sat between the two groups. All of the foster carers knew each other and gave warm greetings. Simon's foster carers also gave a warm greeting to John as he entered the room.

Louis began by outlining the aim of the contact session. This was to help both Simon and John come to a better understanding of their past together and to begin to understand some of the hurts and confusions that had happened and, in particular, so that John could answer some of the questions Simon had about the things he had done.

Louis then suggested that he would read out Simon's questions one at a time and started with Simon's 'memory questions'. John was able to answer the first of these and explained why he thought Simon might have believed in the ghost. This led to some further reminiscing between both Simon and John while they recalled various of their older siblings' friends and things they did, or asked one another 'Do you remember when?' Louis and Elsie gently steered the session back to answering the questions, with Elsie able to say to John, 'When we were talking about Simon's questions, do you remember you said how worried and angry you got when Simon cried in case your mum heard and you would get into trouble?' John nodded and Simon said he also worried when their baby sister cried. Elsie then told Simon that John also remembered being very hungry sometimes and on the session went until Louis read out the final question. 'Did John know it was wrong to do those things to people even if they are your brother?' With tears in his eyes, John said he did know it was wrong and that he was sorry he had hurt Simon and made him feel so scared. Simon was watching John intently while holding the hand of his female foster carer. After a short silence, Elsie asked John if he remembered thinking how children who get hurt by someone in the way he hurt Simon might feel about who is to blame. John said he did and that he wanted Simon to know that what happened was not his fault and that he was really very sorry. John then said that if Simon would give him the chance sometime in the future he would like to make it up to him and be the kind of brother he should have been when they were living together. Simon looked at John and then at his foster mother (whose hand he was still holding) then looking back at John said, 'Thank you John.'

Simon's foster mother then asked him if he was saying thank you for what John had said or thank you because he wanted to start seeing John again in the way they had before. Simon looked again at John and said, 'No thank you, not right now.'

John looked sad, and Elsie then said to Louis, 'I can see this is difficult for John. I understand that he would like everything to feel OK between him and Simon now, but I can also understand that from Simon's point of view he needs some time to think through the things John has said today and work out how he feels and what he will need to have happen to feel safe in the future.' Simon nodded.

Louis then began to draw the session to a close, thanking John for taking responsibility and saying sorry to Simon, and acknowledging Simon's courage in being able to meet with John and ask him his questions. Both boys had shown courage by not keeping secrets that had harmed them and this was the beginning of their journey into healing.

Elsie then led John and his foster mother back into the room where they had first met so that they could debrief. This left Louis with Simon and his foster carers to give Simon space to reflect and debrief.

Paper and writing and drawing materials were available for both boys in anticipation of the debrief. They and their foster carers were also offered snacks and drinks.

Questions to help prompt reflection:

· How does it feel now you have met with your brother?

· What do you think are the most important things he said or did in the meeting?

· What did you like the most and the least about the meeting?

· Is there anything else you wish you could have asked or said that was not possible during the meeting?

The boys' foster carers were also asked to comment on how they felt their foster children had managed the meeting.

There was also space to think and talk about how each boy imagined how the other might have felt about the meeting.

Simon was relieved and said he would remember John saying it was not his fault and that he was sorry he hurt and scared him. Also significant for Simon was that he was still anxious about the possibility of having to see John again too soon. He was reassured by both his foster carers and Louis that this was understandable as he needed time to settle and feel safe. He would not have to see John until he felt it was the right time for him.

John was also relieved and said he would remember that he had faced the truth and done the right thing by saying sorry to Simon. He was sad that Simon did not want to see him again at the moment. With support, however, he was able to reflect on the possibility that Simon might still have a lot of confused feelings about the past and needed time to work these out and feel safe.

Both sets of foster carers had also been prepared in advance that while the meeting would be helpful in supporting both boys in beginning to integrate and process some of the traumatic events from their pasts, it was also possible that both Simon and John might experience further 'memories' related to abusive experiences. This possibility was also explained to both boys (who had already experienced this kind of recall following on from life story work or in relation to other environmental triggers). Both foster carers encouraged the boys to let them know if this happened so that they could give them support in making sense of these experiences and help them feel safe again.

## Conclusions

Enabling positive sibling relationships when children share a history of developmental trauma and maltreatment should include supporting them in developing a shared understanding of their history and the experiences that led to the need for placements with substitute parents, whether or not they are placed together or separately. However, such work becomes imperative if siblings have been placed separately and, particularly, where one or other of the children has been abused by a sibling. Each sibling is in need of support to enable them to address their traumatic experiences, abusive re-enactments and victimisations. They need to be empowered to develop a coherent narrative and potential for developing healthier ways of relating to one another, so that their ongoing availability as supportive family members throughout the life cycle will be enhanced. There should be an aim to support regular ongoing contact that helps keep siblings connected and abreast of the changes in one another's lives. However, depending on the developmental stages and changes in the understanding of the children, therapeutically facilitated contact that helps address their concerns and questions may need to be revisited.

## Contact between siblings following disrupted placements or where one sibling is in care

There are of course occasions when following the placement of a sibling group for adoption, one (or more) of the siblings has to return to foster care due to the difficulty for the adoptive parents of sustaining the placement; for example, the behaviour of a particular child becomes too difficult to manage.

This naturally evokes overwhelmingly strong feelings for all concerned. The child going back into the care system may feel rage, despair, abandonment and a rejection that confirms the child's innermost fear of being unlovable. For the adoptive parents, they may also feel rage, despair, hopelessness and an immense sense of failure. For the sibling(s) remaining in the adoptive placement, there may be anger at the departing child for not managing, grief for the loss of their sibling, relief at the end of what may have been a terrible experience and a nagging fear that they themselves may be 'the next in line' to leave the family home. The sense of frustration, anger and self-chastisement can be transferred to professionals, such as social workers, who can feel somehow responsible for the disruption to the family. Maybe there was something I could have done better? Could things have been different? These questions may be wondered by all parties involved.

The implications for foster or adoptive families having contact where one (or more) child remains in care are wide-ranging.

## Case study: 14-year-old girl

Louis once worked with a girl, aged 14, who was adopted aged 4½ years old. Her three older sisters (aged 6, 8 and 11 when she was adopted) all remained in the care system. The girl was adopted by a wealthy and successful family for whom it was common to attend independent school, travel around the world, dress in designer clothes and speak two or three languages. For the girl's siblings, the future was less glamorous and all of the sisters struggled in their own way. One spent four years in a residential home after the disruption of seven foster placements. Another was pregnant at the age of 17 – the same age as Louis' client's birth mother. The last sibling had mental health issues and was on medication. The sisters had face-to-face contact once a year at a neutral venue organised by the adoptive parents. The girl Louis worked with was well able to recognise the increasingly vast cultural chasm opening up between her and her siblings. Things became difficult when one sister asked for money to buy clothes for her baby. This scenario is just one of many that foster and adopted children confront and it is all too easy to see how difficult it must be to navigate these deep and troubled waters of discontent.

It is the role of social workers, contact workers, psychotherapists and, where possible, adoptive parents and foster carers to enable children and young people to be more able to make sense of such situations and attempt to facilitate more meaningful contact and shared understandings. Many adoptive parents and foster carers report to Louis and Elsie how frustrating it can be to witness children at a loss as to what to say or, more often, be seen to 'glide over' anything that is perceived as difficult or upsetting to talk about. To be more able to have resilient relationships that are of substance and depth, and are long-lasting, children (and young people) require adults who are willing to enter the realms of more challenging conversations in order to create a template that communicates 'this is difficult to talk about, yet we can do this!'

## Case study: When adopted siblings are separated and one child is returned to care

Amir and Ephra were adopted aged 3½ and 5 years old respectively. Their background was of extreme neglect and it was suspected that Ephra may have been sexually abused by a family relative, as well as physically abused by her father. From the outset, her adoptive parents had struggled with the placement, particularly in terms of managing Ephra's aggression, control issues and sexualised behaviour. Amir, on the other hand, presented as overly compliant, adaptive and withdrawn. The adoptive parents, with the support of therapeutic services, did their best to maintain the placement, yet, after eight years, the adoptive parents felt they could no longer cope with Ephra and social services received her back into care. She was placed with long-term foster carers. By this time, she was nearly 14 years old and Amir was 12½. It was agreed that the siblings would have monthly face-to-face contact, as well as contact by phone on a weekly basis.

Meanwhile, Ephra had re-made contact with her birth mother with the support of her social worker. The birth mother's life had significantly changed over the last four years and she appeared to be managing relatively well. Meanwhile, Amir's behaviour began to spiral downwards and he soon became more oppositional, began to steal and, at one point, threw a knife at his adoptive mother. Louis and Elsie were contacted to explore the situation and, amongst other things, make an assessment of the contact issues in relation to the children. At this point in the intervention, the adoptive parents had been advised not to have contact with Ephra who continued to make clear her anger towards them. Her foster carer noted though that Ephra did talk to her about them, asking if she knew what they were doing and 'was Amir OK?' There were times when the foster carer was sure that Ephra would cry herself to sleep.

When Louis and Elsie met Amir's adoptive parents, it was clearly apparent that they wanted the best for Amir and Ephra and were willing to reflect on the story of Ephra's disrupted placement and its impact upon the family as a whole. Elsie spent time reflecting on their loss, acknowledging how hard it must have been to parent a child with such a traumatic history. Their initial frustration and anger with social services shifted to a deeper sense of helplessness and shame at not being able to parent Ephra in the way they had longed to be able to do. The parents described their anxiety around Amir's contact with Ephra, particularly in relation to her newly established contact with her birth mother. Social services had informed Elsie that the birth mother had indeed made progress in terms of her mental health, yet there were still significant concerns regarding her ability to be a predictable, constant figure in Ephra's life.

When Louis met Amir, he was impressed at his ability to reflect on being adopted, the loss of his sister and his ongoing concerns about his sister's safety and wellbeing. Amir worried that Ephra might get hurt by his birth mother and he wondered if she would come back to the family to live. Amir also admitted that he 'felt bad that I am the one left living with mum and dad!'

When Louis met Ephra at her foster carers', she was anxious about his visit. At first, she was very distracted and controlling and then she began to relax as Louis acknowledged how she had suffered so many changes of home and parents for a girl of her age and how sad this must be for her. Louis used Dan Hughes' model of PACE (Playful, Accepting, Curious and Empathic)[9] to engage Ephra and convey that he had her best interests in mind. The process of relating in this way enabled her to be more co-regulated and receptive in their discussions. At times she needed to dash to the kitchen to fetch food, yet she returned to take part in another manageable chunk of discussion.

Louis and Elsie concluded that all of the family had questions they wanted to ask, things that they feared others may ask and a profound yet fragile wish for things to be different. Louis and Elsie felt hopeful at the overriding sense of compassion offered by the adoptive parents towards both children. The disruption to the family of Ephra returning to care had created a barely masked fear and paranoia that this could happen again. It seemed to Elsie and Louis that none of the family members felt secure in their place in the family and Ephra needed further help to make sense of what had happened to her.

Elsie and Louis agreed the following structure with the adoptive parents and Ephra's foster carers.

- Prior to a contact session involving the children it was agreed that the adoptive parents and Ephra's foster carers, who had never met, should have a short facilitated meeting to help them explore how they would work together to support the children in what could be a very emotive meeting.
- The process of working with the family involved:
  - preparation of Ephra, Amir and the adoptive parents
  - exploring what each person wanted to ask or say to one another
  - establishing a context and purpose for the contact
  - preparing the adoptive parents and Ephra's foster carers to be more able to contain the children's thoughts, feelings and behaviour
  - planning of the contact session between the adoptive parents and Ephra's foster carers
  - planning for the contact session involving the children
  - planning for the potential consequences of the contact
  - facilitating the contact session
  - debriefing of the contact session.

The areas outlined above followed a basic framework that can be shaped to each family, yet there are unique aspects to working with children who have one or more siblings that are in care. For adoptive families who have suffered the experience of a disruption and return to the care system of their child, the unbearable and unspeakable feelings evoked need to be explored and expressed. As there are so many conflicting thoughts and feelings involved, it can be helpful for professionals to use 'parts' language in order to make exploration more possible. A parent can be supported to explore the part of them that feels devastated, the part that feels relieved, the part that feels angry, and so on. A similar approach can be used for children and young people which assumes that a person is more than the 'part' being explored. Therefore, one can ask an adoptive parent, 'Tell me about the part of you that feels devastated about your daughter returning to care.' Then one could ask, 'And what other parts are there…is there a part of you that feels relieved?'

There are, of course, certain areas that may be of use to a family to explore in this situation:

- What do the adoptive parents think they could have done differently to prevent their child going into care?

- Is one of the parents feeling different to the other, such as relieved when the other is feeling distressed?

- How able are the parents to reflect upon what has happened?

- How do the parents' attachment styles impact upon the process?

- Has the remaining child(ren) been allowed to discuss a range of feelings such as anger, relief, sadness and fear about the departing sibling?

- Does the remaining child(ren) have any guilt over what has happened?

- Does the remaining child(ren) fear that they may not manage in some way and have to leave the family?

- How does the child(ren)'s attachment style impact upon the process?

- What early life trauma issues related to the children's past may need to be considered in the children's current lives? What situations may be 're-enacted' from the past?

- What needs to be acknowledged to the departed child?

- Have the adoptive parents been able to express how sorry they are that they could not care and keep the child and how this must remind the child of not being cared for in their birth family?

- If the remaining child is somewhat adapted, compliant or caregiving, is there a need for an expression of healthy protest or ambivalence?

- What needs to be expressed and acknowledged between the siblings?

- Do they need support to say explicitly that they miss one another and think about one another?

- How can the foster carers be integrated into the dialogue in order to ensure that the child returning back to care has a template for open and reflective discussion?

- How has the facilitated discussion shifted the perspective of future relationships and contact into the future?

- If the child returning to (or already in) care has contact with birth family members, what worries, fantasies or questions are there being held by the adoptive family members? Do these need to be expressed to the child who has returned to living in care?

- What could be the trajectory of progress for all involved? What could be the potential obstacles for family relationships?

- In terms of the child in care's contact with birth family members, what needs to be explored and made explicit with the remaining child(ren)?

- Would any arts or creative mediums support and enable the above discussion?

- What could be the benefits of a period of further life story work?

- Do the contact arrangements support the children's unique ways of coping with meeting one another?

- Are there any issues around social networking, Facebook, etc. that need addressing?

- What would be the best way of evaluating the contact arrangements?

## CHAPTER 9

# Contact for Adopted Children with Adoptive Parents who have Separated or Divorced

It is a sad fact that both Louis and Elsie have experience of supporting a number of adoptive families where adoptive parents separate following the process of adoption. We have also consulted or supported several colleagues who have had to deal with this issue. It is not possible to say that parenting children with early life trauma is always the cause, yet in our experience many adoptive parents report their struggle to care for children with multiple needs and attachment-related issues as at least part of the cause for the increased disharmony in their relationship.

In the same way that contact for children from non-adoptive families can be deeply stressful, the situation is potentially made all the more difficult by the evocation for adoptive children of the themes of disharmony between adults/parents, broken homes, rejection, separation and an often muddled story regarding why the couple have separated.

## Case study: Tom and Emma

Alex and Lorraine had been married for over 12 years and had adopted Tom (6 years old) and Emma (8 years old) over four years ago. A year into the adoption, the couple's relationship became strained as Alex and Lorraine began to argue over their differences about how to parent the children. Alex believed that they needed to be stricter with the children while Lorraine wanted to be more nurturing. They received some couple support from an adoption organisation which helped for a while. However, it was not long before Alex and Lorraine grew apart, resulting in Alex having an affair with a colleague at work. The couple soon separated and told the children that they would not be together any more as they were not happy together. For the first few months, Alex made little contact and then told Lorraine that he'd like to see the children and, if they wanted, they would be welcome to stay overnight.

Since the parents' separation, Emma had become more clingy and Tom's behaviour and work at school had deteriorated. Emma had told Lorraine that she 'hated' Alex and 'never wanted to see him again'. She was also angry that it had been Tom's birthday the previous week and Alex had not phoned or sent him a card. Each member of the family had begun to polarise in their opinions of one another, although Lorraine believed that, if possible, it would be beneficial for the children to have a father figure in their lives.

When assessing the family and the contact issues, the 1:1 meetings with each child revealed their mutual anxiety around 'people going or staying in the family'. There was concern from the children that social services involvement meant that they may have to return to their birth family or go to another foster family. Emma was also worried that Alex would 'take mum away, as he never liked us and wants her all to himself'. A part of Emma also believed that Lorraine could not manage parenting alone and may choose Alex ahead of the children. It was agreed that a 'facilitated contact' between Lorraine, Alex and the children would help them to discuss their situation and, importantly, diffuse the notion that Lorraine would leave the children for Alex. In a session that involved the children and Lorraine, she was supported to make clear to the children that she could manage parenting them both and was not going to leave them. Both children listened intently as she explained this and you could see tangible relief on their faces as they heard that she loved them in a way 'that could fit all of them into her heart' and she was not going to leave them. This facilitated conversation allowed for a deeper integration of their life story as it was acknowledged to the children that given their history of rejection and loss, it was understandable that their minds would expect the worst to happen. Dan Hughes refers to this as 'normalisation' of a child's experience.[1]

Alex was also prepared for the facilitated contact. An initial meeting confirmed his own anxiety and grief regarding the children and the break-up of his marriage.

Like Annie in a previous contact scenario, both Tom and Emma were prepared to think about the contact in advance (with Lorraine present). Importantly, *the context and meaning* was explored with the children. It was more than being about meeting with Alex, which Emma had already made clear she did not want to do; it was about having the opportunity to develop a narrative and make sense and meaning for the children, who needed to know:

- why Alex and Lorraine had separated
- that they were deeply sorry for any distress this has caused and still causes the children
- that it was not the children's fault that they had separated. This could also be put into context (integrating life story work) with perceptions the children may have about themselves and their lives: *that parents always leave them in the end!*

- that Alex still wants to be a father to the children
- that Alex and Lorraine will do their best to have a shared plan for caring for the children and that the children's needs will come first.

To enable Emma and Tom to invest in the facilitated contact, it was necessary to acknowledge that it would be understandable if they had 'big feelings' about meeting Alex and that it was not surprising that Emma had already said that she hated Alex. This strong statement was both affirmed and explored, with Elsie sharing that if she'd been in Emma's position and thought she had been abandoned by her adoptive father, a part of her would also feel hateful. This allowed Elsie to attempt to reframe Emma's experience into 'a part' of Emma feeling hateful rather than the whole of her (feeling hateful), thus allowing a greater possibility of not being overwhelmed by her feelings and making room for other feelings. Elsie empathically wondered aloud whether a part of Emma also felt abandoned and hated by Alex when he left the family. Elsie reflected on knowing that Emma's birth father had left her birth mother when she was young and how tough it must be for Emma that it had happened all over again. Maybe a part of Emma wondered, 'Am I never going to have a dad like some other children?'

Emma became tearful and cuddled her mother and Tom energetically said, 'Yes! She said to me that we'll never have a daddy!' Both children were then supported to share their fears, hopes and sadness about Alex and Lorraine's separation and the echoes of losses earlier in their lives. At the end of the session, both children expressed their interest and readiness to meet Alex. However, if it had been the case that they maintained a wish *not* to meet Alex, this would have been respected. Elsie would have supported and invited the children to create a message to Alex, if possible, expressing that they were not yet ready to meet him.

Emma and Tom were also prepared to think about what they wanted to say and ask Alex with Lorraine, who provided a wonderful, nurturing and thoughtful presence. The seating arrangements were taken into account, as well as how each child wanted to say hello and say goodbye to Alex. For this facilitated contact, the children were seated between Lorraine and Elsie with Louis being the person who would be supporting and guiding Alex, sitting next in line. Last, it was explained to the children that for this meeting, there would be no time for play and that it would be quite a short meeting.

The children were already familiar with the room in which they would meet Alex, as they had done their preparation work there.

With Elsie's support the children created a list of questions and statements for Alex:

- Why did you leave us?
- Was it our fault?
- Will you be coming back?
- Do you still love us or just mummy?
- Do you think about us?

- We remember when you shouted at mummy.
- Why didn't you get Tom a birthday card? Can you promise to try to remember from now on?

Alex was prepared by Louis to meet with Lorraine and the children. They worked through the children's questions which, unsurprisingly, brought up strong feelings of guilt, grief and anxiety for Alex. It was important for Louis not to move too quickly into reassuring Alex and metaphorically 'putting a lid on his feelings'. Therefore, Alex was assisted in exploring and experiencing his distress in order to widen his capacity for managing the facilitated contact. It was likely that these difficult feelings would be triggered during the contact and Alex had to begin to learn to tolerate them, not feel overwhelmed and to be able to respond to the children's deepest concerns. This session also operated in some ways as an assessment of whether Alex would be able to manage the contact and whether he was willing to put their needs ahead of his own. If he had been unwilling to respond to their questions, then we would have questioned the potential of the contact. It is crucial that adults (often with support) are able to rise above their own anxieties. This preparation work alleviated some of Lorraine's concerns and led to a brief facilitated meeting between her and Alex as the last stage of preparation for the facilitated contact. It would not have been wise to expect the parents to work together in the interests of the children had they come together for the first time with the children. Both needed an opportunity to experience being together and processing feelings the children's questions would generate for them, so that they would not be taken unawares when they did meet with the children. Lorraine and Alex were able to commit to the process and appeared to appreciate the structure and purpose to the contact.

The facilitated contact between Alex, Lorraine, Emma and Tom lasted no more than an hour. Sometimes, the initial facilitated contacts are planned to last just 30 minutes if the participants' feelings are highly charged. In this case, Alex had been prepared to answer all of the questions and with Louis' help was able to take time to respond and even expand on what needed to be said. On one occasion, Emma asked Alex, 'Do you love us as well as mummy?' Alex responded by saying that he loved them all. Louis and Elsie developed this conversation to support Alex to wonder what may be behind Emma's question. Elsie wondered aloud whether Emma wanted to know if Alex had room in his heart for the children and Lorraine. Alex movingly described how even as an adult he was still learning about love and that the one thing he had recently learnt was that his heart had more than enough space for many people, including family and friends, and there would always be a special place reserved for them.

At the end of the contact, when all of the questions had been asked, Alex left the room first with Louis, so that Lorraine and the children could remain in their familiar environment to debrief. Emma said that she could tell that Alex was nervous when he came into the room by the way he 'did not have a real smile' but she could see him relax 'when Elsie gave him a cup of tea'! Emma was 'really, really glad' they'd had the facilitated contact and asked when the next one would be.

Tom was also pleased that Alex 'had remembered to come' and was pleased that Alex had said sorry for the difficult argument between him and Lorraine that resulted in Alex shouting furiously. Tom was also pleased to hear that Alex had said that it was not the children's fault that he had left the family; Emma agreed energetically. Last, Tom was pleased that Alex (at Louis' suggestion) had brought 'Sorry' cards and a belated birthday card for Tom.

The family were supported by having a further three facilitated contacts. Each one lasted a little longer and the parents were supported to pay particular focus to noticing the children's non-verbal body language in order to attune to and practise their understanding of the children's feeling states. Conversation was focused on a high level of engagement, interest and praise for the children.

Relational play was encouraged, in which the parents used themselves more as the objects of play (Theraplay games were very useful in this area) rather than board games, DS or phone games.

## CHAPTER 10

# Where Contact is not Possible

## Contact for Children who are not Able to Meet their Birth Parents or Family

There are some children who are 'looked after' or adopted who for various reasons are unable to have contact with their birth family. This may be due to the fact that:

- the birth family members are acknowledged to be a risk to the children and their new carers' safety

- the birth parents may have died

- the birth parents may be missing or absent

- the birth parents' current condition or life situation may be such that it is considered 'too distressing' for a child to encounter (the parent may have serious mental health issues, be hospitalised or terminally ill)

- the child may be an inter-country adoption where birth parents are missing, dead or unknown.

This particular area of contact can be very distressing for children affected by the knowledge that they can never have contact with their birth parents. As a result, children may develop fantasies, questions and beliefs about themselves that can remain dormant. Over the course of their lives, children may pick up intuitively that thoughts, questions and worries about one's birth family should be suppressed. All being well, children and their parents can learn that exploration and discussion of their histories throughout their lives will enrich self-understanding and promote a sense of mutual openness about why they were adopted and taken into care. If carers and parents are fearful or anxious about their foster or adopted children's curiosity about 'making contact', then there is the increasing risk that a child's interest will spill into the realm of social networking. This unmediated exploration of contact poses a potentially much greater harm: that the child will be without adequate support in this process. Sometimes, a significant family event or setback may precipitate a 'wondering' about one's past life. This charged *pendulation* of a child's thoughts between past and present life presents further possibility for self-integration and making deeper meaning of one's loss of birth family. It may also relate to the process of letting go of the wish for reunion with one's birth family. The demand for parents or carers supporting their children with such loss-related issues are that painful feelings and experiences can be accepted and explored. This is understandably difficult for many parents whose intuitive response may be to make things better, offer reassurance and point attention away from the past towards 'what there is to be grateful for'. However, this masks an attempt in ways to 'put a lid' on or discount their child's experience.

## Case studies: Mali and Joseph

What follows are two case studies which high light ways of working with and supporting children who have to manage such complex situations and painful feelings.

For Mali, a 9-year-old girl adopted from Thailand when she was 1½ years old and for Joseph, an 11-year-old boy adopted at the age of 3, contact with their birth parents was impossible.

Mali was relinquished by her birth mother in Thailand after only seven days. Even her actual birth date is unclear. She was brought up in an orphanage until she was seen and subsequently adopted by Aaron and Sheila. Mali had been taken to Thailand to visit three times and was absorbed by the country in which she was raised. She had also met one of the carers at the home who remembered her well. However, despite their efforts, nothing more could be discovered about her birth mother or father.

Joseph was taken into care aged 1¾ years old with his two siblings. All of the children had been placed with different families. Joseph had yearly contact with his older sister, and they had been provided with life story work to make sense of their traumatic life history. Their birth parents had been involved in a criminal gang and drug use, and the birth father had been suspected of being linked to a paedophile ring.

Both children had begun to ask about their birth parents at home and at school. Mali had drawn images of ghosts and written question marks over a piece of school work that explored children's beliefs about their families.

Joseph had become very upset just before his birthday and had experienced a sequence of ongoing nightmares in which hooded men would creep into his home and take him away and torture his parents.

Both Joseph and Mali's adoptive parents were at a loss to know how to talk to their children and each approached their local social work teams for advice. Each family was then referred to Louis and Elsie. Typically an initial meeting will take place with the parents of the child to begin the process of assessment and planning for a therapeutic intervention. What each family had in common were children who for different reasons were unable to have direct or letterbox contact with their birth family and it was likely that this could remain the case into their adult lives. It could also be said for both children that they were confused and distressed about this prospect.

## Working with Mali

When Louis first met Mali, she presented as a witty, playful and engaging child. At first, she was quite shy yet after a while she was able to explore some of her thoughts about being adopted and the absence of contact with her birth family. Louis had already acknowledged to Mali that he had met her parents and was now meeting her, as they were all too aware of the recent questions she had begun to ask them about being adopted and contact with her birth family. Mali had only just returned back from holiday to Thailand and on the plane home she had asked her adoptive mother 'Will I ever meet my tummy mummy?' She had also asked over the last month:

- Do you think she's alive? (Her mother had answered yes.)
- How do you know?
- What if you're wrong?
- What would happen to me if something happened to you?
- Maybe she had other children...brothers and sisters after me that I don't know about! (after seeing what appeared to be a Thai woman in the street)
- Do you think she might have moved to England?

Louis wrote down with Mali the questions she had been asking lately and then acknowledged that no wonder she had been feeling confused and cross recently with all of these questions in her head! Louis said, 'I think I'd be cross and worried too if these thoughts were in my mind about my mummy!'

Louis then invited Mali to work with him using the sand tray. Sand trays allow children and adults to work non-verbally in relation to thinking about contact. In order to understand more about Mali's experience of contact and being adopted, he asked her to draw a line in the middle of the sand and to find objects or figures from a nearby shelf to represent her current adoptive family and her birth family and/or life in Thailand. Sand tray work involves the use of toy figures, cars, animals, dolls house pieces, mythical creatures, scary beasts and natural found objects to enable a person to create symbolic representations that can be mutually explored.

Mali looked at the shelves with the figures quizzically for a few moments and then worked at pace. On one side of the tray she placed figures representing her adoptive family, pet dog, maternal aunt and paternal grandparents. On the other side of the tray she placed a dragon, a small house and a black woman figure. She then used her finger to draw a question mark in the sand. Joining the two 'sides' of the tray was a bridge with a figure of a baby underneath.

What followed is what can simply be described as a 'show and tell' by Mali as she described 'my family *now*'. Louis asked her to introduce him to each figure and who they represented. (Note: it is helpful when working with sand trays to try not to attach one's own feelings or perceptions to what has been chosen when working with children or adults. For example, if a child has chosen an animal such as a tiger, try not to say 'What a scary/lovely tiger!' If a person has chosen a scary-looking witch to be the birth mother, try not to say 'Tell me about this evil witch!' The aim is to elicit the sand tray user's perceptions of what they have chosen.) Mali described the members of her family with warmth, placing them fairly close together and facing one another.

For her birth family side of the tray, she spoke more hesitantly and looked sad as she described the dragon as reminding her of Thailand's temples and the black woman figure as representing her birth mother who was 'sad and lonely'. Mali could not describe why the figure was sad and lonely. The question mark drawn in the sand was there as she did not know who the rest of her family are or indeed where they are. Mali's finger slowly traced the outline of the question mark as she spoke. She acknowledged that she felt confused about why she had been 'given away' (for adoption). An emergent issue was that she wondered if she had been left at the orphanage by her birth mother, who then planned to come back later (when she was better) to take her back.

The figure of the baby beneath the bridge, placed between the current and past families, was 'sleeping and waiting for her mummy'.

## Working with Joseph

For Joseph, his sand tray of his current and birth family was quite different. Like Mali, Joseph chose benign figures for his adoptive family yet surrounded them with tanks, fencing and a policeman. The sand separating the two worlds was divided to the base of the sand tray. Joseph chose scary mythical creatures, a witch and a brutal, muscular-looking male figure to represent his birth family. All of these figures were turned towards the adoptive family.

Joseph described his adoptive family one by one and said that the tanks and fencing were for protection, placing them even closer to the family. It was hard for Joseph to talk about the birth family yet he was able to say that they had all broken out of jail and were stealing, lying and murdering. The scary male figure was waiting 'for the right time to get the gang together and make an attack'. The birth family needed to build a secret bunker to hide in. He then placed a warship and two sharks in the water space between the families as guards.

These images provide a graphic representation of children's inner worlds and thoughts, feelings and beliefs about their past and current families. Of course, these perceptions can and will change yet, as an initial tool for exploring experiences of being fostered or adopted, there is an opportunity for gaining valuable data.

## Working with the adoptive parents

During their individual meetings both sets of adoptive parents shared their concerns about their children. The common theme was how to address the children's increasingly open thoughts and feelings about their birth family. Searching online for Mali's birth family did not pose a threat or offer any possibility of finding them. The situation was very different for Joseph and his parents already suspected that he had been searching online about his birth family after a school teacher had shared 'how easy it is for families to trace one another' during a history lesson involving a timeline and family tree. The parents had noticed that Joseph's anxiety had transferred to more challenging behaviour as well as him wetting the bed on the day of the school lesson. Further meetings with both sets of parents and their social workers led to a decision to explore the children's concerns about contact using a therapeutic intervention. The idea was to discuss the children's hopes, fears, wonderings, anxieties and curiosity about their formative lives and the impact on their thoughts, feelings and behaviour now. We worked with both families in a similar way. The plan was to have up to six sessions to:

- explore with the family their current thoughts and feelings about the birth family
- acknowledge to the children how the anxiety caused by this process may be connected to their recent changes in behaviour
- acknowledge the unique aspects of being adopted and how there will be ongoing times during the children's life course that they will wonder about contact with the birth family, even if it takes the form of a fear of being taken
- make conscious links with the idea of 'being taken' as infants and any fear of 'being taken' now. To work with Joseph in particular to develop a greater sense of safety within his family
- assess whether a deeper level of understanding of the children's early life story is required
- facilitate a session where the children and adoptive parents would be supported to write 'letters not to be sent' to their respective birth families
- integrate and reflect together what sense has been made of the above process.

The exercise of writing a 'letter not to be sent' involves a person being helped to write to someone in mind to whom for various reasons is considered inappropriate to write an actual letter. The aim of writing such a letter is to allow for a greater range of expression, which includes thoughts and feelings that one would normally inhibit or suppress.

## Writing the letters

Louis worked with Mali to write her letter. Mali wanted her adoptive mother to be present. Given Mali's age (9), she was less confident at writing and liked the fact that her adoptive mother would write for her as she thought about what she wanted to say. When asked how she would like to start she decided, 'Dear Tummy Mummy'. She also knew immediately that she wanted to say, 'I wish that I could see you again!' Louis was simply thinking aloud with Mali about what she wanted him to write, paying mindful attention to making sure that no thoughts were imposed upon her. It was vital that Mali be the author of what was being written in order to give it more meaning. Following the lead of the child can mean that what is composed may be relatively short: maybe four to six lines. Some children become immersed in writing one or two pages.

Louis made sure that he helped Mali to integrate earlier questions to her adoptive parents into the letter: Did you have any other children? Did they go to an orphanage? I wonder sometimes if you have moved to England? I sometimes worry if something has happened to you. The whole process took about 30 minutes.

Some children, young people and adults benefit from being offered a framework for beginning sentences. Here are a few that we have used:

- I am writing this letter because...
- This letter is difficult/easy to write because...
- One thing I remember was...
- One thing I would rather forget is...
- The thing that makes/made me angry is...
- A happy memory was...
- Something that made me feel sad was...
- Something that made me feel scared was...
- The thing I have to say is...
- The one thing I wish was that...
- I want to tell you that my adoptive parents are...
- What they give me and you couldn't is...
- One thing I have to say/ask before I finish this letter is...
- The way I'm going to end this letter is...

The plan was for Mali and her adoptive parents, with Elsie and Louis, to read the letters aloud to a drawing or photo of the birth mother.

Elsie supported each adoptive parent to write their own letters. In the same way that writing a letter for children allows an opportunity to speak the unspeakable, adoptive parents and foster carers can feel liberated to enter the same process, using the same framework to encourage writing. For Mali's parents, her adoptive mother found it easier to write, saying 'I've often thought these things and never had the chance to say them!' With kind permission, this is her letter:

> Dear Mali's mum,
>
> I am writing this letter because I've always wanted to tell you some of the many thoughts and feelings I've had about you since we adopted Mali. I want to thank you for giving us such a beautiful, playful and loving girl. If I had wished for the perfect kind of girl for me, Mali would be that girl. I feel blessed. However, life is not without its problems and sometimes Mali worries lots about you and why you gave her up for adoption. I heard that it was because you were young and fragile and could not look after her. One thing I wish is that you'd written her a letter to tell her more about you. We have visited the orphanage where she was taken and they know nothing about you. This is the one thing that makes me feel sad...and angry I suppose...the fact that Mali has so little information about her birth family. Naturally, she thinks about whether you have had other children. I hope (if you have) that you've been able to look after them this time. The one thing I want to tell you is that this makes me all the more determined to give Mali a life where she will always know that she belongs to our family, that she is loved and that I will always try to keep what she needs in my mind. I'm sorry that you will probably not get the chance to see her as it is unlikely that you'll move to or visit England.
>
> Good luck for your life in the future,
>
> Sheila (Mali's adoptive mum)

This letter was relatively straightforward for Sheila to write and she welcomed the occasional prompt from our suggested list. It is important to remember to remind parents that they hold the children in mind when writing their letters as they will hear them later on. It is a chance for a potent form of advocacy on behalf of one's child. The momentum gained in the therapeutic intervention with Sheila led to an idea that Louis and Elsie had not planned. Sheila asked if she could write a letter to the birth father. This was interesting as Mali had rarely mentioned her birth father, of which nothing is known, and it was interesting to note that he had remained out of the therapeutic frame. Within the birth family system he had not been mentioned, yet this is not to say that he should not be included in the process of letter writing. It felt significant to acknowledge his absence as well in relation to Mali. Sheila's letter to him was more brief:

> To Mali's birth dad,
>
> I am writing this letter to say that I am sorry you have not been able to see what a wonderful, special girl Mali has turned out to be. I can only imagine that you too had your own reasons for not ever meeting Mali yet this is your loss more than Mali's. I hope you are doing OK and I wish the same for Mali's birth mum. I also want to say that I hope this has not happened to any other women you have been involved with. Like

Mali's birth mum, I guess you'll not visit England. She is safe with us and we will love her and enjoy seeing her grow up into a wonderful woman.

Goodbye and good luck,

Sheila (Mali's adoptive mum)

Elsie and Louis used a session to sit with the parents and they each took turns to read their letters to one another. Mali's adoptive father, Dave, was visibly moved. Louis explained that the next session would involve the reading of letters to either a drawing or photograph of the birth mother. There was no image of the birth father. Sheila imagined that Mali might draw a question mark to represent him. The family possessed just the one photograph of the birth mother taken by an astute member of staff at the orphanage. It is often the case that children can be simply left outside the orphanage gates in order to deal with the shame.

## The facilitated contact

The facilitated contact with birth parents of whom there could be no contact was planned a week after Mali had written her letter. It was seen as helpful to proceed while the letters were still fresh in the family's minds. Mali appeared understandably nervous on the day and had elected to sit very firmly squeezed in between her parents on a sofa. The parents had brought a copy of the photo of the birth mother and, as expected, Mali had drawn a large red question mark to represent the birth father. The images were placed on a chair in front of the family. Louis explained how each parent was going to read their letter and then Mali would be last. Although the order of reading letters can be fluid, it was felt in this case that Mali would benefit from seeing her parents go first. Mali was invited to choose which parent went first and she chose Sheila who was encouraged to take her time and compose herself before reading. It is the facilitator's responsibility to ensure that the process is given time and space in order that everyone involved can fully absorb what is happening.

Sheila and Dave read their letters starting first with the birth mother and then with the birth father, making great efforts to speak with affect and clarity. Dave's letter was the shortest, so he was invited by Elsie to read his letter twice. Mali was transfixed by the process and after each letter smiled widely, hugging her parents. Elsie described how pleased she looked with what her mum and dad had written and Mali nodded. These moments hold great potential as attachment building, serving as 'glue' to the sense of feeling connected with one another.

Louis read Mali's letter twice on her behalf. He asked if there was anything else she wanted to add, change or say. She shook her head and said, 'What do we do with the letters?' A good question!

A conversation began about what to do with the letters and how to end the session. Some families:

- · want to simply say goodbye to the images and tidy things away
- · want to create some form of ritual and burn the letters
- · want to release balloons to represent a sense of 'letting go'
- · like to put the letters into a special place or folder to be read again
- · like to leave the letters behind in the room, not to be seen again
- · need help from the facilitator about what to do with the letters.

There are no rules about what should be done and it is central to the intervention that the family (and particularly the children) should be heard.

In the debriefing after the reading of the letters, Louis asked each member of the family what it was that they most remembered. Mali said, 'Reading the letter to my tummy mummy and hearing my mummy say how special I am...and my daddy!'

Elsie's follow-up telephone calls and e-mails to the parents revealed that Mali had often talked about the session. Both parents had noticed that she had presented as more relaxed, affectionate and wanting to play more with Dave.

Also, the intervention served to provide the family with a healthier template or model for communication and relating more openly. It was now more permissible to talk about Mali's past with curiosity and compassion.

A similar process occurred for Joseph and his adoptive parents with their letters. Joseph needed much more help at first and his adoptive parents were astonished at the intensity of his anger towards his birth family. Behind his fear was rage. At the end of the letter reading, Joseph wanted either to bury or burn the letters. The adoptive parents asked if they could make copies just in case Joseph wanted to see them again in the future (another creative suggestion). Joseph was content with the idea and then the family gathered their letters and burned them in the yard outside. Like Mali, Joseph was noticeably happier and less guarded and aggressive. He still felt slightly anxious about the idea of being 'taken away' yet his parents now were able to gently remind him of the session and that even though a part of him felt worried, they were going to make sure they would keep him safe and protected.

Facilitated contacts with children and their families where contact is not possible can be a powerful therapeutic intervention that can be provided by contact workers, social workers, counsellors and psychotherapists.

# A framework for facilitating the reading of letters to birth parents with whom there can be no contact

- Assessment or evaluation of the child and family.

- Formulation of therapeutic intervention to explore absence of contact.

- Separate meetings with child(ren) and parents or foster carers.

- Meeting with parents and social worker (where appropriate) to plan and agree facilitation of session.

- Preparation of the child and writing of the letter.

- Writing of the letter and preparation of the carers for reading of letters. If there are two carers, this will involve sharing of the letters they have written.

- Facilitation of reading of the family's letters to a drawing or photograph of the birth parents. Parents read their letters first and then the child. Facilitator manages the pace of the session and can suggest that a letter be read twice. Facilitator can read on behalf of the child (leaving the parent free to attend to the needs of the child).

- Closing of the exercise and agree plan on what to do with the letters (this could involve a further meeting).

## Debriefing with the family

- What was at least one thing each person will remember? (Facilitator to include what they will remember about each member of the family.)

- Follow-up phone call or visit to the parents.

- Potential meeting with the family after one to three months.

## CHAPTER 11

# Contact with Young People

## The Long Shadow of Adoption

Working with young people who are adopted or living in foster care provides some unique challenges for those involved with contact arrangements.

As well as involving changes in our hormonal and physiological make-up, adolescence is also the second most significant stage of neurological change, which includes an increase in our capacity to think abstractly.

The transition from adolescence into young adulthood can be a bumpy road as young people navigate the desire to have more responsibility, autonomy and choice, and engage in more 'grown up' activities. This natural wish to gather experiences, try out new identities and to develop romantic attachments can also propel adolescents towards more risk-taking behaviour such as drug and alcohol use, sexual exploration, gang initiation and boundary challenges towards their primary carers. Despite some young people's life defying propensity for resilience and making 'good enough' choices, many young people who have travelled through the care system are confronted with a multitude of potential triggers of their early life trauma.

Forming and maintaining relationships, establishing intimate connections with others, creating robust friendships with peers and making use of 'wise elder figures' who may serve as mentors to a person's emerging identity are not easy tasks for growing adopted or fostered children. As if this wasn't complex enough, there is the conflicting need to be the same (as others) and different to others. This is, of course, the adopted child's life challenge: to explore how they are the same as other children with parents and how they are different.

Living in foster care or being adopted as a teenager casts a long shadow over one's present and future life. Helping young people to explore what is the same and yet uniquely different about their lives enables light to enter what may be hidden or buried in the shadows of their experience. If carers, professionals and adoptive parents are willing to enter the murky and painful shadowland of a child's past and present experience then there is a greater potential for the emergence of hope for the future. James Hillman (1990)[1] (in his essay 'The Great Mother, Her Son, Her Hero, and the Puer') states that 'Youth is the emergence of spirit within the psyche.' This awakening *spirit* contains an elemental hunger for experience, more extreme states of being and a 'sense of calling'. For adopted and fostered children, this may involve a curiosity to uncover what is left of their history as a way of being more able to make sense of their present lives in order to move out of the shadow of their history. To engage young people in this process, adults need to be willing to pay attention to their imagination and creative interests. Frankel (1998)[2] describes in his excellent book, *The Adolescent Psyche* how 'we must attend to how the adolescent's imagination is fed through the music, movies, television, literature and poetry that adolescents are attracted to and actively seek out'. These creative interests may point to a profoundly deep need to better understand one's life story. As a consequence, the young person's relationship to contact (whether they are having it or not) is re-evaluated.

The issue of contact is imperative for foster carers, adoptive parents and professionals to reflect on as the likely or possible trajectory of family lives collide in the future, as the young person negotiates their way through issues of separating and belonging and identifying with two families. If our gaze is not willing to enter the shadows of an adopted adolescent, then there is the risk of unmediated, unstructured contact in the future that may, sadly, cause distress and emotional turmoil to those involved.

In our experience of working with foster carers, adoptive parents and professionals, the more common recurring themes are the beliefs that adolescents should be encouraged to move on, make choices, stay out and 'grow away' from parents. Our experience has been, surprisingly, the opposite. Many fostered or adopted children want and need to be around their parents or carers for significant periods of time.

Over recent decades, professionals working with adopted children and young people have had to learn to take account of and attend to cultural and racial perspectives. These are particularly important areas to consider when working with the adolescent as they strive to make sense of their identity and begin the process of separation. The growing number of inter-country adoptions, the ongoing integration of multiracial and cultural communities and an increasing number of same sex parents means that assessments need to embrace a curious and inclusive approach to assessing these dimensions with children and families. Louis has also noted that there appears to be a very significant number of adoptive parents who have religious or spiritual beliefs. Therefore, professionals may want to explore the impact of adoption on the parent's faith, spiritual practice and how meaning is made of a child's struggles on the path of adoption.

The following case study includes a number of the issues mentioned above such as race, heritage and sexuality. It is also a case study in which Louis and Elsie supported the work of a youth worker by engaging in team and individual meetings for reflective practice, offering e-mail support and using regular telephone debriefing calls.

## Case study: Andy

Andy was a 15-year-old boy who was adopted aged 6 by a single carer, Tess, who described herself as 'a single, gay woman who loves shoes!' Andy was also of dual heritage. His birth mother was African Caribbean and his birth father was Swedish. His father had died when he was 5 years old and Andy had always felt responsible for his birth mother's wellbeing. Tess had adopted Andy to fulfil a long-standing wish to be a parent.

Andy's early life history told a story of domestic violence, neglect, and drug and alcohol using parents. Andy's birth mother had been singing in a band when she met Andy's father. She had her own troubled history having experienced a protracted period of sexual abuse as a child and she experienced ongoing struggles with her mental health. Andy's birth father, a gifted artist, was prone to violent outbursts and manic behaviour. It was not surprising that Andy grew up with a fierce temper, poor ability to regulate and a tendency to quickly turn his anxiety into an onslaught of challenging behaviours.

Tess had managed well for the first two years of the adoption and had (by her own admission) begun to relate to Andy at times as if he was a friend. This suited Andy's precocious behaviour and tendency to avoid being cared for in ways that other children of his age might enjoy. Andy had been involved in some delinquent behaviour and was allocated a youth worker via the local youth offending team. At home Andy's behaviour had begun to test Tess's ability to cope. A number of issues had begun to surface:

- Andy had become increasingly aggressive towards Tess.
- He was stealing money and personal objects.

- He had shouted at Tess, 'You're not my mother...you're a dried up fake of a mum!'
- He had also taunted Tess about her sexuality in front of his friends by saying 'Say something that's gay mum!' Worryingly, he had told his teacher that Tess had asked him to 'sex her'.
- Tess had become increasingly anxious and considered asking for antidepressants from her GP.
- As a single carer, Tess was finding it increasingly difficult to hold down her job as she had to react to ongoing crises with her son.
- Andy had begun to experiment with self-harm by scratching his arms with sharp objects.
- Andy had asked Tess whether his birth mother had ever sent letters that mentioned their shared family history or his birth father's history.

The situations listed above occurred over a period of four to five months. They seemed to illustrate all too clearly Andy's conflict around his attachment to Tess and birth family, his identity issues and his need for a more coherent narrative about his past.

At the point of referral, Andy, along with Tess, was having face-to-face, once/twice yearly contact with his maternal aunt, Pam, who was considered a benign figure within the birth family system. In this instance, Louis and Elsie were asked to offer consultation and supervision to the youth worker, Jamal, who was allocated to the case. It was agreed that the youth worker would make independent assessments.

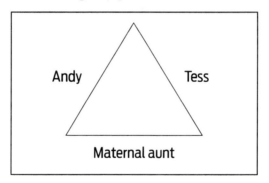

FIGURE 11.1 THE ADOPTION QUADRANGLE

## The tasks and role of agency professionals

The youth worker, Jamal, was prepared via an initial meeting and then a series of Skype consultations. Jamal was supported to individually prepare Tess, Andy and Pam in the same way as outlined in previous chapters:

1. Gathering paper information and reports.

2. Liaising with relevant professionals.

3. Evaluating the impact of early life trauma, attachment-related issues and developmental concerns.

4. Meeting with Tess, Andy and Pam independently and meeting Tess and Andy together.

5. Establishing each person's hopes and fears regarding contact.

6. Reflecting on any need for life story work as a means of integrating and working with the momentum of contact arrangements. In this case, a later life letter had been prepared for Andy, but not yet shared with him by Tess, who worried about the impact the difficult information contained within it might have on Andy. This proved very helpful in that it held a lot of neutral and positive information about his father's background, interests and culture. With Jamal's support Tess was able to share and help process the information in the letter with Andy.

7. What are the blind spots within the arrangements so far and wishes of the individuals?

8. Creating a therapeutic contact plan.

9. Assessing and managing contact venue details.

10. Applying Theraplay domains of Structure, Nurture, Challenge and Engagement.

11. Facilitating contact where appropriate.

12. Providing opportunity for debrief and re-evaluation of contact arrangements.

13. Reflecting on what worked best. What obstructed, hindered or negatively impacted the contact? What could be improved?

Jamal's meeting with the maternal aunt revealed a woman who was torn by split loyalties – to Andy's birth mother (her sister), to Andy and towards Tess, who she acknowledged as the ongoing stable factor in Andy's life.

The meeting with Andy demonstrated the muddled ideas, perceptions and beliefs about his birth mother, as well as helping to clarify his questions about his birth father. A significant part of Andy, like many adopted children, still held on to a fantasy of reunion with his birth mother. He imagined a mother who was stable, well, loving, consistent and available at last to offer Andy the kind of love and care he had longed for all of his life. Louis had encouraged the youth worker to explore with Andy whether a part of his heart had been 'kept in reserve', just in case his birth mother should return to claim him? Andy tearfully admitted that he had always hoped this, even though another part of him knew that his birth mother could not give him what he longed for. Andy could see that Tess had always been there waiting to provide the deep level of love and care she felt, yet his deeply held loyalty to his birth mother meant that he could not yet allow himself to accept what he so desperately wanted.

The meeting with Tess showed her to be a compassionate, reflective, loving mother to Andy who only wanted the best for her child. At times, her selflessness meant that she struggled with boundaries and could minimise her own deeply held wish to claim Andy as her own son.

It was clear that Andy was on a developmental trajectory towards making unmediated contact with his birth family. Therefore, it was all the more necessary that he could be supported to have a more meaningful, real conversation with his maternal aunt, who made clear her commitment to help Andy make sense of his early life history, discuss his birth mother's current condition and mental health and to giving her blessing to Tess as Andy's mother. Andy needed permission to live and be happy with Tess. Louis, Elsie and the youth worker were not sure if the aunt's blessing would be enough for Andy.

Louis and Elsie were also intent on helping Andy with his troubled thoughts and feelings around his identity. There were a number of areas to address explicitly:

- Any curiosity Andy might have about his racial and cultural background. His mother was of African Caribbean descent and his father was of Swedish origin. How did they arrive at a point where they were using drugs? What was their early life history?

- How could Andy be supported in developing a positive sense of his own identity as a young man with a dual cultural and racial heritage?

- Did Andy need to enter a cycle of further grieving for his father? Now that he was older, was he grieving at a deeper level for the father he 'never had'?

- How was Andy processing the issues of difference in terms of how he looked different to Tess who had always tried to communicate that 'this made no difference to her'? Maybe Andy's concerns needed to be heard and acknowledged rather than reassured and moved away from his true feelings?

- How was Andy making sense of his adoptive mother's sexuality being a gay woman? Was this yet another area where Andy felt 'different' to Tess and thus even more marginalised? Andy had said already that Tess had 'sexed' him; was there a part of Andy that was muddled around his emerging sexuality being 'contaminated' by Tess? How could this fantasy be explored so that their human similarities of knowing about love, loss and discrimination provide a point of connection?

- How could Andy's behaviours of lying, stealing and aggression be explored between Andy and Tess and seen as a communication of his inner turmoil and struggle to find words to say that he needed help?

Most importantly, the overriding theme of the intervention was to make explicit the issues of race, gender and cultural difference between Andy and Tess. Only by making clear their struggles and differences could there be an opportunity to find a place of connection or mutuality.

Initially, Jamal focused on Andy's need as a 15-year-old to become more autonomous and independent. Were there developmental tasks beckoning? However, Louis cautioned against promoting this too strongly on Andy's behalf and instead considered a conflicting developmental need for Andy both to grow and separate and also be more dependent and connected to Tess.

It soon became clear that Andy's birth mother would not be able to manage an appropriate contact. However, the maternal aunt, Pam, was willing to help Andy make more meaningful sense of his past and its influence on his current life. Pam admitted that she did not want Andy's life to follow that of his birth mother's. Upon hearing that his birth mother could not manage contact, Andy appeared somewhat relieved. He initially said that there was 'no point having a facilitated contact with Pam coz I see her anyway once a year'. Jamal had been prepared for such a response and replied that the meeting with Pam was going to be a special kind of contact that would try to help Andy understand why his birth mother could not look after him or come to contact now and why that might make him feel the way he did now.

Pam revealed herself to be very committed to the facilitated contact as she was worried about Andy's current behaviour. Like most birth family members, she feared being disloyal to her sister (Andy's birth mother) yet the youth worker emphasised the primary focus was on enabling Andy to retrieve memories and gather a more coherent narrative about his life. The object of the therapeutic gaze was on assimilating unflinching facts about his history and not to allocate blame to the birth parents. However, there might be the opportunity to acknowledge culturally agreed perceptions such as 'all children are entitled to love and care' or 'all babies deserve to be fed, protected and loved'.

The key aspects of this contact work was ensuring that the issues of gender, race, difference, sexuality and fantasies about 'what was the same and what was different' (about Tess and Andy's relationship) were explicitly explored with Andy and Tess, and that these issues were viewed through the prism of Andy's attachment issues, early life trauma and being adopted. Therefore, proactive discussion with Andy about the impact of his troubled life history on his perception of himself as being of dual heritage enabled him to voice hitherto suppressed concerns. Likewise, direct exploration of his thoughts and feelings about living with a single, gay mother also enabled him to acknowledge the part of him that struggled with his friend's discrimination and verbal abuse. It proved important to allow expression of the part of him that 'wanted all of this to stop and for my life to be normal!' This created the possibility of a further conversation that helped him to acknowledge the sense of relief and appreciation of being 'special' to Tess and his fear of Tess leaving him in the same way he had been abandoned before.

Whilst we generally advocate the inclusion of adoptive parents in these kinds of contacts there may be situations when the young person's current needs for exploration may be best served by not involving the adoptive parent directly and having a neutral figure offer the support. Andy's conflicted feelings of wanting to attack Tess verbally in the presence of Pam led to a decision that Jamal would support him.

## The contact

Pam was able to express her wish that Andy be happy, allow himself to settle and be taken care of by Tess. Jamal was also able to encourage a mutual expression of sadness that Andy's birth mother had not herself learnt how to parent Andy or manage contact. Louis and Elsie had encouraged Jamal to support Pam to make clear that she herself was also unable to care for Andy and once again to give Tess her blessing as the primary carer. Andy listened very carefully, looked sad and after a long sigh asked for a hug from Pam and said, 'It's OK now...I'm OK now. I didn't want to let you or mum down. I promised myself that when I was taken away...Tess will be totally over the top if I tell her she's my mum now...oh my god! She'll love it!'

Pam smiled and said, 'All children need a mum...you need a mum. You weren't taken away Andy, your mum (my sister) was never really able to give you what you needed; I should have done more myself to help you get safe sooner... Tess is a lovely mum, so let her be a mum to you.'

Andy smiled widely and said, 'Probs...'

Following on from Jamal's discussions with Pam, she approached her sister to ask if she had any positive mementos or memories of Andy's birth father that could be shared with him. Together they decided to develop a play list of what had been some of his birth father and mother's favourite songs and singers. There was also a small sketch which the birth father had made of Andy as a sleeping toddler on which he had written 'my beautiful boy'. Pam put all of these things together and wrote a note to Tess explaining all of this and saying that she was so happy that Andy had the loving mother he so deserved. After discussion with Tess, Jamal and Tess then shared these with Andy, who was very moved, particularly by the sketch his birth father had made of him. One of his comments was, perhaps, revealing what had been a negative self-belief in response to the sketch 'so that means he thought I looked alright'.

## CHAPTER 12

# Contact in Kinship Care

The potential for kinship placements to offer long-term stability for children who cannot live with their birth parents has become increasingly recognised. However, the understanding of the permanence and stability these placements offer is 'obscured because most children living away from their birth parents with friends and relatives are not looked after and so are not counted within local authority statistics'.[1]

Organisations that have campaigned for research and offer support and representation to kinship carers, such as Grandparents Plus, The Who Cares? Trust, Family Rights Group and Buttle UK, advocate for the recognition of the needs of the children and their kinship carers and argue cogently that there should he access to payments and services offered to non-related carers.

In March 2011 the government published *Family and Friends Care: Statutory Guidance for Local Authorities*, which includes some guidance on the issue of supporting and managing contact arrangements in kinship care. For example:

> 5.24 There is a greater complexity in the relationship between foster carers and parents when the carers are family members or friends. Whilst family and friends foster carers are just as likely as unrelated foster carers to safeguard and promote the child's welfare, this is sometimes at the cost of the loss of their relationship with the child's parents, who may be the carers' own child or sibling. Additionally, if parents are felt to be a potential threat, it can be easier to safeguard unrelated carers, by keeping their location secret from the parents. Family and friends foster carers may experience hostility from the parents of the children they are raising, who may blame them for taking the child away from them or for not supporting them against the local authority. This hostility can make managing contact particularly difficult for family and friends foster carers.[2]

It is estimated that between 200,000 and 300,000 children are cared for full time by a relative, friend or someone else previously connected with the child, and that the legal status of the arrangements will vary and many will be viewed as informal.[3] Seven thousand two hundred looked after children are placed with family members and friends who have been approved as their foster carers.[4]

Family and friends carers step in to care for children who cannot safely live at home with their parents. This may be because of parental difficulties, mental or physical ill health, domestic abuse, alcohol or substance misuse, imprisonment or bereavement.

Many children being cared for by kinship carers involve situations where birth parents are involved in substance abuse with many of the children experiencing consequent maltreatment involving neglect and abuse.[5]

Children whose futures are being decided by the courts and are placed with relatives, (frequently grandparents) because of neglect and maltreatment will have the same complex needs and behaviours as children placed with people who are not related (this may also be the case for 'informal arrangements'). During the care proceedings, expectations about frequency and supervision of contact will be similar to those where children are placed with non-related carers. There may also be expectations that the grandparents and other relatives take on responsibility for the supervision of contact in their homes. However, the circumstances leading to the placement and the kinship carers' attitude towards the mother and/or father of the child impact upon the quality of the contact experience for both the child and the parent(s).[6]

Just as with children placed with unrelated carers the issues for maltreated children living with members of their extended birth family are complicated and carry significant concerns that need to be addressed. For the kinship carer there is the added dimension of confronting the fact that the people who did this to these children are also relatives and, frequently, their own adult child.

## The impact of neglect and maltreatment

When a child has been neglected or maltreated and taken into care, we can assume that a significant level of trauma has occurred. The levels of stress and anxiety may have been intolerable for all involved. Many professionals involved in child protection work are familiar with reports and assessments that describe the reality of stress involved in traumatic experiences. Children may have lived with parents whose growing dependency on drugs and alcohol fuelled a co-dependent relationship that was characterised and punctuated by alternating periods of euphoria, depression and anxiety. In these circumstances, domestic violence can also have been a recurring event, during which children bore witness, as parents or their partners shouted, screamed and hit each other. Children may have gone hungry, experienced being fed a diet of crisps and sweets, eaten scraps of food left on the floor. A child's day-to-day routines may have been chaotic and unpredictable leaving a child fearful and hypervigilant. Children may have lacked stimulation or been barely played with and left unattended for long periods of time. They may have been left in dirty nappies, cots or beds and been cold because of inadequate clothing. Visitors to the home may have been experienced as frightening and intrusive; sometimes these same visitors may have abused the children. School-age children may have gone to school late, hungry and poorly clothed. The local neighbourhood may have been unpredictable, threatening, noisy, and without nurture, support or opportunities for play. However, what we also know is that the children will have an attachment to their parents, who are unlikely to have been consistently neglectful or abusive and who during more stable periods may have been able to attune to their needs for love and care.

For grandparents of such children (or aunts, uncles and some friends) it can be extremely difficult to go through the process of recognising and being witness to such poor care of children and, at the same time, grapple with mixed feelings in relation to the children's parents. Extended family members may be highly distressed, confused, angry, frustrated and feel impotent when seeing children treated badly. Many families are torn apart in such circumstances. There are some family members whose loyalty to the parents may override the fundamental needs of the children and these adults can deny, dismiss or collude with the maltreatment, doing all they can, under difficult circumstances, to try to keep children with their parents. On the other hand, we also know that many grandparents and relatives either at the parents' request or on their own initiative step in and take the children to live with them (keeping it in the family), hoping the parents will use the time and space this offers to sort themselves out. Many of the informal kinship arrangements may begin in this way.

Comprehending the enormity of coming to terms with the realisation of this level of dysfunction in the lives of one's own (adult) children, brothers, sisters or grandchildren can be overwhelming.

David Pitcher (2002) commented that, 'Some grandparents try hard to find a sensitive way of telling their grandchildren about why they are living with them… Some grandparents deal with the pain of the situation by becoming severely critical of their son or daughter: "She's a druggie, not my daughter anymore."'[7]

What professionals need to hold in mind is that research into the attachment status in non-clinical populations shows that as only 59 per cent of us have a secure attachment style,[8] we need to understand therefore that an insecure attachment style does not of itself mean that we cannot parent effectively, otherwise far more children would be in need of alternative parents! Those who struggle most with parenting in a way that is 'good enough' are people who have unresolved experiences of trauma and loss and have a limited capacity for reflective functioning and ability to understand the thoughts, feelings and behaviours of others.

Many professionals have experience of families where there has been evidence of trauma and abuse being passed down through the generations. Some of the case studies we have used in other chapters of this book give testament to this. In these cases, grandparents, even if putting themselves forward to care for a child who has become the subject of care proceedings, are highly unlikely to receive a positive assessment. However, even where there are no social services records relating to their adult children's development while growing up in their care, social workers will usually proceed with caution; for as we know not all abused and neglected children come to the notice of child protection services. A major question for professionals must be what factors led this child's parents to become so dysfunctional, and inevitably they will need to consider the role their developmental experiences have played.

On this issue, the *Family and Friends Care: Statutory Guidance for Local Authorities* looking to approve relative and friends as foster carers for looked after children states:

> 5.37 The carer's past experiences of parenting will need to be assessed as part of a fuller picture of their capacity to care for the child. It may be that the looked after child's parent has been the only family member to experience difficulties, or these may have been part of a broader pattern within the family. The carers may be able to draw positive learning out of previous difficult

experiences and it will be important to understand their level of insight into these.[2]

Many grandparents and other kinship carers in this situation will themselves feel perplexed as to why their adult daughter or son went so far off the rails, and frequently make sense of the situation through pinpointing events during adolescence, the romantic sexual partner they became involved with and their involvement with street drugs or increasing use of alcohol.

Grandparents who might undergo assessments to become kinship carers are frequently left feeling they are being judged negatively, and have to fight tooth and nail to obtain the right to bring up their grandchild. Many spend thousands of pounds on legal fees. Not surprisingly, grandparents who have these kinds of experiences are left feeling resentful and mistrustful of social services and social workers.

However, research into kinship care shows that the majority of children appear to benefit and that in time their challenging behaviours settle. Often children move to relatives with whom they are already very familiar. Kinship placements also offer the possibility of ongoing and regular contact with birth parents *and* the extended family.

A recent Grandparents Plus research study (2013) showed that:

- The majority of children (79 per cent) have contact with at least one parent.

- Thirty-four per cent have contact with both parents, a further 34 per cent have contact with only the mother and 11 per cent have contact with just the father.

- Four in ten (37 per cent) said the contact is beneficial for the children.

Worryingly, one in seven (13 per cent) of kinship carers report that children find contact distressing. Forty-two per cent say children find it unsettling.[5]

Because of the frequency of contact that can take place in kinship placements, the child's attachment to their birth parents and, particularly, their mothers is actively promoted. This is an aspect of kinship care that is very different to adoption and to a degree is also different to permanent foster care. While there are clear arguments for the benefits of contact, contact and, particularly, high levels of contact can also activate the child's attachment wounds. Some of children's experiences during such contacts may be unsettling and, as the research above highlights, some children experience distress. These children need and deserve as much as any other child coming to terms with maltreatment: informed support that helps them make sense of their history, feelings and relationships, with the aim of enabling them to develop a coherent narrative. As with children placed for adoption or in foster care, children in kinship placements need reassurance that it was not their fault that their birth parents were unable to look after them or keep them safe.

Kinship carers may feel alienated from, or fearful of, the implications of trying to access professional support for themselves and their children. Those who are open to trying to access such a service may, however, find that there are few services or professionals available or able to offer the informed and nuanced support they need.

Louis and Elsie were asked to evaluate the contact arrangements for a girl who was nearly 10 years old and who was being cared for by her maternal grandparents.

## Case study: Bella

Bella was a gregarious, feisty girl who had been living with her maternal grandparents since the age of 4 years. Bella's birth mother Diane, who had a degree of learning difficulties, was only 17 years old when she had given birth to Bella. Sadly, Diane had become involved with gang culture and the birth father was one of the gang members. He and Diane had an off-on relationship, and although Diane had put his name on Bella's birth certificate he later denied paternity. The grandparents worked with social services and tried to find ways of helping Diane to move out of the gang and were supportive of her in parenting Bella. However, Diane was resentful of what she saw as their interference and this only served to drive a wedge between them. Towards the time that Bella was received into care Diane had taken to leaving Bella with them for long periods of time. The grandparents, Dave and Angela, who were in their 50s, had resolved to care for Bella themselves. They were approved as foster carers for Bella, and their hope was that one day their daughter would find a more stable path back to Bella and family life. Unfortunately, Diane had remained enmeshed with gang culture and her use of alcohol and drugs gradually increased. When Bella was 6 years old Diane had her second child by a different father removed at birth and taken into care. This process had upset Angela and Dave immensely. It was made all the more difficult as they were aware that they were unable to care for another child, as Bella was already a challenging child to look after and Angela's health had deteriorated during the period they had been caring for her.

Bella's grandparents and social services had agreed weekly contact at the beginning of the placement but Diane's unreliability around contact eventually led to an agreement that it would be reduced to six times a year. Diane was better able to manage this level of contact but could still be unreliable. During Diane's second pregnancy, she, Dave and Angela had agreed that once the pregnancy was showing Bella would not have contact with Diane, as they wanted to protect Bella from experiencing the loss of her sibling. The grandparents supervised the contact and they would usually go to a nearby park or play area.

During the last year, Bella had begun to ask more questions about her mother. The grandparents had told Bella that her mother 'loved her but could not look after her' because she 'was unwell'. Like many family members (foster carers and adoptive parents), they had intended to try to let Bella know that she was loved by her mother. Bella had now reached a stage in her life when this left her with more questions than answers about why she was being cared for by her grandparents. She also had experience of seeing Diane in various states of intoxication. Understandably, like many children in care, she found it too hard to ask Diane at contact meetings why she was not able to live with her. Maybe she worried that her mother was still too fragile to hear such a question. Maybe a part of her feared that she might hear an answer that was too difficult to bear. However, Bella did feel safe enough to ask her grandparents:

· Is mummy still unwell? When she is better, can I live with her again?
· Does she have a new boyfriend?
· Is he kind to her?
· Why does she always forget my birthday card? Is she sick again?
· Will I always live with you?
· Has mummy had other children?

The above questions express the typical trains of thought that can occur within a child's mind who is fostered, living in kinship care or adopted.

When Elsie asked Dave and Angela what they thought worked well with the contact arrangements, they replied that they thought it was important for Bella to see that her mother was OK. Elsie then asked why they thought Bella still worried about her mother even though she could see her mother was OK. Dave said, 'Now that she's older she can probably tell when her mum is having an off day and sometimes her behaviour might seem a bit odd because she was on drugs or drink.' Angela said that she sometimes felt upset because of the way Diane was looking and behaving and that Bella may have noticed this too. Both Dave and Angela worried about how to speak with Bella about her mother and her problems.

Louis eventually made contact with Diane and arranged to meet to discuss contact with Bella. Louis needed to be persistent as Diane's anxiety led her to not attending and cancelling the first two appointments. When they did meet, Diane was late and clearly anxious. She admitted that she 'may have had a drink to calm her down'. It was clear that a part of Diane desperately wanted to think about her daughter and how to make contact more rewarding and meaningful. However, her ability to manage her own levels of stress was low. This was understandable, as by her own account, her daily life was continually hazardous and threatening. Louis also observed that Diane either seemed preoccupied and distant, or would bring the conversation back to her own needs and worries, and was unable to think about Bella's troubles. A further three meetings enabled little or no change in Diane's presenting style. An offer to include her parents (Dave and Angela) only served to agitate her further.

Louis and Elsie met the grandparents (with Bella's social worker) once more to evaluate the situation and discuss what could be done about contact. Everyone agreed that, for now, Diane was unable and, on one level, unwilling to manage a facilitated contact and explore the important questions Bella had been asking of late. Dave and Angela were deeply saddened by the fact that Diane was continuing to struggle to such a degree. Louis and Elsie acknowledged that both Dave and Angela had entered another cycle of grief as they recognised at a more profound level their daughter's struggle with survival. Louis suggested that each grandparent write a letter 'not to be sent' to Bella, thus allowing them to express the full range of thoughts and feelings that had been suppressed for so long. Dave and Angela were reluctant at first but decided to try as they were all too aware of their need to deal with their increasingly strong feelings. Each worked apart and then Louis brought them together to share their letters by taking turns to read them to one another. The process of verbalising their thoughts and feelings and experiencing an attentive, supporting other as witness was particularly moving. It was important not to rush the process, and as Dave's was somewhat shorter than Angela's, Louis asked him to read it again.

Louis also suggested to Dave and Angela that they each write a 'not to be sent' letter to Diane expressing whatever thoughts and feelings they had about their past and present relationship with their daughter. They clearly continued to love and care about Diane, while also feeling angry, dismayed and in some way guilty about the way she had failed as a mother.

Louis made a follow-up telephone call to the grandparents two days later. Angela, but not Dave, had taken up Louis' suggestion of writing out her thoughts and feelings about Diane and told Louis that she had cried a great deal while doing so. During this conversation Angela made a request for Louis and Elsie to help her and Dave talk to Bella about her mother (their daughter Diane). Almost intuitively, Bella had asked Angela if they had been talking about her mum to Louis, which had left Angela stuck for words. Angela recognised in a way she hadn't before that 'Bella needs us to give her the whole story…I think in ways she has been giving us clues for a few years…it's just that *we weren't ready*! She needs to know the answers to her questions, otherwise she'll blame herself for all that's happened.'

Soon after, while preparing for the facilitated contact, Angela and Dave began to see that they were ready to 'claim' Bella symbolically as their own daughter. They had begun to free up their inhibitions around claiming and attaching to her and wanted Bella to know how much they loved her. In the past they had withheld the fullness of their love and commitment (refusing social services' suggestions that they apply for a special guardianship order) to Bella, worrying that it was somehow 'wrong' or disloyal to their daughter Diane. Now, both grandparents saw how much Bella needed them.

Louis and Elsie met Bella with her grandparents to discuss the plan for a facilitated meeting with Dave and Angela to talk about 'all the important questions she had been asking them about her mum'. Elsie made clear that both grandparents had wanted to do this before, yet had found it difficult to do. Bella watched attentively. She was quieter than usual and made very good eye contact, nodding occasionally.

Louis asked Bella if she had other questions about Diane. 'Sometimes,' said Bella, but she could not remember what they were.

Louis agreed a time and date to visit Bella with her grandparents to prepare her for the meeting, after which there would be the facilitated family meeting. Meanwhile, Elsie would visit Dave and Angela in order to prepare them. This meeting would happen after Louis' visit to Bella so that they would have feedback and all the questions that Bella wanted answering. The family agreed that they would try not to explore the questions in conversation, although they could write down in notebooks Louis had provided any further thoughts or questions. Louis would collect the books before the contact meeting occurred.

Last, Louis told Bella that she could always change her mind about the contact meeting. It could be 'paused' and happen at a later date or even not at all. However, Bella did not change her mind about the facilitated meeting, although she did say it was a 'bit weird' to have such a formal meeting with Dave and Angela. During the week of the meeting, Louis met Bella alone to help her prepare. Bella still wanted to discuss the same questions she had asked her grandparents before. She was happy to ask them herself, although she seemed grateful when Louis mentioned that if she were to feel as if she couldn't or did not want to ask the questions, then Louis could do so on her behalf.

Bella added two questions:

- Can I stay with you forever?
- Do I need to change my name?

The questions may have reflected Bella's processing of her attachment and identity needs in relation to her grandparents. Maybe recent weeks and experience had led her to feel closer and more connected to them. Bella's earlier question of 'Will I stay with you forever?' seemed to be an expression of her wondering exactly where she would be in the future. Her more recent question of 'Can I stay with you?' appeared to be an expression of an inner wish to belong and attach to her grandparents in a more meaningful way. It is often the case that in the process of exploring more meaningful ways of experiencing contact, a path is created that allows those involved the potential to develop individually and interpersonally. Last, Louis explored with Bella where she would like to sit. This simple reflection of the positioning allowed for the *orientation* of her most primal defence responses. Louis used five seats with toys chosen by Bella to represent Dave, Angela, herself, Elsie and Louis. Bella was then encouraged to move and change where people were seated and to *sense in her body* what felt right.

Elsie met the grandparents to prepare them for the facilitated contact. Angela was able to reflect on the letter she had written to Diane who had experienced a difficult birth. Angela had always wondered if this was the reason for Diane having had some learning difficulties. When she was Bella's age Diane had been very sad and confused following the sudden death of her grandmother – Angela's mother with whom Diane had a very close relationship. Looking back, Angela was able to reflect on how unavailable she had been to offer Diane comfort as she had been in shock and was grieving the sudden loss of her mother. Angela said that in some ways writing the letter had helped her to think about how she could explain Diane's difficulties in a sympathetic but honest way to Bella. Both Dave and Angela were committed, yet nervous, about the idea of answering Bella's questions, yet the meaningful purpose of supporting Bella in developing a deeper and more truthful understanding about her past, current and future life motivated them. Elsie explained that in many ways their key role in the process was simply to focus on what Bella was saying, be attentive and try to keep reassurance to a minimum. The aim of the contact meeting was to 'open up' areas of concern or anxiety for Bella and explore them more fully. This would in turn *normalise* Bella's current feelings. For example, as Bella had been displaying more anger and challenging behaviour of late, Elsie and Louis were hoping to contextualise this by acknowledging: 'No wonder you've been more cross recently as you've been worrying about these questions you have had in your mind...I'd be grumpy myself if I had questions like "will I be staying with you forever" whirling around in my mind...poor you!'

Elsie worked through each question which Bella had carefully written down, and thought with the grandparents how they would answer. For the first time they were going to acknowledge how hard life had been for Bella with her mother, how scary it had been, as well as share a few of the incidents that would have occurred before she joined them.

Elsie explained how both she and Louis would gently support the discussion. Dave announced suddenly that he was worried he might cry and this led to an exploration of his fears about being vulnerable. Many parents need support in this area. For children, it can be a powerful experience to see their parents express deep levels of feeling for them. It shows children that they matter. Parents may need time to process their feelings and it is important to make clear that this is an expression of how much they care and is to be included in facilitated contacts, as long as parents are not *overwhelmed* by their feelings of course. If parents do appear to be too worried about the depth of their feelings, there may be a need to have a signal to pause the session briefly to allow them to have a break and compose themselves. Ideally, a team member or supporting professional should be with them in order to ensure that the experience is contained and integrated.

## The contact

The contact venue was a family centre that was familiar to Dave and Angela and Bella had a chance to see it on the centre's website.

The family arrived on time and Bella knew that the plan was for no more than one and a half hours for the meeting. The family were positioned in the seats Bella had chosen, with her sitting between and fairly close to Dave and Angela, with Louis to Angela's right and Elsie to Dave's left.

After making clear again why the family had come to the meeting (to work through the important questions Bella had been asking about her birth family and living with Dave and Angela), Louis and Elsie worked through Bella's list of questions.

Bella was at times transfixed by what her grandparents were saying (both had noticed this during the contact meeting). It was Louis' job to read out Bella's questions on her behalf.

It was a very moving contact meeting and on two occasions Bella needed to seek a cuddle and comfort from her grandparents who offered this in the most loving of ways.

When it came to the questions about staying forever with her grandparents and changing her name, Dave and Angela each wanted to take turns to tell Bella how there was nothing in the world they would love more than to have Bella live with them forever. She began to cry, clutching on to Angela. Louis wondered aloud how a part of Bella must have so wanted to know that she could be with people who would love and care for her forever. Bella clutched on to Angela even tighter.

Dave and Angela agreed that the question about Bella's name would be taken seriously, yet required more thinking about and talking with the social worker. Bella, still emotional from the last question about living with her grandparents forever, seemed content to come back to this question at a later date.

At the end of the contact meeting, Louis and Elsie brought the family drinks and some food. Bella had described what she would like after the contact: apple juice (fizzy drinks like Coca-Cola are discouraged), a chicken wrap and an ice cream. Elsie had pre-bought the food for the occasion.

This facilitated contact meeting had forged new and meaningful bonds of attachment within the family. In fact, it had given Bella, Dave and Angela a greater sense of being and belonging as family, and permission to become closer and to express feelings of affection. Until now, they had indulged in 'psychic love', the kind of love where one might say, 'I don't need to say I love her, she knows I do!' Children in and around the care system need more overt expressions of love and affection than more secure children.

## Clinical conclusions

When thinking about the clinical appraisal of Bella and her grandparents, the following framework was applied:

**Attachment:** Bella was assessed as having a more ambivalent style of attachment. Dave and Angela were relatively secure in their attachment styles, although both did show some avoidant/dismissive traits. Children with an ambivalent attachment need a lot of reassurance that their carers will be there for them and will meet their needs.

**Trauma:** Bella's history was clearly traumatic and her struggle to self-regulate could be attributed in part to the lack of a co-regulating other. Much of Bella's more aggressive behaviour carried an underlying element of fear and anxiety. Both grandparents were actively encouraged to attune to Bella's fear which would in turn reduce the aggression. Bella showed signs of developmental trauma in terms of having cognitive (educational), relational (with peers) and attachment-related concerns. Bella's physiological concerns also masked long-standing attention deficit.

**Neuroscience:** As mentioned, Bella's attention deficit was connected to impaired executive functioning and processing ability. If using the model of the triune brain, in which the brain is viewed as having evolved in stages, from the brain stem/primitive brain, which is the first area of the brain to mature and regulates basic functions such as arousal, reflexes and the cardiovascular system; the Limbic system or mid-brain, often referred to as the 'emotional brain' because it is the source of urges, needs and feelings; and finally the Cortex or 'reflective brain' which involves reasoning, reflection, communication and planning, one could argue that Bella was functioning more from her 'primitive' or reptilian lower brain, resulting in behaviour that was largely fear-based. The triune brain theory was first developed by Paul MacLean, the former director of the Laboratory of the Brain and Behavior at the United States National Institute of Mental Health.

**Theraplay domains:** Following paper assessment, meetings with the grandparents, discussions with her school teacher and social worker and personal observation, Bella presented as needing:

- **A medium to high level of structure:** Bella needed regular monitoring and containing by her carers and was the kind of child who needed to know 'what was happening when'.

- **A high level of nurture:** Like many children within the care system, nurture should be considered a high priority, particularly when therapeutic intervention is planned.

- **A medium to low level of engagement:** Bella is a child who actively seeks attention so there is less of an onus on the grandparents to seek and engage her (as she is often seeking them!).

- **A low level of challenge:** Bella struggled with competition and although desperate to win games, hated losing herself. Bella also struggled with the academic demands of her school's curriculum and needed to work at a level that still allowed her downtime and time to feel connected to her grandparents before doing homework.

- **Developmental issues:** The impact of Bella's early life meant that she presented in ways that were developmentally younger than her chronological age. When under particular stress, Bella could seem like a 3- or 4-year-old.

General advice to all kinship carers who are taking a child into their home following neglect and abuse would be to focus on putting in place high levels of structure and nurture.

Dave and Angela tried to protect Bella from the painful reality of her mother's way of life, perhaps not realising the incongruity of this approach given Bella had lived that life with her mother during the early years of her own. Other children living within their extended families may be all too well aware of the painful details of what their parents do that they should not or don't do that they should. Their kinship carers may be openly critical about one or other or both of their parents whose behaviour and unreliability creates stress, disappointment and frustration. Contact visits may be tense if taking place in their kinship family home. Older children may continue to visit their parents at their homes and see for themselves what is or is not right. Sometimes they are visiting a parent, usually a mother who has given birth to a younger half-sibling and is living with that child's father. Whatever a child's parents may have done, children often remain loyal and want to see them, and the way that kinship care enables ongoing contact promotes their attachment and facilitates these feelings. It is important, therefore, that children feel able to talk with their grandparents or kinship carer about their feelings and experiences of the contact. As David Pitcher states, 'Many grandchildren felt inhibited about mentioning their parents in their grandparents' presence. The fear of disloyalty was as great as for children with non relative carers.'[9] If children are worried that talking with their carers about confusing experiences or worries will upset or anger them, then they may feel they must not, otherwise the contact may be stopped altogether.

Kinship carers need as much support around managing contact and the feelings this generates, as do adopters or foster carers. Helping them to find safe people and spaces where they can express their anxieties and frustrations, and gain advice and support, is equally as important. Just as adoptive parents and foster carers can benefit from advice about how to talk with children about their history and the reasons their birth parents are unable to look after them, kinship carers should also be given this kind of advice and support.

Natalie Salaman, an Enfield adoption support social worker, has contributed a very helpful guide on ways of explaining and talking to young children about their history and birth parents issues. Her advice is available online via the North London Adoption Consortium Adoption Support Handbook, *Difficult Stories* – Appendix 4.[10] These ideas could be adapted to share with kinship carers so that they are empowered to talk with their children in truthful and age-appropriate ways. Making life story books with or for children in kinship care may not be a priority for professionals as many of the reasons for doing so are to give children who are living away from their families of origin an understanding of their identity and family history. It may be assumed that through living in kinship care, they will have access to this information. However, professionals involved in kinship care could offer meaningful support to kinship carers and their children by helping the child make sense of their history through the use of life story work. This, of course, may prompt the child who is having contact with their birth parents to ask questions. If you are embarking on this kind of work, it would be helpful to try to engage with the birth parent and explain to them the kinds of explanations you intend to give to the child. This could include offering them support in thinking through how they could support the child should they ask them questions, for example, about their drug and alcohol dependency.

Being sensitive to children's developmental needs is also important. Young children experience the loss of their parental relationships in very different ways than do older children and teenagers. Kinship carers will need to revisit what they tell the children in their care as they grow and develop. What is acceptable and appropriate to tell a younger child about why they are not living with their parents, or why their parents present as they do, is unlikely to address the level of insight an older child requires. Offering ongoing access to support that is sensitive to the issues and experiences of kinship carers is a prerequisite to maximising the potential for them to meet the ongoing and changing needs of their kinship children.

# Developmental Stages of Understanding and Adjustment

## Assessing and reviewing contact issues and needs in adoption and foster care

Our understanding of the development and psychological adjustment of the adopted child has been informed by the research conducted on the relinquished adoptee. Whilst some of these developmental tasks are relevant to the growing child who is placed with adoptive or other substitute parents due to maltreatment, there are some important differences that need to be considered when thinking about contact issues and updating life story work.

A child's understanding of themselves and their relationships is changing throughout their development and occurs within the context of the family and community within which they live. Relationships with peers and the school community play a huge part in how all children develop their sense of identity and self-awareness. All children will have views, feelings and reactions about the fact that some children do not live with their birth parents or families.

Much that has been written about the child's development and adjustment to adoption has been based on research of relinquished babies. Whilst the psychological tasks highlighted from such research are pertinent to all separated children, the experiences of maltreated children need specific recognition when considering the impact of contact arrangements on the child.

| Child not adopted, fostered or in kinship care (or maltreated) | Child relinquished for adoption | Child removed due to maltreatment |
|---|---|---|
| | **0–36 months** | |
| Trust vs mistrust, issues relating to attachment security and parental/caregiver sensitivity. | Plus… | Plus… |
| Preferential attachment by 6 months by which time secure attachment relationships result in normal cortisol levels: therefore less stress upon development of the brain. | The earlier the baby is placed the higher the probability of developing a sense of trust and attachment security. | Pre-birth experiences, early abuse and neglect will challenge babies/toddlers in developing a sense of trust and safety. |
| Environmental experiences including attachment relationships impact upon neurological development, including the stress response system. | However, even the newborn can experience the loss of relationship with birth mother as traumatic.[1] | Depending on how contact is supported, experiences may unsettle or traumatise and regular separations from foster carers as well as birth parents, along with experiences of multiple escorts and supervisors can undermine the potential for building trust and an improved sense of security and regulation of stress. |
| Environment and routine is likely to be predictable, consistent with available carers. Proximity seeking with primary carers and internalisation of secure base. | If relinquished babies/toddlers are having contact with birth parents, contact will be infrequent and adoptive parents will be present, acting as secure base. | Toxic stress can cause developmental damage. Contact plans should address supporting babies and toddlers in reducing exposure to stressful experiences. |
| Can develop attachments to more than one parent/caregiver in order to maintain sense of safety. | | |

---

1   Verrier, N. (1993) *The Primal Wound: Understanding the Adopted Child*. Louisville, KT: Gateway Press.

| Toddler through to 4 years | | |
|---|---|---|
| At age 4 secure attachment experiences will have established a normal pattern of cortisol level; this has taken from the age of 4–6 months. | Plus… | Plus… |
| | Sense of self and others may be impacted by awareness of difference, e.g. transracial placement. Contact with same race birth family/community can support a positive sense of racial identity. | Sense of self may be negatively impacted by early maltreatment, fear, loss and separations. Capacity for stress regulation may be compromised. Developing sense of autonomy can become a *need* to control. This may begin to manifest in play with others. |
| Increasingly develops physical skills and personal control. Develops a sense of autonomy/shame. | | |
| From 3 years sense of self and others is developing – 'Who am I' 3-year-olds can tolerate short separations more readily. | If having contact with birth family it would be likely to be relatively infrequent and include adoptive parent(s) as secure base'. | Contact with neglectful or abusive parents, or parents unable to attune can reinforce negative experiences of mistrust and insecurity, reinforcing negative 'internal working models' about self and others. |
| Begins to perceive differences and if notices them points them out. Tends to feel OK about adoption and difference in family structures. | | Supporting young children through reducing exposure to prolonged stress should be one of the aims of all contact plans. |

*cont.*

| Child not adopted, fostered or in kinship care (or maltreated) | Child relinquished for adoption | Child removed due to maltreatment |
|---|---|---|
| | 4–7 years | |
| Development of independence continues. Imaginative, magical and egocentric thinking develops, leads to beliefs that wishes can make things happen and that they are responsible for everything that happens to them and others who are important to them.<br><br>Fearful thoughts and dreams. Fears being lost, or that parents will not be available when needed. Lots of questions about babies.<br><br>At age 6 beginning to understand the difference between adoption and birth. Accepts adoption as a way to form a family. | Plus…<br><br>Tends to like adoption story but does not understand adoption concepts. Tells most people they are adopted. Feels some difference, especially if in a multicultural transracial placement. Usually receives and accepts a simple but positive story about why they were relinquished for adoption. Need an explanation that helps understanding that they were born *and* adopted.<br><br>By age 7 fears of parental loss or abandonment may begin to include worries about being given away again or being reclaimed by birth parents. Any contact will be inclusive of adoptive parents. | Plus…<br><br>Children may believe they caused the maltreatment and loss of their birth parents. Even if no longer having direct contact with birth parents, fearful thoughts and dreams may link to experience of maltreatment. Children need security and reassurance, support in managing and contextualising fears that have a basis in reality.<br><br>A simple and honest story about why they are in need of foster care or adoption which puts the responsibility of why and how with adults. May continue to be vulnerable to stress and have limited capacity for self-regulation. Support of an adult(s) who the child knows and with whom they feel safe is essential if having direct contact – ideally adoptive/foster parents. |

| 7–11 years | | |
|---|---|---|
| From around 6/7 mastering situations outside of the family is the major task; learning, developing motor skills and social interactions with peers are the major preoccupations. Success leads to a sense of competence and failure to a sense of inferiority. There is an incorporation of family values, development of conscience and an increasing capacity for self-control.<br><br>Begins to understand that adoption/foster care means a child is given or taken away. Reactions to adopted and fostered peers depend on information from adults and the media. Will react to the status of adopted and fostered peers based on whether they like them or not: 'adoption is OK because I like you'.<br><br>May wonder if their parents could give them away *and* have fantasies about living with different parents. | Plus…<br><br>Thinks in a more complex way about adoption. Although may stop asking questions. Increasing interest in birth parents and starts to consider/evaluate the factual reasons they were 'given away' and consider the feelings of the birth parents. 'Why did they give me away?', 'Did I do something wrong?', 'Not everyone is adopted like me.' Fears loss of adoptive parents, e.g. through illness or of being reclaimed by birth parents. This is age/ stage of adaptive grieving process. May feel confused or uncertain; certainty of permanence with the adoptive family means loss of the birth family. Need to mourn their losses and acknowledge the positives.<br><br>May also have fantasies about living with different parents.<br><br>If direct contact has been an ongoing feature adoptive and birth parent(s) are likely to have developed a co-operative relationship. | Plus…<br><br>The development of academic learning, peer relationships, social and emotional skills may be delayed as a consequence of neglect and abuse. Children may experience significant levels of shame, self-doubt and low self-esteem. Insecure relationships with adoptive or foster parents may add to fears that they will be abandoned. Adaptive grieving may include thoughts and feelings about 'why did it happen to me?', 'the reason I was abused is because I was bad'. Interest in birth family may include concerns for the parents' wellbeing, fear of reprisals and being reclaimed.<br><br>Contact can confuse and exacerbate insecurity if it does not support the child in making sense of their abusive history, placing responsibility for their removal from birth parents' where it belongs. Any child involved in direct contact needs the support of adults who know them and their history, needs and current concerns. For the adopted child this is their adoptive parent(s). There should be a similar expectation of support from foster carers. |

*cont.*

| Child not adopted, fostered or in kinship care (or maltreated) | Child relinquished for adoption | Child removed due to maltreatment |
|---|---|---|
| | Early adolescence 12–15 years | |
| The beginning of the period of transition from childhood to adulthood. | Plus… | Plus… |
| Research points to significant transformations in neurological structure and function which is not believed to be completed until mid 20s. | Adaptive grieving may include angry reactions. May be angry over loss of control over adoption decisions, wants more control in life. | Adolescents who have experienced early loss and trauma can experience difficulty with leaving their secure base to explore the world, or can find returning or reconnecting with their secure base difficult. |
| Ability to think abstractly is developing. | Has capacity for a more complex reasoning about adoption story and needs a more nuanced understanding. | Adolescence can also offer opportunities to redo/ understand early experiences of attachment and loss – maltreatment. |
| Emotional control may be volatile/angry, may resist authority, try on different identities. | | |
| Onset of more risk-taking behaviours. | Sense of permanence with adoptive parents may reassert itself. | Can understand the concept of child welfare, the role that outside authorities play in removal and that their needs were better met by adoption. A good time to revisit life story work…if having direct or letterbox contact, may benefit from an opportunity to ask for information from birth parents/family. Will need the empathic support of adoptive parents and birth parents for such contact to be beneficial. |
| Wants more control in life. | Understanding of biological reasons for adoption becomes more complex. | |
| Growing sense of self-awareness and identity issues. | Generally does not talk about being an adoptee. Adoptive parents need to be proactive. | |
| Tendency to reject peers who are different. | | |
| May be negative about what adoption and foster care reflects about peers. | Is beginning to separate from two sets of parents. | No contact/discussion risks adolescent initiating own searches. |

| | | |
|---|---|---|
| Begins process of separating from one set of parents.<br><br>In adolescence the search for romantic relationships begins to influence the continuing need for affectional bonds. | May begin to want more control over any ongoing contact arrangements, e.g. opt out or have them in a different way. If adoption has been closed then may initiate own searches/exploration, e.g. through use of the internet. | The adolescent in foster care may have little opportunity to review their history (frequently do not receive life story work or have later life letters) and may have relatively high levels of contact during which historical reasons for removal have not been addressed. Therefore, may struggle to manage a healthy sense of identity and be vulnerable to being drawn to identification with dysfunction. |

## Later adolescence

| | | |
|---|---|---|
| Both *parent* and adolescent can agree the same objective for the young person in late adolescence: to learn to act more 'grown up'. They may differ, however, in the meaning they attach to this objective. For parents it may mean learning to take on more adult responsibilities. For the teenager it means taking more adult adventures to confirm that they are officially old enough to do so. | Plus…<br><br>Is taking the next psychological steps in separation/individuation with two sets of parents in mind.<br><br>Fear of abandonment can transfer to romantic relationships. | Plus…<br><br>Romance and sex are powerful triggers for activation of attachment issues, and early maltreatment can impact upon the young person's self-image and sense of self as worthy and lovable. Emotional maturity may be delayed and the task of separating from adoptive/foster parents more complex. |

*cont.*

| Child not adopted, fostered or in kinship care (or maltreated) | Child relinquished for adoption | Child removed due to maltreatment |
|---|---|---|
| Neurological changes are ongoing.

Separates from one set of parents. May face concerns about leaving home but usually feels secure about its permanency. | As understanding becomes more sophisticated, more awareness emerges about physical and personality identity.

A lack of information/contact can lead to idealising birth parents.

At age 18 the adopted young person can legally and independently seek information about birth history and initiate search and reunion, although they may begin this process much sooner given access to information via the internet. | If adopted young people have not had contact they may seek out information/contact independently.

Increasingly fostered young people may be having unsupervised contact with birth family who may be anticipating their return aged 18 or before. Those who took a 'parentified' role when younger may struggle to resist this expectation, while those who experienced rejection by birth parents may encounter further rejection and hostility.

Whether adopted or fostered these young people need continued opportunities to discuss/receive support, in managing contact/no contact and the meaning of their early life experiences. |

# Endnotes

## Chapter 1

1.  Loxterkamp, L. (2009) 'Contact and truth: The unfolding predicament in adoption and fostering.' *Clinical Child Psychology and Psychiatry* 2009 *14*, 423–435.
2.  O'Regan, T. (2012) 'Contact within care proceedings: the legal framework.' *Seen and Heard* 22, 2, 46–59.
3.  Baynes, P. (2010) 'Interim contact.' *Seen and Heard 20*, 4, 33–42.
4.  Collier, C. (2012) '"Papers! Papers! Papers!" Contact notes in care proceedings.' *Seen and Heard 22*, 4, 7–8.
5.  Rella, M. (2010) 'Therapeutic access: From supervising access to building parent-child relationships.' *OACAS Journal 55*, 4, 19–31.
6.  Schofield, G. and Simmonds, J. 'Contact for infants subject to care proceedings.' *Adoption & Fostering 35*, 4, 70–74.
7.  Humphreys, C. and Kiraly, M. 'High-frequency contact: A road to nowhere for infants.' *Child and Family Social Work 2011*, 16, 1–11.
8.  Howe, D. and Steele, M. (2004) 'Contact in Cases in which Children Have Been Traumatically Abused or Neglected by their Birth Parents.' In E. Neil and D. Howe (eds) *Contact in Adoption and Permanent Foster Care*. London: BAAF.
9.  Lucey, C., Sturge. C., Fellow-Smith, L. and Reder, P. (2003) 'Parental visiting, conflicting allegiances, and emotional and behavioural problems among foster children.' *Family Relations 52*, 1, 53–63.
10. Dale, P. (2012) Response to DoE/Narey consultation document on contact arrangements for children. Available at www.peterdale.co.uk/wp-content/uploads/2011/08/ContactPaperResponseAug2012.pdf, accessed on 7 May 2014.
11. Lindsey, C. (2006) 'Contact with Birth Families: Implications for Assessment and Integration in New Families.' In J. Kenrick, L. Tollemache and C. Lindsey (eds) *Creating New Families, Therapeutic Approaches to Fostering, Adoption and Kinship Care*. London: Karnac Books.
12. Brown, R. and Ward, H. (2013) *Decision-Making within a Child's Time Frame. An Overview of Current Research Evidence for Family Justice Professionals Concerning Child Development and the Impact of Maltreatment*. Available at www.gov.uk/government/uploads/system/uploads/attachment_data/file/200471/Decision-making_within_a_child_s_timeframe.pdf, accessed 2 May 2014.
13. Schore, A. (1994) *Affect Regulation and the Origin of the Self*. Hillsdale, NJ: Lawrence Erlbaum Associates.
14. Hertsgaard, L., Gunnar, M., Farrell Erickson, M. and Nachmias, M. (1995) 'Adrenal responses to the strange situation in infants with disorganized/disoriented attachment relationships.' *Child Development 66*, 4, 1100–1106.
15. Perry, B.D. (2003) *Effects of Traumatic Events on Children*. The Child Trauma Academy. Available at www.ChildTrauma.org, accessed on 16 May 2014.

16. van der Kolk, B. (2008) 'Developmental Trauma Disorder: A New, Rational Diagnosis for Children with Complex Trauma Histories.' In D. Benamjer and K. White (eds) *Trauma & Attachment*. London: Karnac.

17. Golding, K. and Hughes, D. (2012) *Creating Loving Attachments: Parenting with PACE to Nurture Confidence and Security in the Troubled Child*. London: Jessica Kingsley Publishers.

18. Hughes, D. and Baylin, J. (2012) *Brain Based Parenting: The Neuroscience of Parenting*. New York, NY: W.W. Norton.

19. Kaniuk, J., Steele, M. and Hodges, J. (2004) 'Report on a longitudinal research project, exploring the development of attachments between older, hard-to-place children and their adopters over the first two years of placement.' *Adoption & Fostering 28*, 2, 61–67.

20. Kanink, Steele and Hodges (2004).

21. Howe and Steele (2004).

22. Logan, J. and Smith, C. (2004) 'Direct Post-Adoption Contact: Experiences of Birth and Adoptive Families.' In E. Neil and D. Howe (eds) *Contact in Adoption and Permanent Foster Care*. London: BAAF.

23. Thoburn, J. (2004) 'Post-Placement Contact between Birth Parents and Older Children: Evidence from a Longitudinal Study of Minority Ethnic Children.' In E. Neil and D. Howe (eds) *Contact in Adoption and Permanent Foster Care*. London: BAAF.

24. Macaskill, C. (2002) *Safe Contact? Children in Permanent Placement and Contact with their Birth Relatives*. Dorset: Russell House Publishing.

25. Wilson, K. and Sinclair, I. (2004) 'Contact in Foster Care: Some Dilemmas and Opportunities.' In E. Neil and D. Howe (eds) *Contact in Adoption and Permanent Foster Care*. London: BAAF.

26. Selwyn, J. (2004) 'Placing Older Children in New Families: Changing Patterns of Contact.' In E. Neil and D. Howe (eds) *Contact in Adoption and Permanent Foster Care*. London: BAAF.

27. Neil, E., Cossar, J. and Lorgelly, P. (2011) *Supporting Direct Contact after Adoption*. London: BAAF.

28. Sants, H.J. (1964) 'Genealogical bewilderment in children with substitute parents.' *British Journal of Medical Psychology 37*, 2:133–141.

29. Triseliotis, J., Feast, J. and Kyle, F. (2003) *The Adoption Triangle Revisited: A Study of Adoption, Search and Reunion Experiences*. London: BAAF.

30. Bifulco, A., Jacobs, C., Bunn, A., Thomas, G. and Irving, K. (2008) 'The Attachment Style Interview (ASI): A support-based adult assessment tool for adoption and fostering practice.' *Adoption & Fostering 32*, 3, 33–45.

31. Kaniuk, Steele and Hodges (2004).

32. Howe and Steele (2004).

33. Logan, J. (2010) 'Preparation and planning for face-to face contact after adoption.' *Child & Family Social Work 15*, 3, 315–324.

34. Palacios, J. (2009) 'The Ecology of Adoption.' In Wrobel, G.M. and Neil, E. (eds) *International Advances in Adoption Research for Practice*. Chichester: John Wiley & Sons Ltd.

35. Logan, J. and Smith, C. (2004) 'Direct Post-Adoption Contact: Experiences of Birth and Adoptive Families.' In E. Neil and D. Howe (eds) *Contact in Adoption and Permanent Foster Care*. London: BAAF.

36. Harris, R. and Lindsey, C. (2002) 'How professionals think about contact between children and their birth parents. *Clinical Child Psychology and Psychiatry 7*, 2, 147–161.

37. Conway, P. (2009) 'Falling in between minds: The effects of unbearable experiences on multi-agency communication in the care system.' *Adoption & Fostering 33*, 1, 18–29.

38. Conway (2009), p.21.

39. Grotevant, H., McRoy, R. and Ayers-Lopez, S. (2004) 'Contact After Adoption: Outcomes for Infant Placements in the USA.' In E. Neil and D. Howe (eds) *Contact in Adoption and Permanent Foster Care*. London: BAAF.

40. Howard, J. (2012) *Untangling the Web: The Internet's Transformative Impact on Adoption.* New York, NY: Evan B. Donaldson Adoption Institute.
41. Fursland, E. (2013) *Facing Up to Facebook: A Survival Guide for Adoptive Families.* London: BAAF Publications.
42. Howard (2012), p.4.
43. Wilson, K. and Sinclair, I. (2004) 'Contact in Foster Care: Some Dilemmas and Opportunities.' In E. Neil and D. Howe (eds) *Contact in Adoption and Permanent Foster Care.* London: BAAF.
44. Schofield, G., Beek, M., Ward, E. and Sellick, C. (2011) *Care Planning for Permanence in Foster Care.* University of East Anglia: Centre for Research on the Child and Family.
45. Schofield *et al.* (2011), pp.9, 10.
46. Schofield, G., Ward, E. and Young, J. (2009) *Parenting while Apart: Experiences of Parents of Children Growing Up in Foster Care.* University of East Anglia: Centre for Research on the Child and Family.
47. Sturge, C. and Glaser, D. (2000) 'Contact and domestic violence – the experts' court report.' *Family Law 30,* pp.615–629.
48. Sturge, C. and Glaser, D. (2000) p.618.
49. Siegel, D. *Trauma, Brain and Relationship: Helping Children Heal.* [DVD] Santa Barbara Graduate Institute. Available at www.healingresources.info/emotional_trauma_online_video.htm, accessed 1 May 2014.

# Chapter 2

1. Neil, E., Cossar, J., Jones, C. and Lorgelly, P. (2011) *Supporting Direct Contact after Adoption: Supporting Post-Adoption Contact in Complex Cases.* London: BAAF and Ari.
2. Neil *et al.* (2011), p.3.
3. Neil *et al.* (2011), p.5.
4. Levine, Dr. P.A. *Somatic Experiencing Trauma Institute.* Available at www.somaticexperiencing.com, accessed 16 May 2014.

# Chapter 3

1. Howerton, C.L., Morgan, C.P., Fischer, D.B. and Bale, T.L. (2013) 'O-GlcNAc transferase (OGT) as a placental biomarker of maternal stress and reprogramming of CNS gene transcription in development.' *PNAS 110,* 13, 5169–5174.
2. Bergman, K., Sarkar, P., O'Connor, T.G., Modi, N. and Glover, V. (2007) 'Maternal stress during pregnancy predicts cognitive ability and fearfulness in infancy.' *Journal of the American Academy of Child and Adolescent Psychiatry 46,* 11, 1454–1463.
3. Perry, B.D., Pollard, R.A., Blakley, T.L. and Vigilante, D. (1995) 'Childhood trauma, the neurobiology of adaptation, and "use-dependent" development of the brain: How "states" become "traits".' *Infant Mental Health Journal 16,* 4, 271–291.
4. De Gangi, G. (2000) *Georgia Pediatric Disorders of Regulation in Affect and Behavior.* Waltham, MA: Elsevier.
5. Perry *et al.* (1995).
6. O'Regan, T. (2012) 'Contact within care proceedings: the legal framework.' *Seen and Heard 22,* 2, 46–59.
7. Puckering, C., McIntosh, E., Hickey, A. and Longford, J. (2010) 'Mellow Babies: A group intervention for infants and mothers experiencing postnatal depression.' *The British Psychological Society in Counselling Psychology Review 25,* 1, 33.
8. Theraplay Institute (2013) *The Theraplay Institute.* Available at www.theraplay.org, accessed 16 May 2014.

9.  Siegel, Dr. D. (2010) *Dr. Dan Siegel: Inspire to Rewire®*. Available at www.drdansiegel.com, accessed 16 May 2014.
10. Fonagy, P. and Target, M. (1997) 'Attachment and reflective function: Their role in self-organization.' *Development and Psychopathology 9*, 4, 679–700.
11. Taken from the NSPCC report *All Babies Count: Information for Professionals*. Available at www.nspcc.org.uk/Inform/resourcesforprofessionals/underones/all_babies_count_summary_PDF_wdf85684.pdf, accessed 11 February 2014.
12. Scott, D., O'Neill, C. and Minge, A. (2005) 'Contact between children in out-of-home care and their birth families.' Available at www.community.nsw.gov.au/docswr_assets/main/documents/oohc_research.pdf, accessed 2 May 2014.

## Chapter 4

1.  Neil, E. *et al.* (2011).
2.  Schofield, Ward and Young (2008/9) 'Parenting while apart: Experiences of parents of children growing up in foster care.' ESRC End of Award Report, RES-000-22-2606. Swindon: ESRC.

## Chapter 5

1.  Fahlberg, V. (1994) *The Child's Journey Through Placement*. London: BAAF, p.134.
2.  Fahlberg (1994), p.153.
3.  Adapted from Fahlberg (1994), p.171.

## Chapter 6

1.  Neil, E. *et al.* (2011).
2.  Loxtercamp, L. (2009) 'Contact and truth: The unfolding predicament in adoption and fostering.' *Clinical Child Psychology and Psychiatry 14*, 3, 423–435.
3.  Selwyn, J., Frazer, L. and Wrighton, P. (2006) 'More than just a letter: Service user perspectives on one local authority's adoption postbox service.' *Adoption & Fostering 30*, 2, 6–17.

## Chapter 8

1.  Rowe, J., Hundleby, M. and Keane, A. (1984). Long-Term Foster Care. London: Batsford Academic and Educational in association with BAAF.
2.  Burnell, A., Castell, K. and Cousins, G. (2009) *Siblings Together or Apart*. Family Futures Practice Paper Series. London: Family Futures.
3.  Selwyn, J. (2004) 'Placing Older Children in New Families: Changing Patterns of Contact.' In E. Neil and D. Howe (eds) *Contact in Adoption and Permanent Foster Care*. London: BAAF.
4.  See for example: Finkelhor, D., Ormrod, R., Turner, H. and Hamby, S.L. (2005) 'The victimization of children and youth: A comprehensive, national survey.' *Child Maltreatment 10*, 1: 5–25 and Tucker, C.J., Finkelhor, D., Shattuck, A.M. and Turner, H. (2013) 'Prevalence and correlates of sibling victimization types.' *Child Abuse & Neglect 37*, 213–223.
5.  Caffaro, J. and Conn-Caffaro, A. (1998) *Sibling Abuse Trauma: Assessment and Intervention Strategies for Children, Families, and Adults*. Birghampton, NY: The Howarth Maltreatment and Trauma Press.

6. Caffaro and Conn-Caffaro (1998), p.29.
7. Caffaro and Conn-Caffaro (1998), p.33.
8. Bhreathnach, É. (2011) *The Scared Gang.* Ballynahinch: Alder Tree Press.
9. Golding, K.S. and Hughes, D.A. (2012) *Creating Loving Attachments: Parenting with Pace to Nurture Security in the Troubled Child.* London: Jessica Kingsley Publishers.

## Chapter 9

1. Hughes, D. (2009) *Attachment-Focused Parenting. Effective Strategies to Care for Children.* New York, NY: W.W. Norton.

## Chapter 11

1. Hillman, J. (1990) 'The Great Mother, Her Son, Her Hero, and the Puer.' In P. Berry (ed.) *Fathers and Mothers.* Dallas, TX: Spring Publications.
2. Frankel, R. (1998) *The Adolescent Psyche.* London: Routledge.

## Chapter 12

1. Boddy, J. (2012) *Understanding permanence for looked after children: A review of research for the Care Inquiry,* The Fostering Network. Available at www.fostering.net/sites/www.fostering.net/files/resources/england/understanding-permanence-for-lac-janet-boddy.pdf, accessed 16 May 2014, p.4.
2. Department for Education (2011) *Family and Friends Care: Statutory Guidance for Local Authorities.* London: Department for Education.
3. Roth, D., Aziz, R., Ashley, C. and Lindley, B. (2013) *Relative Poverty: Study of Family and Friends Care in London.* London: Family Rights Group. Available at www.frg.org.uk/involving-families/family-and-friends-carers-e-publications-and-studies, accessed 16 May 2014.
4. Department for Education (2010) *Statistical First Release.* London: Department for Education.
5. Gautier, A., Wellard, S. and Cardy, S. (2013) *Forgotten children: Children growing up in kinship care.* Survey Findings Report/June 2013. Grandparents Plus. Available at www.grandparentsplus.org.uk/wp-content/uploads/2011/03/Forgotten-Children-0613-4.pdf, accessed 16 May 2014.
6. Pitcher, D. (2002) *Staying Connected: Managing contact arrangements in adoption.* London: BAAF Publications.
7. Pitcher (2002), p.47.
8. Mickelson, K.D., Kessler, K. and Shaver, P.R. (1997) 'Adult Attachment in a nationally representative sample'. *Journal of Personality and Social Psychology 73,* 1092–1106.
9. Pitcher (2002), p.47.
10. Salaman, N. (2014) 'Appendix 4: Difficult Stories' in *North London Adoption Consortium Adoption Support Handbook.* Available at http://cdn-21.create.net/sitefiles/21/4/7/214711/2014_Handbook_doc.pdf, accessed 16 May 2014.

# Index